Five Cities

Modelling Asian Urban
Population-Environment
Dynamics

Five Cities

Modelling Asian Urban Population-Environment Dynamics

Editors

Gayl D. Ness
with
Michael M. Low

For
AUICK and UMPEDP

OXFORD
UNIVERSITY PRESS

OXFORD
UNIVERSITY PRESS

Oxford University Press is a department of the University of Oxford.
It furthers the University's objective of excellence in research, scholarship,
and education by publishing worldwide in

Oxford New York

Athens Auckland Bangkok Bogotá Buenos Aires Calcutta
Cape Town Chennai Dar es Salaam Delhi Florence Hong Kong Istanbul
Karachi Kuala Lumpur Madrid Melbourne Mexico City Mumbai
Nairobi Paris São Paulo Shanghai Singapore Taipei Tokyo Toronto Warsaw

with associated companies in Berlin Ibadan

Oxford is a registered trade mark of Oxford University Press
in the UK and in certain other countries

Published in Singapore
by Oxford University Press Pte Ltd

ISBN 0 19 588693 3

1 3 5 7 9 10 8 6 4 2

In Memory of
Mayor Tatsuo Miyazaki
Mayor of Kobe City, 1969 to 1989
The first President of AUICK, 1989

In appreciation of his dedication and his vision of a better urban life.

Preface

Over the past decades, the momentum of world population growth has decreased as a result of the unflagging efforts of many concerned parties. Due to the high birth rate of the past, however, the world population continues to grow by approximately 80 million people per year, of which 50 million are born in Asian countries.

In the meantime, urbanization is occurring at an even greater rate than population growth in nearly all developing countries. In the advanced countries, more than half the population already lives in urban areas.

According to the United Nation population projections, the urban population in less developed regions will also exceed half the total population by the year 2015. Under accelerated urbanization, much attention has been given to mega-cities in developing countries, especially in Asia. Medium-sized cities, on the other hand, have been relatively neglected although they are facing the same pressures of urbanization. Whether medium-sized cities possess their own unique concerns and problems or face the same problems as mega-cities has yet to be established. This book is significant in that it focuses on the medium-sized cities in Asia, in which much can be done to prevent extreme urban concentration and further environmental deterioration.

It is my hope that *Five Cities* will be used to promote dialogue between cities and towns across national borders. They differ in resource bases as well as in their socio-cultural and political background, but they share the same responsibility in providing people with a more sustainable urban environment. I believe that sharing ideas and experiences affords them a valuable opportunity to learn from mistakes made and foster successful new efforts.

Public authorities should work for and with people. Building a sustainable urban environment requires all local actors, including businesses and civil society, to work in partnership. Without active involvement of the people, local authorities cannot do much to enhance environmental health. It is in this sense that I hope this book will be read not only by administrators, but also by a wide range of other people.

In conclusion, we would like to express our sincere gratitude to Dr Gayl Ness, Professor Emeritus of the University of Michigan and General Director of this study, and to the many other people who took part in this research, for contributing significantly to the publication of this book. We are also deeply grateful to the United Nations Population Fund and the Hewlett Foundation for their support.

Kazutoshi Sasayama
Mayor of Kobe
President, Asian Urban Information Center of Kobe

Acknowledgements

The publication of this volume marks ten years of work in the University of Michigan Population Environment Dynamics Project (UMPEDP), and ten years of collaboration between the Asian Urban Information Center of Kobe (AUICK) and UMPEDP. It also marks 15 years during which I have had the privilege of working with the City of Kobe. For me this has been an immensely enlightening and invigorating time, both professionally and personally. Many people and institutions have helped to make these years so rich and rewarding; they deserve recognition.

My good friend and colleague, Dr Hirofumi Ando, first introduced me to Kobe in 1984, when he asked me to help organize a comparative study of Kobe and Singapore. The study was supported by the United Nations Population Fund (UNFPA) and organized by Nihon University's Population Research Institute, under the direction of Professor Toshio Kuroda. Over 35 years Dr Ando has been a warm and wise friend and colleague. It is difficult to think of this past life without the presence of Hiro and his family. I first met Professor Kuroda in 1972 and we have since worked together on many projects. For wisdom, energy and the ability to grow younger as he ages, Kuroda sensei has no match.

It was Dr Ando's position in UNFPA that helped bring Kobe to the important role it has played in promoting urban planning in Asia. UNFPA is to be credited with a remarkable vision, laid down by its first Executive Secretary, Mr Rafael Salas, and wisely continued by Dr Nafis Sadik. Both have kept UNFPA open to and experimenting with activities in a wide variety of conditions that affect and are affected by the human population. Theirs has become the vision of the organization, and it is a remarkably wise one. UNFPA has supported work not only in the core activity of family planning and fertility limitation, but has looked outward to issues of national and rural development, urbanization, women's status, and more recently, population-environment dynamics. I have worked for many years with UNFPA and have always been impressed with the commitment and quality of its staff.

I have also been much assisted through the years by USAID's Office of Population, and especially by its current director, Dr Duff Gillespie, and his able assistant Joanne Grossi. There is a striking observation to be made about UNFPA and USAID's Population Office. Both have women in half or more of their professional positions. In both cases, they are like lush islands of gender equality in seas of male chauvinism. Perhaps this is why both have been so willing to take an exceptionally broad view of the problems they are designed to address.

In providing long term support to AUICK, the leaders of Kobe have shown that remarkably broad and long-term view we often find in Japan. They see both the possibility and the responsibility for Kobe to play a positive role among the cities of Asia. Former Mayor Miyazaki and current Mayor Sasayama have shaped, articulated and sustained this vision, but it has also been shared and supported by a superb staff and an enlightened citizenry. The leaders and the citizens of Kobe have also been to me the warmest and most hospitable hosts one can imagine.

The UMPEDP was formed in 1988, and received generous grants from the MacArthur Foundation in 1989 and 1990. This was very much due to the leadership of Dan Martin at MacArthur, who saw the importance of finding ways to promote interdisciplinary work on population-environment dynamics. The original MacArthur grant has sustained UMPEDP for ten years. Its last contribution enabled us to provide a publication subsidy for this volume, so that its price could bring it more easily within reach of a larger audience of Asian leaders and scholars.

The authors of the five city studies are people with whom I have had the pleasure to work for many years. They have all provide much assistance in highly professional research, in their deep wisdom, and in their warm friendship. I am much in their debt. That to Professor Wilhelm Flieger of San Carlos University in Cebu City will never be paid. We were all saddened by his sudden death in February this year. The world is a poorer place without him.

The University of Michigan has provided a most supportive and stimulating environment. Our department of Sociology has encouraged and supported an extremely wide variety of perspectives and research strategies. My colleagues in the department have been good listeners, good critics and good friends. The university as a whole is also a remarkable institution, designed, in the words of past President James B. Angell, 1871–1909, "...to give an uncommon education to the common man." (He could have added 'woman' as well, since the university began admitting women in 1870.) It is a superb example of that most American institution, the public university, supported by local taxpayers, with rich and extensive relations between the institution and the society. The university's support of research is a long history of wisdom and generosity. Far from a parochial mid-western institution, it has for long been highly international in its student body, faculty and scholarship. This has made it one of the best places in the world to study Asia, a remarkable flowering in the flat southeastern Michigan countryside. Michigan leads all American universities in the external support it receives for research. This reflects both a structure and a culture that work to support research. That support is centred in its Office of the Vice President for Research (OVPR), but the spirit pervades all units and personnel. The OVPR provided a grant late in the work on this volume to help us host our Thai colleagues and complete the chapter on Khon Kaen. But within this pervasively supportive university are many unsung heroes whose assistance is so critical to making support a reality at all levels. I have found much assistance from Marvin Parnes, associate vice president for research, and Peggy Westrick, in the office of the Associate Dean for Research in the College of Literature Science and the Arts. Elaine Johnson of the Financial Office provided financial reports in a timely fashion. Our support staff in Sociology – Lara Nelson, Sabrina Williams, Julia Mattucci-Clark and Pat Preston – were always there with cheerful competence to help move things along. These people represent the best in the university's spirit of assistance. Rather than throw up bureaucratic hurdles, they consistently worked to find ways to get things done. They would be the first to say 'we're only doing our job', but the way they do their jobs is what makes our university so effective in supporting research.

In addition to the MacArthur Foundation, this project received financial support from the Hewlett Foundation. Dr Joseph Speidel, director of Hewlett's population programme saw the need for work in population-environment issues and the importance of the urban scene. AUICK had originally designed this project to include only three cities – Faisalabad, Surabaya[1] and Kobe. The Hewlett grant allowed us to include Khon Kaen, Cebu City and Pusan, adding greatly to the study's utility. The support of Joe Speidel and The Hewlett Foundation are gratefully acknowledged.

I also had excellent assistance from colleagues at the university, who came together to form an informal advisory committee for the project. This was especially important since we were experimenting with STELLA, the dynamic modelling program used in four of the five city studies. Professors Bobbi Low,

---

[1] Data and logistical problems precluded including the Surabaya study in this volume.

Steve Brechin, Bill Drake, Carl Simon and Steve Lansing (unfortunately no longer at Michigan) provided invaluable assistance. Their friendship and collegial assistance is gratefully acknowledge

I first hired Michael Low as an undergraduate research assistant, because his study of Japanese and creative writing would be useful to this project. Michael soon worked himself into a position as co-editor. We have tried to write well, though we recognize that is often suspect in academic publications. We have tried to use the English language as the marvelously precise and evocative tool of communication that it is. We wanted to expose some of the human reality that underlies population-environment dynamics. To the extent that we have succeeded, Michael deserves much credit.

To all who have assisted in this project, and in the longer years of my work in Asia, I offer my deepest appreciation, but I also absolve others of responsibility for the follies and mistakes I have made. Those are mine alone.

Gayl D. Ness
Ann Arbor, Michigan
July 2000

Contents

Part I

Introduction: Vignettes, Theory, History and Methods

Chapter 1

Five Asian Cities:
Two by Air and Three by Sea

Gayl D. Ness with Michael M. Low

This book examines the population-environment dynamics of five medium-sized cities in Asia. From West to East, they are: Faisalabad, Pakistan; Khon Kaen, Thailand; Cebu City, The Philippines; Pusan, South Korea; and Kobe, Japan.

The aims and methods of this study are detailed in Chapters 2 and 3. Before we embark on that larger voyage, however, we must take a brief look at these five cities themselves. The physical images they provide, their positions in the larger nations of which they are a part, and their own histories provide a glimpse into the rich variety of the relations between the dynamic movements of population and the environment that they represent. We begin with five vignettes, then we lay out the plan of the book.

VIGNETTES

Physically, the cities present two fundamentally different faces to the world. Two are inland cities, approached by air or land. They are laid out in straight lines with fractalized boundaries spreading outward from an identifiable centre. The other three are seaports, approached from the sea. They sit nestled into the base of sharp mountains, giving promise of deep water for a port. These physical images tell much about the cities, but there is more detail in their histories and in the images they present from street level as well.

Faisalabad: A New City under Double Pressures

The flight from Karachi follows the great Indus River north-east toward its source in the Himalayas. Over a flat, arid plain, the broad, brown ribbon of the river winds its way, splitting apart and coming together again in a chaotic pattern of moving waters and shifting sandbars. Dams and canals mark the way, their impact evident in square patches of green and gold: orchards, and fields of grain or cotton. To the east and west, the land stretches in a dull brown expanse to the horizon. The flight stops at Multan, where the Panjand, the 'five waters' of the Jhelum, Chenab, Ravi, Beas and Sutlej Rivers join the Indus, bringing more glacial waters from Kashmir and Jammu.

The river continues. Far ahead it rises in the western Himalayas, where the snowmelt alone fills most of the great river system. The snows are sufficient. The river's catchment area in those high, glacier-filled mountains is over 100,000 square miles, greater than that of any other river in southern Asia. But the snowmelt also varies greatly with the season. Above the dam at the Kalabagh, the summer produces a run of 410,000 cubic feet per second in July, while the winter cold reduces it to a mere 27,000.

Below Multan, the river skirts Mohenjo Daro, one of the two great cities of the Indus civilization, and one of the oldest of the world's ancient civilizations. Exceptional floods of the Indus devastated the city a number of times, but as extreme as the river can be at times, it has always brought life to the land. Nor did it constitute a formidable barrier to the warrior civilizations that crossed this dry, flat land. The first migrants did, however, find it an amazing sight. The Aryans, coming on this vast water system 5000 years ago from their dry home-land, likened it to an ocean – *Sindhu* in Sanskrit. And from Sindhu came the modern name, Indus. Later conquerors crossed easily, from Darius and Alexander the Great to the Persians who brought Mogul civilization to the subcontinent. It was against these same Moghuls that Great Britain fought to conquer India, over roughly 100 years, from 1753 to 1850.

Though the arid land and the great river have known rich ancient civilizations, Faisalabad itself is a new city, established by the British only at the end of the last century. The 19th century imperialists, pursuing the dreams of more and more industrialization, dug a canal from the Chenab River into what they then considered a lifeless plain, that is, one that produced no marketable goods. They drained and watered new agricultural land and founded a market town to serve the region. It was first called Layallpur, in honour of the Lieutenant Governor of the Punjab; after independence it was named for a major benefactor, King Faisal of Saudi Arabia.

Today the city is the second largest industrial centre in Pakistan. Its cheap, new lands and abundant water attracted thousands of farmers to produce cereals and fruits. The nearby Punjab produced cotton of fine quality, and the town became a major centre of Pakistan's modern textile mills. The influx of Muslim migrants from India after the partition and independence of Pakistan in 1947 overwhelmed the city. The migration continues and the town is still struggling, with only moderate success, to keep its infrastructure development up to the burgeoning population growth.

The streets of the city show three dramatically different faces. In one there are broad avenues, shaded by great Eucalyptus trees. Here are the heavily fenced mansions of the mill owners, the 'Club', a large park, and a fine university. Bougainvillea climb walls and fences in a riot of colours. Another face is found in the town centre, a large circular road around the old clock tower, with other roads radiating outward to 'the bazaars', or central neighbourhoods. Here are shops with wares from all over the world alongside those of the local artisans; the newest electronics beside colourful textiles and party decorations. The streets are filled with cars, motorcycles and bicycles; pedestrians, mostly men, move about with serious concentration or sit leisurely in the shade of a coffee shop. Finally there are roads leading to the outer colonies, or neighbourhoods. Filled with a rich variety of traffic from great trucks and buses to camel or donkey carts, these roads are often like tank traps that force the flow of traffic to writhe in chaotic lines to avoid the deepest of the holes. There is poverty, but not the grinding poverty one often associates with Southern Asia. Here there are jobs.

If immigration and high birth rates of the past have produced pressures on the city's infrastructure, the future holds even greater pressures as the twin forces of population and environmental change converge. The influx of farmers made the region rich in produce, but this also meant continued large families with the inevitable consequence of land fragmentation. Now, many plots are too small to support a family, and the migrant stream is swelling into the city. Nor is that all. Irrigated agriculture in an arid climate inevitably increases the salinization of the land, reducing yields, killing fields and driving even more into the urban migrant stream. Seldom has a population-environment dynamic been so clear and produced such unrelenting pressure on a city.

Khon Kaen: Heart of the North-East

The flight from Bangkok to Khon Kaen first traverses the broad plain of Central Thailand. The Chao Phrya River snakes its way from the north, twisting and turning in this old, flat deltaic plain. Bangkok sits astride some of its more radical curves just a few miles up from the sea. The straight lines of the man-made canals, or *klongs*, contrast with the natural twists of the river. The low wooden houses lining the *klongs* are a Thai's dream of a 'house on the *klong*'. Near the river many *klongs* are gone, covered over to form Bangkok's wide thoroughfares, lined with new skyscrapers which now border the river as well. Bangkok has become a great hub of international organizations for South-East Asia. Some of the buildings, however, like the gleaming Sofitel Hotel, will never be occupied. They are sinking and tilting dangerously. All of Bangkok is sinking, faster than Venice, and little is being done about it, except for the few individuals who build small cement dikes around their sinking houses and place new layers on the floors.

Beyond Bangkok the plain stretches to the horizon. Two hundred miles square, the flat green land seems to go on forever. Everywhere, canals run straight lines to the curved riverbanks, marking the extensive irrigation system that supplements the heavy seasonal rains to make the plain the breadbasket of Thailand. Soils help. The rich sedimentary soils, formed over eons of river drainage, lay over a pan of clay, holding the water and making the land ideal for rice planting. With 20 percent of the country's area and 40 percent of its rice land, the central plain produces more than half of Thailand's rich rice crop. Thai rice, long grained, slow-growing and fragrant, draws a premium price on the world market, and from this central plain comes the crop that makes Thailand one of the world's leading rice exporters.

To the north-east, the land begins to rise, rolling gently to fields and forests. Beyond the hills is the high plateau of the North-East, draining farther north and east into the majestic Mekong River that forms part of Thailand's border with Laos and Cambodia. The region's 65,000 square miles hold about a third of Thailand's population, with higher densities than other regions. It is poor. Its sandy soils do not hold the water as well as those of the Central Plain. With such soils and high population densities, the North-East has provided Bangkok with a steady stream of migrants throughout this century. Most have been from the lowest rungs of the labour force, pushing pedicabs, or 'bicycle-taxis', before the motorized *tuk-tuks* took over as all cycles were driven from the roads by the great rush of traffic.

The North-East has long been closer to Laos in language and culture, but is drawn to Thailand by the great magnets of Bangkok, the Central Plain, and the Monarchy. The North-East backwater was invaded, however, during the American war in Vietnam. Airfields and army bases sprang up to support the air offensive against North Vietnam. New roads cut across its hills, plains, swamps and rivers. The global market intruded as well. Soils less suited to rice can still grow corn for the Japanese feed market, and jute to compete with Bangladesh's main export crop. Most recently, the central government has developed a strategy to promote growth in regions outside of Bangkok and the Central Plain. In each case, cities are designated as new hubs for development.

Khon Kaen is the new hub for the region's development, the heart of the North-East. Lying on the rail line from Bangkok to the river border town of Nong Khai, it was until recently a sleepy backwater in this sleepy region. Rapid economic growth, government investments, and a flood of foreign investments have awakened both the region and the city. Built around a large man-made lake and fed by three small rivers, the town is taking on a new vitality. A major regional university was established in the 1960s, and it now boasts thousands of students and a full range of scientific and academic subjects, including a major agricultural research and experiment station.

Although the town has grown rapidly – from 31,000 in 1970 to 150,000 today – the infrastructure development has kept pace. Utilities, energy, water, roads and housing are well developed. Still something of a way station for rural migrants moving from village to town to Bangkok, it has begun to attract more of those migrants for itself, and now one can even find some movement back from Bangkok to the less crowded and more placid regional capital. It helps greatly that population growth has slowed. Thailand's family planning programme has been one of the world's most successful; it has reduced the total fertility rate from traditional levels of six to seven to modern levels of two in less than a generation.

The city centre reflects the recent economic development. Gleaming new high rise hotels and office buildings share the space with sprawling shopping malls and new government buildings. Restaurants abound, from fancy eateries with nightly entertainment to the ubiquitous wheeled food stalls that serve up steaming noodles and buns. The streets are in good condition and the traffic is lively and orderly. Small Japanese cars dominate, but there are also many pickup trucks turned into public transport filled with a dozen or so Thais going about their business. Massive trucks and busses are routed away from the city centre for the most part, reducing the sense of gridlock found elsewhere. The university lies outside the city on a large, tree-filled campus; at the other end the lake is lined with restaurants and cabarets, sleepy in the fierce daytime sun, but coming alive with coloured lights and rock bands in the cool of the night.

Although Khon Kaen was hit by Thailand's economic crash of late 1997, when the value of the currency was cut in half, there is little apparent misery. Readjustment has taken hold. Thailand has emerged more open and democratic and with a better set of financial institutions. The future for Khon Kaen looks favourable. Population growth is well controlled. The urban infrastructure seems healthy and growing. Attention is now being turned toward the technical issues of air quality, and there is a favorable prospect for continued improvement in the quality of life.

Cebu City: Magellan's End

Cebu City lies near the centre of the Philippines Islands, in the Visayas, on the island of Cebu. It is most famous as the site of the death of Magellan on 27 April 1521. After bringing his small fleet out of the fierce straits that today bear his name, in November 1520, the first circumnavigator set out across what he thought to be a small pacific sea. Four months later, on 31 March 1521, he planted a flag on Massava in the Philippines archipelago and claimed the islands for the King of Spain. Shortly after, he found his way to Cebu, made a treaty with the local chief, then foolishly got embroiled in a local conflict. Attacking a much larger force of natives on the island of Mactan, Magellan was killed by the local chief, Lapulapu. It was left to his captain, d'Elcano, to bring the ships back to Spain in 1522, and thus complete the first circumnavigation of the globe.

Cebu City occupies a small rounded plain under the rugged peaks of a string of mountains, reaching 1000 metres and running almost south to north along the spine of the island of Cebu. It is open to the south, but protected from eastern and south-eastern winds by Mactan Island. On its north-east corner, a narrow strait separates the city from the Island. Through generally situated on the Pacific Ring of Fire, neither the city itself nor Cebu Island is threatened by earthquakes or active volcanoes. It is, however, threatened by Tsunami, tidal waves triggered by nearby earthquakes.

When Magellan arrived, the Philippines were beginning to feel the influence of Islam, brought by the same Arab traders that converted Indonesia and Malaysia over the previous centuries. The arrival of the Spaniards would establish a line of demarcation between Christianity and Islam in the central Philippines. Half a century after Magellan, Spaniards came again to make good their earlier claim to the islands. They soon moved their political and cultural centre to the head of the great Manila Bay some 300 miles north of Cebu, but left a fort in the city. In the following years, the Spaniards planted forts along the coasts of Cebu islands against the Moros, or the local warrior-carriers of Islam. Today Cebu City still stands between the more Catholic central and northern Philippines and the southern islands with their higher concentration of Muslims.

Under Spanish rule, Cebu City remained a quiet backwater. From the 16th through most of the 19th centuries, Manila dominated all interests. It lay on the famous 'Galleon' route that brought silver and gold from Spanish Mexico and Peru to trade for Chinese silks and porcelains and South-East Asian spices. Not until the rise of industrial society and its great appetite for raw materials did the Central Philippines awaken to the world. Then it was Chinese mestizos who brought Castillean culture to the central islands, planting sugar and tobacco, mining gold, and cutting logs from the great rain forests. Then Cebu City began to flourish as the trade and commercial centre for the Visayas.

Later in the century came the Spanish American War, when the US took the Philippines from Spain, and fought what can be called its 'first Vietnam war' against a nationalistic guerrilla force that desired independence and forced America to pay dearly for its foray into imperial venture. It was in that war that the southern Muslims, the Moros, were more seriously subdued as Captain (later General) 'blackjack' Pershing 'pacified' the southern Philippines and brought them more closely under Manila's control.

Cebu Island is made up of layers of old volcanic and newer limestone rock. It is porous and does not hold water. In addition, its steep slopes make it unsuitable for agriculture. Extensive deforestation has taken most of the cover from the slopes, leaving the island highly eroded. Short rivers run from the mountain spine into the sea, bringing some water to the city. But a long dry season from March through May turns the rivers into dry beds, exacerbating the city's water problems. Around the city the hills offer some relief from the heat and congestion, and have become suburbs for the wealthy.

Today the streets of Cebu City display a distinctively Philippines culture, alongside something more common to all of Asian cities. Streets are crowded with pedestrians, cars, motorcycles and the unique Philippines Jeepney. Built originally on the chassis of the vintage World War II Jeep, the Jeepney's body is elongated and covered to accommodate a score or so of passengers. Garish colours, vivid decorations, and names of saints mark the individuality of the owners. Jeepneys are private and chaotic, but they provide what must be one of the most efficient public transportation systems in the less developed countries of Asia. Driven completely by the market, they ply from where people are to where people wish to go, with little regulation from the central or municipal government, and what regulation there is can easily be surmounted by a judicious gift to people in control.

The city centre lies along the port, churches and the old fort. The noisy streets are choked with cars and motorcycles, but one can see the hills rising above the town, stretches of parched grey and brown, set with green gems, the well watered compounds of the rich who have taken to the hills to escape the congestion of the central city. Everywhere, in the central city and on the hillsides, houses sprout ugly water tanks, a testimony of the weak public utilities system of the city.

Cebu's major problems today lie in two directions. First, the heavy administrative centralization of all the Philippines in Manila has deprived the city of the long experience of autonomy that might have given it a better government. Second is the basic political culture of the Philippines, in which family ties predominate, thus thwarting the growth of the civic consciousness required for good government. The population continues to grow rapidly through both natural increase and in-migration. Lacking the effective family planning programmes of Thailand and Indonesia, fertility in the Philippines remains relatively high, adding problems of maternal and child health to those of rapid population growth. The weakness of government also means that environmental problems are neither well recognized nor effectively addressed by public resources and services. At the same time, the strong market orientation and entrepreneurial spirit of the city's inhabitants give promise of continued economic growth. The cost to the environment is yet to be known.

Pusan: Rapid Growth Produces Promises and Challenges

The Korean peninsula hangs like an appendix from North-Eastern China, forming a mountainous barrier between the Japan Sea on the East and the Yellow Sea on the West. At the southern tip, separated from Japan by only 150 miles, deep inlets cut into the land. A mere five-kilometre opening leads into one of these inlets, running north-west between a long peninsula and Yong Do island. The inlet narrows to just two kilometres to lead into the bay of Pusan, South Korea's second largest city and largest seaport. Hills rise sharply to 600 metres above the narrow plain of the city. Two rivers, the larger Nakdong and the smaller Suyong Bay, spill out of the mountains, bordering the city on the west and east. For much of the past 1000 years, this area has been a gateway for invading armies moving both outward and inward.

Korean society and culture are very old, with centralized kingdoms emerging more than 2000 years ago. Chinese influence has waxed and waned over the centuries, at times bringing high Buddhist and Confucian cultures. At other times, Pusan was used as a military staging ground, such as when the Mongols launched two abortive attacks on Japan in 1272 and 1281. It was also through this gateway that the Japanese invaded Korea in 1592 as part of an unsuccessful attack on China. The invasion was short lived, and for the next two hundred years, Korea remained closed and independent, though under the protection of the Manchu rulers of China.

Pusan's life as a modern port began under further Japanese intrusions at the end of the 19th century. First as part of Japan's war with China, and later as a full-scale invasion and colonial annexation, Korea was taken by Japan and fully annexed in 1910. Pusan was built by the colonial Japanese government as a major seaport and the southern terminus of a rail line the Japanese built into the north. At the end of World War II, Russian occupation in the north and US occupation in the south divided the country at the 38th parallel. Each became independent and embarked on different political-economic courses. During the Korean War, Pusan again became the bridge for devastating military activity. North Korean forces attacked and drove down to the tiny Pusan Perimeter in 1950, from which United Nations forces fought them back to the 38th parallel and beyond.

South Korea's great leap to export-oriented industrialization began with the military government in 1962. Pusan was promoted as both port and industrial centre, with major economic activities located along the narrow Pusan-Seoul corridor. Before the Korean War, Pusan had grown slowly to about 500,000. Since then it has grown rapidly to 3.8 million, where it is currently stabilized. The economic development of both Pusan and all South Korea has been extremely rapid since 1962.

Development has brought Pusan both benefits and costs. A strong central government in Seoul provided effective leadership in pursuing economic and social development. Education was advanced greatly, producing a skilled labour force. Health and family planning were promoted, and fertility fell from traditional to modern controlled levels in less than a generation. Urban infrastructure and housing progressed, making Pusan citizens well fed and well housed. Environmental concerns gained importance as early as the 1970s, when Pusan was given a large green belt on its perimeter, which now makes up just over half of the city's area. The rivers provide sufficient water, but the quality has deteriorated. Here Pusan faces a not uncommon 'downstream' problem. At the mouth of the Nakdong River, Pusan receives the polluting discharges of industrial towns upriver, especially of the major industrial city of Taegu. This is clearly a problem Pusan cannot solve alone. Although the river water is heavily polluted, successful water treatment has precluded the rise of water-borne diseases. Air quality has also suffered with the growth of both industry and vehicular traffic. But here as well, investments in clean air have been undertaken; levels of sulphur dioxide and suspended particulate matter have declined in the past decade, though levels of nitrogen oxides have increased slightly.

Visually, Pusan is an impressive sight. From the Japan Sea, the approach to Pusan leads into a narrow inlet, with rich green and rocky hillsides rising close at hand. Pusan appears first as a series of great white slabs of concrete rising out of the green hillsides. Apartment buildings, with gigantic letters – each three stories high – painted on their sides, speak of regimented humanity densely packed into small, sterile spaces. At the dockside, however, the sterility gives way to a vast sprawling chaos of buildings, tall and squat, new and old, crammed together and overrun with a swirl of bright human activity.

Roads run out of the port; superhighways six lanes deep, with gridlocked traffic outrun by pedestrians and bicycles. A light changes and the grid moves, slowly at first, then with greater speed, dashing through a bottleneck for a few seconds before the light changes and the gridlock reappears.

The people are as lively and diverse as the buildings and the traffic. Streets are ever crowded: women holding hands, couples kissing, mothers coddling their children, vendors ladling out steaming dishes, performers juggling or singing, and corner speeches all add to the movement and cacophony; here is the noise and breath of life. Night brings neither quiet nor rest. After dusk the city comes alight with neon signs and billboard lights, and the streets are still packed with a population that seems never to sleep. Pusan is a city of bursting energy, always on the move.

Pusan's problems are now those of a city under successful development promotion. Population growth has slowed, as investments in health, education and family planning have been effective. Now new investments are needed in environmental protection. Past successes have brought a high quality of life and promise that the future will also see the effective promotion of the well being of both people and the ecosystem.

Kobe: Well-Managed Population-Environment Dynamics

Through the narrow entrance to Osaka Bay, the course lies north-east, passing Awaji Island on the left and the Wakayama peninsula with its tiny islands off Kada on the right. Just five kilometres across, this mouth accommodates thousands of ships yearly. Off to the right is Osaka; straight ahead 50 kilometres across the bay is Kobe, Japan's largest sea port, backed by the rich green of the Rokko Mountains rising to a thousand metres above the bustling city.

Running this course two hundred years ago, one would have seen only the deep green of the Rokko Mountains. Even a close inspection would have found only a few small fishing boats hugging the shores of Cape Wada. To the right, one could have seen Osaka, its port alive with Japanese junks, its low plain dominated by the sombre black stone and white walled castle, rising only a hundred metres above the city. Under the Tokugawa (1605–1868), foreigners and foreign influences were kept out, but Osaka grew to be the central market place for the country. Receiving goods from all parts of the country, it became a new hub of a new society, a middle class merchant culture that created new forms of drama, music and art, balancing the highly-restrained court society dominated by Tokyo and Kyoto.

Running this course 100 years ago, Osaka would appear much the same, with a few more large buildings rising to compete with the castle for skyline prominence. But the scene around Cape Wada would have changed dramatically. There the new port, opened to foreign ships in 1868, would be a forest of masts and smoke-belching funnels. Sail and steam from all over the world came to call, with new goods and new ideas flowing in and old Japanese goods, silk, lacquer ware, sake and rice, flowing out. Behind the bustling city, the Rokko Mountains now stood gleaming white in the sun, devoid of the forests that once anchored the soils in heavy rains. Trees had been cut for ship-building and for fuel wood, leaving barren slopes that poured water and eroded soils into the city and bay when it rained, and stood cold and harsh in the sun when it was dry. But the city grew, with people streaming in from the countryside to take up the jobs brought by trade and to create a new and vibrant city.

The same course 55 years ago, in 1945, would have given a scene of almost total destruction. Kobe had been levelled by wartime bombing that left only a few buildings standing among smoldering ashes. The population that had risen to one million before the war was down to less than 400,000. Only a few functioning ships could have been found among the wrecks in the port.

When the war ended, Kobe began to grow again. There was new work to rebuild the great port city, making it a gateway for Japanese trade that spread rapidly around the world. Since 1945, the scene has been one of almost constant construction and development. Slowly the green returned to the Rokko Mountains as they became part of the greater Seto Inland Sea National Park. Now the forested mountains are a favourite retreat for the more than one million inhabitants of the new city. The new construction took away tops of some of the Rokko Mountains, dropping the fill into the sea to create two artificial islands for container ships, industries, housing and recreation. Where the tops were taken away, new suburbs emerged with gleaming apartment buildings, shopping areas, schools and health centres, all connected to the city centre by an efficient mass transit system of subways and buses. Today these mountain tops stand as shining rectangular patches set in the lush green of the Rokko Mountains.

Recently Kobe experienced another massive destruction, this time at the hands of nature. At 5:46 a.m., 17 January 1995, the earth trembled. For a mere 20 seconds the city lifted and fell and shook sideways in an earthquake that measured 7.2 on the Richter scale. The devastation was terrible. Over 4000 people were killed, 14,000 injured and 100,000 houses destroyed or damaged. The quake burst gas lines, causing raging fires that could not be extinguished because water mains had also collapsed. Immediately after the quake, however, the city began to rebuild, and plan for better quake protection.

Once again, Kobe emerged from the ashes. Population growth has slowed and the city faces the same problem of an ageing population that plagues all of Japan. But the port activity, industries and flow of traffic have been well accommodated. Environmental quality – air, water and land use – have improved along with the development, and the city provides an exceptionally high quality of life. Population-environment dynamics have been well managed.

It is now just a short hydrofoil ride from Osaka's new Kansai International Airport to Kobe. The 'K-JET' glides quietly over the bay toward the deep green of the Rokko Mountains. Slowly, Kobe's gleaming, tall buildings come into view. The Shin Kobe Oriental Hotel rises in a slim, white column partway up the green hillside. Then the lower level of the city can be seen behind the great container cranes that ring the new artificial islands. The stately new city hall rises 30 stories from the plane near the port, higher than its surrounding buildings. There is the red tower of the port, beside it the white filigree of the new maritime museum.

The hydrofoil docks at Port Island, connecting by bus to the fully-automated Portliner, a computerized train that circles the man-made island and runs into the city centre. It stops at Sannomiya Station, the crossroads of central Kobe. The Sogo Department store rises across the pedestrian bridge, its face destroyed by the 1995 earthquake but restored within months. From the station, one can descend into Santica underground shopping mall, where shops and restaurants ply a busy trade. Running down from the station to the port is Flower Road, passing shopping centres, restaurants and a park whose quiet fountains contrast with the bustle of the city just outside. Along the seaside, the city has built a new town with hotels, restaurants and shops whose lights are reflected in the still waters of the harbour. There are only a few signs of the 1995 earthquake.

The city has recovered quickly and is filled with people and activity most of the day and night. Once more it has risen from the ashes to be a rich and bustling port, giving its citizens a high quality of life.

PLAN OF THE BOOK

A study of population-environment dynamics in these five cities raises a number of critical questions. Why *urban* population-environment dynamics? What is the meaning of population-environment dynamics, and how does one assess or measure this? Finally, why these five cities?

These questions are addressed in Chapters 2 and 3. Chapter 2 examines the longer history of urbanization, industrialization and population growth, which give our current era, the past 200 years, a distinctive position in world history. Urbanization is a fast moving, all-encompassing modern fact of life. The urban-industrial arena is now the major frontier where the human population is interacting with the global environment. There has been increasing research on the links between population and environmental change, but little or none of this has been specifically concerned with the urban arena. Hence the importance of examining urban population-environment dynamics.

Chapter 3 looks to methods and intellectual strategies. This begins with an examination of the history and work of the Asian Urban Information Center of Kobe, or AUICK. AUICK is a distinctive new organization that seeks to *understand* Asian urban conditions through research; to *disseminate* what it learns about those conditions; and to *train* Asian urban administrators in ways to deal effectively with the rising problems they confront daily. In the course of ten years of research and training, AUICK has developed long-term relations with a number of cities in Asia. The five cities included in this book have been subjects of earlier studies and surveys, and the four outside of Japan have had administrators trained in Kobe.

CAUTION: DYNAMIC MODELLING AHEAD

A good friend and a fine scholar, Georges Martine, once told me the world in divided into two camps: those who love modelling and cannot get along without it, and those who despise it and cannot bear it. I suspect there is also a much larger third group: those who have had little or no contact with modelling and have no deep feelings about it.

The discussion of modelling in Chapter 3 is primarily directed at this large third estate. Those who love modelling will need no persuasion, and for those opposed, the arguments in Chapter 3 will be far too weak to change opinions. We urge the third group, however, to pay close attention to the discussion of modelling, because it is the technology on which the five-city studies are based. It is this that allows us to examine the recent past and to use the information as a base from which to make projections (not predictions), or to envisage different scenarios for the near future. We argue that this is an especially useful technology for urban administrators, who constitute a major target of this book. They are also a major interest of AUICK, which aims to assist them in promoting higher quality of urban life.

Gayl D. Ness

Chapter 3 also describes what is meant by population-environment dynamics. A simplified model is developed in which the environment is represented in four sectors: air, water, land use and energy. These interact with three institutional sectors: production, transportation and social services. All together interact with population size and composition. The links can be specified and modelled, a process that receives attention in this chapter. Finally, the chapter describes dynamic modelling and the modelling program, STELLA, which the city research teams used to examine the period 1970 to 2020, looking both backwards and forwards.

In Part II, the five city studies are presented. In each case, local social scientists and urban administrators gathered data readily available for the city. The social scientists then analysed the data and modelled the past and future.

In Part III, the editors present an overview comparative analysis in Chapter 9. A concluding chapter examines the implications for urban planning and policy making, as well as for further research and training needs.

A map and photos

A separate section provides a map (Plate 1) locating the five cities in Asia, and photographs (Plates 2 to 15) showing views of their street life or physical environment.

Plate I Locations in Asia

Plate 2 The Chenab Canal: Faisalabad's life line

Plate 3 Faisalabad's multispeed traffic: A major problem

Plate 4 Faisalabad's donkey cart

Plate 5 Khon Kaen: Busy streets but no congestion

Plate 6 Khon Kaen: New buildings of the past

Plate 7 Khon Kaen: Boyscouts, the city's new immigrants

Plate 8 Cebu: Congested and polluted shoreline

Plate 9 Cebu: Cathedral courtyard

Plate 10 Pusan: Busy streets

Plate 11 Pusan: Korea's largest export shoe factory

Plate 12 Pusan: Busy beaches threatened by pollution

Plate 13 Kobe: Benevolent wind currents

Plate 14 Kobe: The port from Port Island

Plate 15 Kobe: Fully automated Port Liner

Chapter 2

The Long View:
Urban Population-Environment
Dynamics in Historical Perspective

Gayl D. Ness with Michael M. Low

GLOBAL POPULATION-ENVIRONMENT DYNAMICS

It is not difficult to show that our era – the past two centuries – is distinctive in world history. The recent rapid growth of the human population is especially new and dramatic. After thousands of years of very slow growth, the human population has exploded in only the last two hundred years, giving us numbers and rates of growth that are both unprecedented and unsustainable. Growth rates peaked in the period 1965 to 1970 at just over two percent per year, when the world's population stood at about 3.7 billion. Although growth rates have slowed since then (to 1.37 percent in 1999), the world's population still grows rapidly. It is estimated at 5.9 billion for 1998[1], and may reach 8.9 billion by the middle of the next century[2]. Figure 2.1 provides a dramatic illustration of this change.

This recent and rapid population growth has been closely associated with a number of dramatic environmental changes (Ness & Golay, 1997):

- Atmospheric change: a rise in heat-trapping trace gases that threaten global warming;
- Stratospheric ozone depletion that has increased the amount of ultra-violet radiation reaching the earth's surface;
- Environmental degradation, including deforestation, desertification, loss of topsoil, salinization of soils, eutrophication of water bodies, loss of wetlands, and coral reef depletion;
- Pollution of air, earth and water through toxic emissions;
- Loss of biodiversity through habitat destruction and fragmentation.

Figure 2.1
World Population, 1000–2050
(1995–2050 Median Variant Projection)

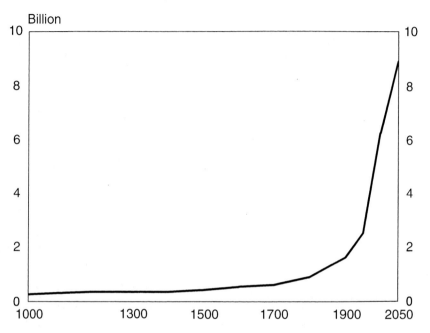

There have been radical environmental changes in the past, of course. Periods of glaciation saw the earth's temperature reduced by six degree Celsius or more for thousands of years, followed by warmer interglacial periods. In the past 500 million years there have been at least five major biotic collapses, with 15 to 50 percent of Families going extinct. Never before, however, has one species had the massive impact that the human species has today. We may be on the verge of a sixth major wave of extinctions, brought on primarily by the work of human beings (Morell, 1999).

This association of human population growth and environmental degradation has given rise to a series of doomsday scenarios. Population growth has been compared to a bomb whose explosion has been responsible for widespread environmental change (Ehrlich, 1972; 1990). Vitusec (1986) estimated that the human species now appropriates some 40 percent of the earth's total photosynthetic production, leading some ecologists to speak of humans as a devastating epidemic on the biosphere.

Figure 2.1 is deceptive, however. This explosion of the human population has not taken place in a vacuum. It has been accompanied by dramatic changes in social organization and technology, which Figure 2.2 illustrates.

Figure 2.2
World Population Growth and Socio-Technological Change, 1000–2025

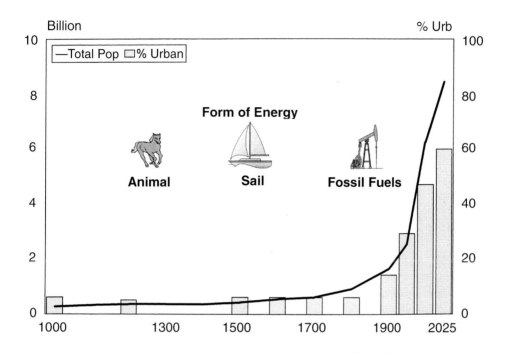

It was an energy revolution, the rise of fossil fuel technology, which permitted the emergence of a wholly new type of society: urban-industrial society. Moreover, that socio-technological change brought with it a process of economic development that increased both human productivity and human welfare. Never before have so many people lived such rich and protected lives as those brought by modern economic development.

Thus it is the new urban-industrial society, with its continuing economic development that lies behind the global environmental change, that we now find so threatening.

This social and technological revolution to urban-industrial society has its roots in previous patterns of demographic change. Population growth from the 16th century onwards, itself induced by prior changes in technology and social organization, brought pressures for even more change (Boserup, 1965; 1981; Livi-Bacci, 1992). The major lesson to be derived from these observations was stated clearly by International Union for the Conservation of Nature – The World Conservation Union (Ness & Golay, 1997):

Population growth, the rise of urban industrial society, economic development and environmental degradation … form a seamless web. Each is both a cause and effect of the other. None can be (treated or) effectively addressed in isolation from the other.

There are also two important corollaries to this observation, which were identified by the IUCN document:

- There is no single, simple and direct link between population and environmental change.
- All population-environment relationships are mediated by some form of human social organization and technology.

GLOBAL URBAN-INDUSTRIALIZATION

Since the rise of agriculture some 10,000 years ago, there have been urban centres: areas of high population density supported by large agricultural hinterlands. For the first five or more millennia of the agricultural era, cities were small and widely scattered. But they existed, and were centres of heightened human inventiveness. Public administration, legal systems, new religious movements, and new forms of technology sprang from these cities, small and scattered though they were.

By the first millennium BC, there were a number of cities with many thousands of inhabitants (Chandler & Fox, 1974; Bairoch, 1988). Thebes, Mycenae, Athens and Mohenjo-daro had between 10,000 and 40,000 residents as early as the 14th century BC. By about 500 BC, cities of over 100,000 existed: cities such as Nineveh, Rome, Athens and a number of Chinese cities for which solid figures are rare, but which are known to have been very large (Bairoch, 1988).

As impressive as some of these ancient cities were, their populations still represented but a tiny portion of the total world population. No more than four, five or six percent of the world's population may have been urban dwellers[3]. As Figure 2.2 shows, the urban proportion remained very small until the advent of the last energy revolution.

Fossil fuels increased human productivity and reduced transportation costs. Moreover, they provided sources of power that were independent of natural conditions. The early textile mills of England, on which its modern industrialization was built, were located in rural areas, along the streams and rivers that provided the needed power. Steam engines were a geographically independent source of power, whose location could be based on calculations of transportation and efficiency. A transportation network was most efficient if goods could be carried in two directions. Thus raw materials and foodstuffs flowing into urban centres were matched with finished products moving out. More people could be supported in more densely settled cities, and this in turn produces more goods by drawing on a larger and immensely more productive hinterland. By the 19th century, the major cities of the burgeoning industrial world could draw on the entire globe as their hinterlands. This globalization, of which so much is made today, is actually only a logical (though exponentially growing) extension of a process begun centuries ago.

Once the energy revolution had made its impact, urbanization became a universal and fast moving process. If world urban proportions in 1800 were not changed much from what they had been for a thousand years, the 19th century saw a radical increase. By 1900 the percentage of Europe's population living in urban areas had risen to 15 percent. It doubled in the next half century, rising to 30 percent in 1950, when the United Nations began what is now a biannual assessment of *World Population Prospects*[4]. By the year 2000, urbanization is expected to reach 47 percent, and 61 percent by 2030. The world is fast becoming an urbanized one and this trend is unlikely to change. By the end of the next century, the great majority of the world's population, perhaps 80 to 90 percent, will be living in urban areas.

In effect, the global population-environmental changes described above represent an interrelated series of transitions. Drake (1993; 1995) identifies nine transitions: fossil fuel, demographic, epidemiological (which is included in the demographic transition), urban, forestry, agricultural, educational and technological. All of these transitions tend to be described by a logistical curve. Changes began slowly, rose to very rapid rates, and finally slowed to near stability. Together they can be called the 'modernization transition', since they identify changes the world is now undergoing from traditional, rural-agrarian societies to modern, urban-industrial societies.

While it is useful to note that all of these transitions exist and are closely interrelated, the primary concern of this work is with the shifts in population and urbanization, though others will not be ignored. The population change is marked by a demographic transition, from high to low birth and death rates. The urbanization transition is marked by a movement from rural-agrarian to urban-industrial society, indicated primarily by the percent of the population living in urban areas.

TWO WAVES: POPULATION-ENVIRONMENT TRANSITIONS

Although all of these aspects of the modernization transition have marked the entire world over the past two or three centuries, they have also shown two historical waves, each of which is located in a different part of the world. The first began in the 'North Atlantic Community', referred to by the United Nations as the 'More Developed Regions' (MDR): Western Europe, with its extensions in North America and Oceania, and Japan, the only country outside of the North Atlantic community now to be included in the MDR category.

In these areas, the modernization transitions were well underway by the end of the 19th century, and for the most part near completion by 1950. But the other regions lagged behind, dividing the world into two major camps. The MDR had low birth and death rates, and more than half their people lived in urban areas. In most of the rest of the world, the 'Less Developed Regions' (LDR), birth and death rates remained high, and less than a fifth of their people lived in urban areas. Table 2.1 summarizes the major characteristics of urbanization and birth and death rates.

Table 2.1
Mortality, Fertility and Urbanization, 1950
by Major World Development Regions

Region	CDR	IMR	CBR	TFR	% Urban
World	19.8	156	37.4	5.00	29.7
More Developed	10.2	43	22.0	2.77	54.9
Less Developed	24.2	179	44.5	6.17	17.8

CDR: Crude Death Rate; IMR: Infant Mortality Rate; CBR: Crude Birth Rate; TFR: Total Fertility Rate.
Source: UN World Population Prospects (1996 Revision) and World Urbanization Prospects (1996 Revision).

Two measures are used for both death and birth rates. The crude birth and death rates are not sensitive to age structure differences. Infant mortality and total fertility rates are presented for greater sensitivity to age structures. The former is generally considered the best single measure of a population's welfare. The division of the two camps is clearly evident. Death rates were much higher in the LDRs in 1950, though they were already beginning to decline. Birth rates were also higher, and they would not begin to decline for almost two decades more.

Both population and urbanization transitions are now underway in the LDRs, but they differ in dramatic ways from the past transitions of the MDRs. These differences are especially important for issues of public policies and programmes designed to address the major problems of population-environment dynamics. To understand the implications of these differences, they must examined more closely.

Two Demographic Transitions[5]

Demographic transition is defined as the change in a population (or society) from high to low birth and death rates. It incorporates both an epidemiological and a fertility transition, which are best considered under a common rubric. This transition has been experienced by all currently industrial societies, and is on the move today in the rest of the world. But to understand more fully the distinctive character of our era, it is necessary to note the historical differences between past and present demographic transitions. Figure 2.3 displays these differences.

The Past Demographic Transition

England and Wales illustrate the past demographic transition. From about 1700 to 1750, the death rate began a long, gradual decline. This was caused by a trade revolution that made new foods from the Americas available to Europe, an agricultural revolution in Europe that increased local food production, and an industrial revolution made new goods available. There was also some global warming, as Europe and Asia came emerged from what is known as the little ice age, from 1400 to 1700. Average temperatures after 1700 appear to have risen about one degree Celsius. All were gradual changes that increased the carrying capacity of the earth and the general standard of living of the human population, with no major medical breakthroughs[6]. While death rates fell, birth rates remained high, for reasons understandable from an evolutionary biological perspective.

Given the long periods of gestation and infancy, and the small number of offspring per birth, the human species is in a relatively precarious situation. Like many other animals, it has evolved powerful mechanisms to keep fertility high

Figure 2.3
Two Demographic Transitions

Past

The Past Demographic Transition occurred more gradually from lower original levels, bringing slower rates of population growth

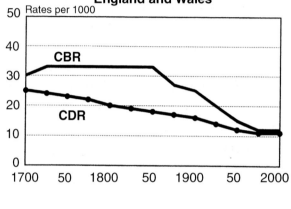

Past Demographic Transition
England and Wales

and

Present

The Past Demographic Transition occurred more rapidly, from higher original levels, bringing higher rates of population growth.

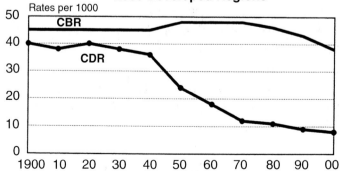

Present Demographic Transition
Less Developed Regions

and protect newborn. Such universals as kinship and the sex drive are important forces for keeping fertility high[7]. Thus, while reductions in the death rate can be easily accepted by societies, reductions in fertility required changes in the physical and social environment of the human species. Those changes came when fossil fuels transformed societies from rural-agrarian to urban-industrial, which basically changed the economic value of children from an asset to a liability. In rural-agrarian societies, children contributed to household income early and supported parents in their old age. In modern urban-industrial societies, children must be educated, thereby postponing productivity for many years, and cannot be counted upon to support aged parents. Thus, with urbanization and the changing value of children, the birth rate declined over one or two generations[8]. The intervening period saw a dramatic rise in the annual rate of population growth, to about one percent per year.

Although England and Wales are the specific examples used here, this same transition took place in every industrialized country in the world. Though the dates and rates of change varied considerably, all of Europe and Russia, North America, Australia, New Zealand and Japan went from high birth and death rates of traditional, rural-agrarian societies, to the low birth and death rates of modern, urban-industrial societies. The last of the MDRs to complete this past demographic transition was Japan, in which fertility began falling slowly in the 1920s, then dropped precipitously after the World War II (Muramatsu, 1984).

The Present Demographic Transition

The same demographic transition is occurring today throughout the world's LDRs. As Figure 2.3 shows, however, there are some dramatic differences from the past transition. First, for reasons that vary and are not all clear, birth and death rates started at higher levels than they were in the past of the MDRs. Second, when the death rate fell, it came down quickly, moving as much in one generation as it previously had in two centuries.

The cause of this new mortality decline lay in the development of new medical and public health technologies based on anti-bacterial chemicals and insecticides that cut disease vectors. These were accompanied by important social changes, such as the emergence of large-scale international organizations that could apply this technology throughout the world. The happy marriage of the new technology and new organizations was facilitated by the 'bureaucratic portability' of the new technologies (Ness & Ando, 1984). In other words, their use did not require deep changes in human behaviour. Rather, they could be applied in a standardized, bureaucratic fashion in many different settings. The consequence was a much more rapid mortality decline, and much higher rates of population growth than had been experienced in the past. Where growth rates reached one percent per year in 19th century Europe, they have recently reached over three percent per year in parts of Asia, Africa and Latin America.

Finally, in the late 1960s, the LDR birth rates began to fall. And when it did so, as it has in parts of Asia and Latin America, it very rapidly declined from traditional to modern levels in a decade or two, rather than in a generation or two. Moreover, like mortality declines, the current fertility declines are facilitated by a new medical technology: non coital-specific contraceptives transported throughout the world by new global organizations. Unlike mortality declines, however, fertility declines required a major change in public policy.

It was in large part mortality declines and the new contraceptive technology that produced the needed, and quite revolutionary, changes in public policy. Up until 1952, most governments of the world were pro-natalist, and were actively opposed to any form of birth control. In 1952, India became the first country to adopt an official policy of reducing population growth by reducing fertility within marriage. This 'anti-natalist policy revolution' (Ness & Ando, 1984) called for the formation of a national family planning programme to spread the new contraceptive technology. Since 1952, almost all LDRs have undergone a similar policy change: officially permitting or actively attempting to reduce population growth by reducing fertility within marriage. To implement these new policies, international and national family planning programmes grew rapidly after 1965.

The results have been mixed. Some countries have experienced very rapid fertility decline accompanied by a substantial improvement in the health of women and children. Other countries have made almost no progress. They continue to show high fertility and population growth, high levels of maternal and child mortality, and very low levels of education and social welfare. Overall, however, the record for the LDRs has been positive and dramatic. Fertility has fallen, and maternal and child health have improved.

The following charts display another aspect of these mixed results. They show the Total Fertility Rate, or the number of children a woman will bear in her reproductive life[9]. China and Thailand demonstrate how rapidly the fertility rate can fall, especially when a country establishes a strong and effective family

Figure 2.4
The Total Fertility Rate

Declined raidly in China and Thailand, due to effective primary education, primary health care and family planning programmes

Has declined only moderately in Latin America, and remains high in Africa. Weak government health, education and family planning programmes are main causes.

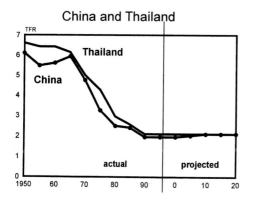

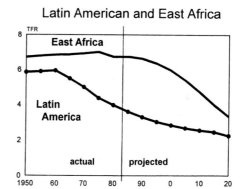

planning programme[10]. Today, all of East Asia has low fertility. South-East Asia is close behind, as is most of Latin America. Africa, especially south of the Sahara, is further behind, with high levels of fertility that are only now just beginning to decline. Weak government programmes in primary health care and family planing are the main causes of both high fertility and high mortality.

The current demographic transition is moving more rapidly than the past, involves far greater numbers, and is driven by distinctive new, bureaucratically portable, technologies, which help to control both mortality and fertility.

Two Urban Transitions

Like the demographic transition, the urban transition has come in two waves. The major differences between the two include speed, magnitude, the character of the urban-rural differentials, and the regional distribution. In addition, there

Figure 2.5
European Urban Population and Percentages, 1500–2030.

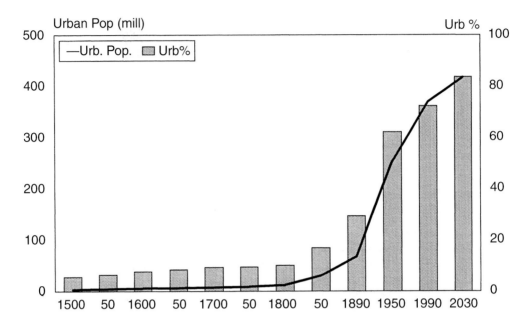

are interesting observations to be made on the issues of population density, and the relation between urbanization and democracy.

Increased Speed and Magnitude

Like the demographic transition, the urban transition was somewhat slower in the past, and involved smaller magnitudes of increase. From 1500 to 1800, the European population doubled from 61 million to 122 million (deVries, 1984). In the same period, the population in urban areas doubled twice: from 3.4 million in 1500 to 6.2 million in 1650, and to 12.2 million in 1800. The increase of about nine million urban inhabitants raised the proportion from about five to ten percent of the total European population over three centuries. The relatively slow growth of this period then gave way to a much more rapid growth of urban populations and proportions after 1800. That pattern will likely continue through into the early 21st century, by which time Europe will be almost completely urbanized, and both total and urban populations are expected to stabilize or decline. This long term European pattern is shown in Figure 2.5.

Figure 2.6
Less Developed Regions: Urban Population and Percentages, 1950–2030

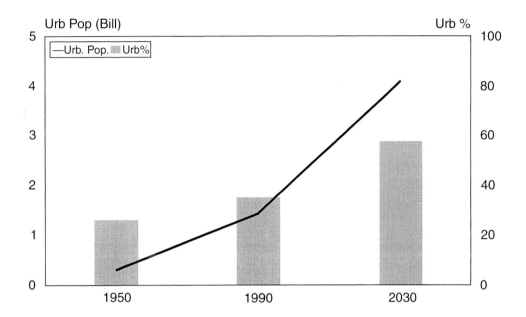

The magnitudes are also important. Europe's urban population grew from 12.2 million in 1800 to 66.9 million in 1890, adding nearly 55 million new urbanites in that century. In the next half-century, to 1950, about 190 million were added, giving a growth rate of about 4.6 percent per year. For the rest of the 20th century, i.e. 1950 to 1990, another 110 million were added, but the growth rate slowed to 1.1 percent. The projected growth of about 48 million over the next 40 years will produce a growth rate of about 0.3 percent. The urban transition is fast coming to a close in the MDRs.

The current urban transition in the LDRs is proceeding far more rapidly, with substantially larger magnitudes, and it is just beginning. Europe added 50 million urban dwellers in the 19th century, the first century of its transition, for an annual growth rate of about 4.5 percent. The LDRs will add about 1.1 billion urban dwellers in the first four decades of its major transition, for an annual growth rate of over 9 percent. In the next 40 years, they will add 2.6 billion urbanites for a growth rate of 4.6 percent per year. The rate is slowing, but the numbers are staggering. Figure 2.6 shows this massive increase. (Note that the left vertical scale in Figure 2.6 encompasses ten times the magnitude of that in

Figure 2.5. If the same scales were used in the two graphs, the European urban population numbers would scarcely be visible.)

Individual city size is also showing a remarkable change. By 1800, Peking had become the first city to surpass one million in population. In 1825, London joined Peking in the million category. By 1900, London was the largest with about 6.5 million, and the next largest 16 cities were all over one million people. In 1950, New York led the list with 12 million, London was second with 8.9 million, and 95 cities with populations more than one million were ranked behind. Today, however, the smallest of the 100 largest cities is 2.35 million (Pune, India). The 15 largest are all above ten million (Population Crisis Committee, 1990). The second urban transition is being marked by the rise 'mega-cities'.

The current urban transition is moving faster and with far greater numbers than that experienced in the past.

Urban-Rural Differentials

Urban-rural differentials – the differences in various rates between urban and rural areas – have also shown a significant change. Many measures are typically used to examine the differentials: birth and death rates, diseases and causes of death, sex ratios, literacy, access to clean water and sanitary services, political activity and others. Of greatest interest here, however, are the differences between death and birth rates, or mortality and fertility differentials. Mortality differentials have reversed from the past. Fertility differentials remain the same, though the potential for rapid reduction of the differentials has increased dramatically.

In the past urban transition, cities were far more deadly places than the rural areas from which immigrants came. Extensive individual studies show urban death rates above urban birth rates for most of the 19th century. Cities grew and were kept alive by rural immigrants, who often paid with their lives for voting with their feet for the city. Kearns (1989) shows an example of this in the mortality rates of Stockholm, and cites Omran (1982) to the effect that similar vital rates can be found for many European cities. The cities of the past transition witnessed first hand the epidemiological transition. Populations moved from high and erratic death rates, caused primarily by infectious diseases, to low and stable death rates, caused by degenerative diseases.

The same new bureaucratically portable technology that brought the rapid mortality decline in the current demographic transition is reversing the urban-rural differences seen in the past. New technology has made people in modern cities healthier than those in the rural hinterlands. The modern decline of mortality in the LDRs came first and more rapidly in urban areas, and only later, more slowly, and in some cases not at all, to rural areas. Indeed, one of the sensitive measures of overall national economic and social development is the degree to which urban rural mortality differences are reduced in the developing regions (UNDP, 1996).

Fertility differentials in the LDRs today, on the other hand, are similar in the less developed regions today to what they were in the earlier demographic transition. Fertility declines in the past and present began in urban areas, then moved to rural areas. There is, however, an important difference in the current declines, which are closely tied to the new 'bureaucratically portable' fertility control technology. With this technology, urban-rural fertility differentials can be reduced very quickly, if a local programme adapts the new technology to the distinctive circumstances of the country[11]. This implies, among other things, that the effectiveness of family planning programmes can be assessed in part by the extent to which they reduce the urban-rural gap in contraceptive use and fertility (Ness & Golay, 1997b, p. 114). South Korea and Taiwan, for example, had two of the earliest and most successful national family programmes. In both cases, the urban-rural difference in contraceptive use and fertility decline was almost completely eliminated. Even relatively poor and predominantly rural nations are able to reduce the differentials. Sri Lanka and Thailand, for example, have had effective family planning programmes, and their urban-rural differentials in contraceptive use and fertility were reduced to zero over a span of less than two decades.

In the current urban transition, urban-rural mortality differentials have been reversed from the past; fertility differentials remains the same, but can be reduced very quickly.

Regional Shifts and Differences

Another difference between the past and present urban transitions lies in their regional distribution. For much of the world's history, Asia, the Middle East and North Africa contained most of the major urban centres, few and scattered though they were. Of the world's 25 largest cities, 13 were in Asia and nine in the Middle East-North Africa until 1800. By 1900, the dominance had shifted to Europe. Figure 2.7 traces the regional movement of the world's 25 largest cities from 1100 to 1950 (Chandler & Fox, 1974).

For this analysis, countries from Persia through Turkey and Egypt to Morocco are included in the Middle East-North African (MENA) category. The Asian urban concentrations occurred primarily in China and India, then later in Japan and Korea as well. In 1100, when Europe had only one of the world's largest cities, Palermo, even Angkor in Cambodia, were included in the top 25. Paris joined the list as number 18 by 1200. By 1300, Milan, Genoa and Venice were added, and Palermo fell off the list. London did not join until 1600. American cities did not appear on the list until 1900, when New York, Chicago, Philadelphia and Boston appeared (and are included with Europe in Figure 2.7). By 1950, eight of the largest cities were in Europe and six in the US. But as a preview of what was yet to come, 1950 also saw the entry of four Latin American cities to the list (Buenos Aires, Mexico City, Rio de Janeiro, and Sao Paulo). There was only one on the list (Buenos Aires) in 1900.

Figure 2.7
Regional Distribution of the World's 25 Largest Cities, 1100–1950

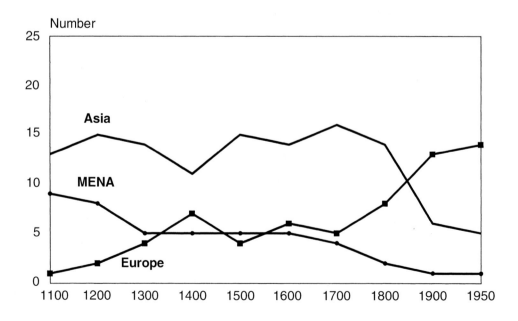

If the first transition wave saw a shift in the world's centre of urbanization from Asia to Europe, we are currently witnessing a globalization of the mega-city phenomenon. If the 100 largest cities today are examined, no continent is without a representative. Asia has regained its earlier dominance, but the distribution of mega-cities is clearly a global one, as Table 2.2 shows.

Table 2.2
Regional Distribution of the World's 100 Largest Cities, 1990

Region	Number	Region	Number
Asia	34	N. America	16
East	14	Latin America	12
South	12	MENA	8
South-East	8	Africa (Sub-Saharan)	2
Europe	21	Australia	2

Source: Population Crisis Committee, 1990

Since 1950, the pace of urbanization has increased throughout the world, but there remain important regional differences. Asia is regaining its lead in urban population numbers. The basic data for this observation are shown in Table 2.3.

Table 2.3
Regional Trends in Urban Populations and Percentages, 1950–2030

Region	1950		2000		2030	
	N (mill)	%	N (mill)	%	N (mill)	%
World	750	30	2890	47	5117	61
MDR	446	55	903	76	1015	84
LDR	304	18	1986	41	4102	57
Europe	287	52	546	75	572	83
N. America	110	64	238	77	316	84
L. America	69	41	386	75	599	83
Africa	32	15	379	38	864	54
Asia	244	18	1387	38	2736	55

Source: UN 1996b

Latin America and the Caribbean have caught up with the industrialized world, with roughly three-quarters of their populations living in urban areas. Africa and Asia are proceeding at the same pace, moving from less than 20 percent urban in 1950 to 38 percent today, and are projected to reach 55 percent by 2030. But in numbers of urban dwellers, Asia dwarfs the other regions. Even with just 38 percent of its population urbanized in 2000, it has almost half of the world total urban population. By 2030, when Asian urbanization is expected to reach 55 percent, it will have about 54 percent of the world's total urban population. Asia's sheer size gives it a position of major importance in the issues of urban population-environment dynamics, but there is another weighty aspect of Asia's distinctiveness as well: its high population density.

Urbanization and National Population Density

Data on average national population density divide the world into two major categories: high and low. Today Asia and Europe (Western & Southern) both have average population densities just over 100 persons per square kilometre. Densities are much lower in Latin America (23), North America (14) and Africa (24). Historically, clusters of urban centres have been found in high-density regions. Densely-settled hinterlands have been important bases of support for their cities.

But though Asia and Europe share historical urban clusters and high densities, they show an important difference. The urbanization of Western and Southern Europe has been supported by extensive trading networks, where urban centres used a large part of the world as supportive hinterland. The urban centres of Asia have been far less trading posts than major administrative centres for their immediate hinterlands. It was primarily these hinterlands, densely settled and highly productive, that supported their cities.

This remains true today, even in the rapidly expanding global market place, which is drawing more and more of the world into a single trading network. Moreover, the rising urban centres in Latin America and Africa appear in part to be outposts of the North Atlantic industrial-capitalist trading system. Asian urbanization is still supported by a more immediate, densely-settled and productive hinterland. Consider some extreme cases. In Western Europe, the 15 million people of the Netherlands are the most densely settled, with some 379 persons per square kilometre in 1995 (UN, 1996). They are, however, supported by the entire world, on which they leave their environmental footprint.

In Asia, there are population densities of over 700 persons per square kilometre for the 118 million people in Bangladesh and 160 million in Java. While their urban centres are also centres of worldwide trade, they are far more completely supported by their own hinterlands. While less extreme, the same pattern is found throughout Asia, where population densities are higher than they are in Europe.

Urbanization in the MDRs is supported much more by a worldwide trading system. Asian urbanization is supported by a densely settled, highly productive, immediate hinterland. MDR cities leave their environmental footprint on the entire world; the Asian urban footprint is more local.

Urbanization and Democracy

There is another product of urbanization that is as powerful, subtler and, at least historically, region-specific. Western urban systems created a new set of interests that both supported and pressed upon central governments, paving the way for a distinctive form of liberal democracy. One of the earliest and most important of this interest mobilization is found in Portugal, Europe's oldest nation-state.

In 1143, the first meeting of the Portuguese Cortes took place in Lamego, a well-fortified hill town in the upper Douro Valley. At this meeting, the Cortes included representatives of the Nobility, the Clergy and the towns, signalling what was to be an important alliance throughout Portuguese, and Western, history. This alliance between crown, church and urban merchant class served Portugal well in supporting the 'great explorations' from 1415 to 1521[12], by which Portugal and Spain discovered the seas and tied the world together into a single ecosystem. Unlike China, in which the merchant class was despised and restricted by the Emperor and the Bureaucracy, the European merchant class became an important ally in the expansion.

In Northern Europe, a similar alliance emerged. The urban movement produced a distinctive public, a variably organized group of people who came to have a collective opinion, which produced some pressure on government. This was seen especially in England and France, two of the leading new urban-industrial societies of the 18th century (Stokes, 1959; Roche, 1999). In the 18th and 19th centuries, new theories of government were proposed, in which people were transformed from subjects to citizens, and the government from officials to civil servants.

Eric Stokes (1959) has defined this as the 'transformation of political legitimacy from the divine right of kings to the divine right of the masses'. It can be seen in the gradual extension of the franchise on the one side, the rise of a class of bureaucratic functionaries who were transformed into servants of the civic body on the other, and between them the rise of the idea of 'civil rights'. It was a long and bitter struggle, and it did not move in perfect lock step in all countries. But in the end, urban society meant the emergence of a public opinion, a force that influenced government from below. In time, governments in Europe learned that it was cheaper and more practical to try to influence than to squelch that opinion. That is a lesson many governments of the less developed regions have yet to learn. Rising urban populations in the LDRs generate a new and powerful voice. Some governments listen, progress and survive. Others try to repress that opinion, at an increasing cost to both efficiency and security.

That raises another delicate issue. Was European urbanization in some way unique? Did European urbanization follow a different trajectory, and define a different future, from that experienced in the rest of the world? More precisely, was it different from that in Asia, the only other region in which from early times, urbanization was a dominant phenomenon of cultural and political life?

Max Weber answers in the affirmative: Western urbanization was different (Weber, 1958). It was different in that European cities constituted distinct geographic and social communities. China, he argued, was composed of people fundamentally committed to the place of their ancestors. Cities were places of sojourn for most of the population. They were places of local administration strongly directed by the central government (Bairoch, 1988). They never developed a civic community that could act collectively on its own behalf, even against the central government. That was, however, something European cities developed par excellence, especially after the tenth century and the general rise of trade and cities throughout Western Europe (Pirenne, 1952). European cities were chartered by a Lord or Bishop, and given rights of self-government. With the expansion of European trade after the tenth century, cities grew up rapidly on major rivers and points of break-in-cargo. These places were local points with distinctive political interest and initiative, often growing to be centres that could contest rights and initiatives with higher powers.

There was also a geographic or ecological source of this emerging independent urban community. The European landmass is highly fractionated. It is cut by major rivers running into the Baltic Sea, the North Sea, the English Channel or

La Manche, the Atlantic, and the Mediterranean. This fractionated landmass allowed and encouraged the emergence of local centres of power, especially after the growth of trade in the tenth century. There were other social organizational roots as well, but European geography was dramatically different from the highly centralized river systems of Egypt or China that gave rise to highly centralized and autocratic political systems[13].

The roots of the European urban community can be traced back to early Christianity, which Weber labelled a 'non-tribal' religion. People are not 'born' Christians. To become Christians and be accepted into the Christian community, they must accept Christ as the savior and be baptized. This fundamental idea had important implications for the newly emerging cities of feudal Europe, where urban dwellers came to be a distinctive community, into which they entered voluntarily. Urban community members held rights and obligations much like those of citizenship itself. The city even offered a refuge from the constraining rules of landed lords. This gained general expression in the German phrase, *stadt luft macht frei* (The air of the city makes one free). For example, serfs were legally tied to the land and forbidden to emigrate, but a serf who ran away and lived in a city for a year and a day became a free man. Thus the city generated a local community, a small 'citizenry' that could be mobilized to protect itself. And protect itself it did in the protracted struggle between the emerging bourgeoisie and the feudal lords. It was this struggle between rising urban interests and the landed interests of the 'ancien regime' that provided an important basis for the rise of parliamentary democracies in Europe.

Many scholars, including Karl Marx, have seen the power of the emerging urban communities as the force that destroyed Europe's feudal structure. Thus the rise of the new urban-industrial society in the 18th to 19th centuries, with its bourgeois democratic forms of government, has roots that go back seven or eight centuries. Those roots lie in the growth of cities, a long term, pervasive and powerful urban transition.

The democratic forms of government in the new wave of urbanization are far less evident. To be sure, many new nations that gained independence after 1945 professed to be democratic, claiming legitimacy on the Western notion of the consent of the governed. Since this was the legitimizing formula for the ruling metropolitan powers, it was the argument to which they were most vulnerable. Once independent, however, the democratic aspects of governance quickly fell to more autocratic forms, even, or especially, in urban areas. Rights of association, free press, and free speech, once used effectively by nationalist leaders to wrest power from the Western metropolitan rulers, have often been abridged as governments seek to control flows of information and people. There is, however, a crude form of public that is still evident in urban areas of the LDRs. That public recently toppled President Suharto from power in Indonesia. In addition, new information technologies, such as the fax and internet, are fast providing the tools by which new publics can be mobilized even against powerful central governments[14]. It remains to be seen where the political processes will flow in the future. No doubt they will be, as in the past, varied.

IMPLICATIONS

Global population-environment dynamics are driven by a variety of conditions that can be drawn together under the rubric of the emerging urban-industrial society. This emergence has come in two historical waves that are distinguished by significant differences. The earlier transition in Europe and its extension in North America were relatively slow, and involved moderate numbers of people. The current transitions, taking place in Africa, Asia and Latin America, are moving much more rapidly and involve numbers of people many times those of the past.

Both waves of transition involved major technological breakthroughs. First, it was the fossil fuel revolution, followed quickly by electrical, electronic and nuclear revolutions in energy technology. The technological breakthroughs of the second transition were of a different nature. One of the most important was the development of a revolutionary new set of mortality and fertility controlling technologies. Along with these there have been dramatic extensions in organizational development. Large-scale bureaucratic organizations have come to dominate the modern world. They have earlier examples in all ancient civilizations; the roots of modern development can be traced as far back as 12th century Europe. But it was only in the 19th century that their position in the world became truly dominant.

Since 1950, that dominance has become overwhelming. This has been especially important in national and international governments, as well as in business and non-governmental organizations (NGOs). It was these groups that helped spread the new mortality and fertility controlling technologies around the world so rapidly. Along with this spread came a series of changes in public policy, in which national and international governments adopted policies that took on increasingly greater responsibilities for directing the course of social and economic as well as political events. In addition, these policies increasingly identified economic development and human welfare as major goals of government.

This places the current and future course of population-environment dynamics in a distinctive position. The central role of urban centres – directing greater attention to urban planning as an integral part of promoting sustainable development – is clear[15]. New technologies and new organizations also give governments more capacity to address population-environment dynamics. The capacity to reduce mortality and fertility, and thus effectively manage problems of population growth, is clearly evident. There is also an increased technological capacity to control environmental degradation through such actions as building more efficient and less polluting energy sources and filtering noxious emissions from industrial production. In effect, we now have greater technological and organizational capacities to address population-environment linkages in such a way as to promote the welfare of both people and ecosystems.

The question remains of what is to be done to more effectively manage modern population-environment dynamics. To address that question, it is necessary to turn from a view of history to a view of action.

Notes

1. *United Nations, World Population Prospects*, 1998 Revision.
2. This new estimate is down slightly from the 1996 estimate of 9.4 billion for the year 2050, using the median variant projection. Both the MDRs and LDRs show this reduction in projected numbers.
3. This was the world average. There were countries or regions with urban proportions as high as ten or 15 percent, but the world average was quite low (Bairoch, 1988).
4. *United Nations World Population Prospects*. The latest available revision is from 1998, providing data for the period 1950–2050. There is also a *World Urbanization Prospects*, the latest version of which is 1996. This provides data for the period 1950–2030.
5. This presentation is based upon similar analyses found in Ness, 1993; 1997 and 1997b.
6. This has been recognized for some time; see, for example, McKeown & Browne, 1955.
7. The power of sex drive is well known. It has often been the cause of great scandal; most communities and religions attempt to control it; and it has been an enduring source of drama and comedy throughout human history. Without that drive, however, it is not likely that the human species would have survived.
8. There is much discussion and debate on the causes of this transition, but there is general agreement that children were more an asset in traditional, rural-agrarian society, and are more a liability in modern, urban industrial society. As the economic value of children declined, people reduced their fertility (Coale & Watkins, 1986; Caldwell, 1976).
9. More specifically, the TFR is the sum of all age-specific fertility rates, or a cross-section snapshot of the fertility of women of all ages today.

10. China's programme is noted for its draconian measures, which includes forced abortions. This is not uncharacteristic of a highly totalitarian regime. But even that regime could not have achieved this rapid fertility decline without having previously established a strong and effective primary health care programme that dramatically reduced infant mortality in the 1950s. Thailand's family planning programme is well known for its development of an effective distribution system to the rural areas, with no trace of any form of coercion.

11. International government agencies and NGOs have often tried to create and manage fertility limitation programmes in less developed regions. The result has usually been failure. Programmes are effective when local leaders build them to suit the political, cultural and economic realities of the country.

12. The dates are those of the Portuguese successful attack in Ceuta in Morocco, in 1415, to the Spanish circumnavigation of the globe under Magellan and Del Canto, in 1522.

13. Karl Witfogel, in his classic *Oriental Despotism,* proposed this thesis of the close relation between major river systems and highly centralized political systems. His highly ideological anti-Marxist orientation unfortunately generated much accurate criticism, but the basic elements of the theory have stood the test of time. See, for example, Worster (1986), *Rivers of Empire.*

14. At this time Mr Stanley Sesser, former staff writer for the New Yorker and now Senior Fellow of the University of California, Berkeley, Human Rights Center, is studying the impact of the internet on authoritarian governments.

15. See for example the UN Center for Human Habitat (UNCHS) 1996 publication, *An Urbanizing World,* and David Drakakis-Smith (1995 and 1996) for reviews of this process.

Chapter 3

The Methodological View: Addressing Asian Urban Population-Environment Dynamics

Gayl D. Ness with Michael M. Low

INTRODUCTION

In the mid-1960s, the air above Pittsburgh was visible and noxious; the river was so laden with chemicals that it caught fire. Today, the air is clear and can be breathed without serious threat to health. The river, while not drinkable, is clear and sweet smelling, and it washes banks that are alive with green parks and restaurants.

Mexico City and Santiago are set in lovely valleys surrounded by majestic peaks. But they are also therefore bereft of air currents that could carry away pollution. The rising numbers of people and automobiles have made the air heavily polluted. In Mexico City, the drawing of underground water for urban use is undermining the city's base: it is sinking.

Singapore and Curitiba have more than doubled their populations in the past generation. Nonetheless, they have become models of cleanliness, providing their citizens with schools; jobs, needed to develop their individual talents; and clean air, parks and gardens to keep their spirits alive.

Kobe's population grew from almost nothing in 1850 to one million people a century later. By 1900 the mountains around the city had been cleared of trees, cut for timber and fuel wood. They stood gleaming white in the sun, and were heavily eroded during the rains. Today, the mountains are green: the rich forest cover provides air for the city and pleasant walks for the inhabitants. From a small fishing village, the city has grown into Japan's largest seaport. The movement of goods and vehicles has grown exponentially, especially in the past four decades. Despite the growth of population and enterprise, however, traffic moves smoothly, and Kobe's citizens enjoy a high quality of life.

Karachi is a well laid-out city on the shores of the Arabian Sea, just north-west of the Indus delta. Despite its excellent design, public services have been overwhelmed, its weak government unable to confront the city's rapid population growth, which stems both from natural increase and in-migration. Even in wealthy neighbourhoods with multi-million dollar homes of the rich from the oil states, home-owners must install deep cisterns and contract with private companies to deliver the water that public services cannot supply. In one of the world's largest slums, Orangi, the local population has organized itself to provide the schools, health centres, police and public services that the government is incapable of delivering.

Faisalabad is a new city, founded on the Indus plain near Lahore a century ago. Canals dug from the nearby Chenab River water the empty plain, producing a rich agricultural hinterland for the city. This area has become a bustling industrial town, famous for the export of its high-quality textiles. Irrigated agriculture in this arid climate, however, is running into problems. Soils are losing productivity through salinization, and the city is threatened with a massive influx of people from the dying agricultural outskirts. The question of how the city will deal with a doubling or more in size in the next 25 years is a serious one.

These brief examples could be multiplied a hundred times, and increased in complexity even more, yet they represent common experiences of urban population-environment dynamics that were addressed in different ways. In Pittsburgh, Singapore, Curitiba and Kobe, the governments have recognized growing problems, developed an understanding of their causes, consequences and possible future outcomes, and created policies and programmes to protect both their populations and environments. In Mexico City, Karachi, and Faisalabad, there has been some recognition of problems, but little understanding of them and even less ability to act to avert their growth.

A critical difference between these two groups of cities appears to be the capacity to *recognize* problems, *understand* them by discovering their causes and consequences, and then *act on* that understanding. In this chapter we focus on methods of recognizing and understanding population and environmental problems. This requires developing a model of these dynamic interactions and some ways to assess both the strength and the direction of relationships. In order to attempt to see where forces are taking a city in the near future, we adopt a dynamic modelling technique, based on the STELLA program, which four of the five cities used in their analyses, and which we shall see in Chapters 4 through 8.

While these chapters will provide details on our approach to the issues of recognition and understanding population-environment dynamics, it does not address the capacity to act. In Part III, we attempt to address that problem.

RECOGNITION AND UNDERSTANDING

Until it was known that lead in paint, water pipes and gasoline could be severely detrimental to the health of children, there was no reason or pressure to exclude lead from these and other products. Until we knew that chlorofluorocarbons (CFCs) destroyed the stratospheric ozone layer, there was neither reason nor pressure to curb their production and use.

Technological history is awash with examples of developments that at first appeared highly beneficial to humans and their environments, but were only later found to have debilitating impacts. Benefits of technological change are often easily perceived, but problems appear with time and often require specialized capacities for monitoring and observation. Automobiles and CFCs represent only two of the more dramatic examples.

When automobiles were introduced around the turn of the century they were heralded as an efficient, safe and clean form of transportation. Even today, it requires only a cursory backward glance for that judgement to be reaffirmed. Think, for example, of what life would be like if modern cities had the same ratio of horses to population as existed around the turn of the century. Without the automobile, the rivers of our cities would be filled with almost pure horse urine, the suburbs would be piled high with horse manure and the flies would be thick enough to blot out the sun. Clearly, the automobile cleaned the environment, especially in urban areas.

But only when the automobile had taken over cities were its own problems recognized. Its noxious fumes pose a threat to life and health, and its exponential growth threatens to produce gridlock, making urban transportation less, rather than more, efficient. Some aspects of these car-induced problems could be recognized readily on the streets; but others, like the impact of leaded gasoline or suspended particulate mater on human health, required detailed and specialized scientific research.

CFCs are another excellent example. Discovered in the 1930s, they were the urban technologist's dream come true. Colourless, odourless and non-corrosive, CFCs were superb insulants and refrigerants. Without them, the development of cheap and efficient air conditioning and refrigeration would have been impossible. And without those developments, cities in the desert or the tropics as we know them now would have been impossible. The best thing about the gases, it was thought, was they *appeared* simply to go away, harming nothing. Only in the early 1970s did theoretical research establish the possibility that CFCs destroy the stratospheric ozone layer, which protects the earth's surface from harmful ultraviolet radiation. And it was not until more than a decade later that empirical research established what these theories proposed: CFCs are indeed destroying stratospheric ozone.

These two examples illustrate different historical trajectories in processes of recognition and understanding. With the automobile, many of its problems of congestion and emissions were readily apparent, recognizable by people on the street. It required specific scientific research, however, to identify health problems. Even more research was needed to understand both how emissions produced health problems, and how they could be controlled. With CFCs, the understanding of potential stratospheric ozone destruction came first, and that only from *theoretical* developments in atmospheric physics and chemistry, which *suggested* that there might be a problem. Only a decade after these suggestions did empirical research and specialized measurement demonstrate the impact of CFCs on the upper ozone layer.

Recognition and understanding of problems come from many different sources. The growing body of scientific studies in any field provides one base. Thus, in searching for a method or strategy to address a problem, such as urban population-environment dynamics, one typically goes to 'the literature', or research that has been done. For the five city studies included in Part II of this book, there is another distinctive source of information to be tapped: the decade of studies conducted by the Asian Urban Information Center of Kobe (AUICK). We consider this an especially important source of information, since AUICK has attempted to listen to urban administrators and to hear from them both what their problems are, and how they are attempting to address those problems.

AUICK[1]

History

AUICK was formally established in April 1989 in a letter of agreement between the City of Kobe and the United Nations Population Fund (UNFPA). It was designed to do three interrelated things:

- Carry out studies of urban problems in Asia
- Disseminate the results of these studies, especially to urban administrators throughout Asia
- Use the results of these studies to provide training for Asian urban administrators, so that they can be more effective in addressing their own problems

Two significant developments led to the formation of AUICK; both developments had a strong influence on its character and work. The first was a comparative study of Singapore and Kobe, *Population Redistribution in Planned Port Cities* (NUPRI, 1986). This study demonstrated the utility of comparative urban research for identifying major problems of urban growth and population movements, and designing effective strategies for addressing these problems.

The second was the United Nations Conference on Medium-Sized Cities held in Kobe in 1987. This conference was distinctive in that its participants were the urban administrators – mayors and city managers – who led medium-sized cities in Asia. These people were what AUICK refers to as the front line managers of modern urban development. The managers saw the value of discussions from which they could learn from one another how best to address their own problems. They subsequently passed a resolution calling for the creation of some form of network or centre that could bring together and disseminate information on Asian urban problems. That resolution led to the formation of AUICK a year and a half later.

From the conference three major emphases in AUICK's work were outlined. First, it would pay particular attention to medium-sized cities, which were seen to be important for overall healthy urban growth, but were much neglected since the international community tended to turn its attention to the great megacities emerging in this period. Second, it would focus on urban administrators. As the AUICK review stated:

One of the enduring characteristics of AUICK has been its focus on urban administrators as what have often been called the front line managers of the urban scene. AUICK has been concerned with listening to what the urban administrators have to say about their problems, the strategies and tactics they develop to address those problems, and the kinds of assistance they need to do a better job of addressing those problems. It has also been concerned with developing effective training programs for urban administrators throughout Asia.

Third, AUICK would pay close attention to the role that population dynamics play in urban growth and the character of urban life.

AUICK's schedule of urban studies called for a bi-annual survey of urban administrators[2]. These studies have been designed to allow urban administrators to identify major problems, indicate how these problems are being addressed, and the kinds of assistance they needed to address their problems more effectively. To date, there have been five rounds of surveys. Each survey was carried out by means of mailed, self-administered questionnaires completed by 100 to 200 administrators from nine countries, ranging from Pakistan to Japan, and from China to Indonesia.

In the years when a survey was not being done, AUICK carried out in-depth studies of a smaller number of cities. Topics were selected to gain more detailed information of issues by the urban administrators identified in the broader surveys. There have now been four rounds of in-depth studies. The five city studies reported in this book constitute the fourth round of in-depth studies on the topic of urban population-environment dynamics.

In both surveys and in-depth studies, AUICK obtains the assistance of local social scientists and urban administrators. The surveys, for example, pass through a local 'access person', usually a university-based social scientist, who arranges translations as needed, distributes the questionnaires, and receives the returns to pass on to AUICK for analysis. For the in-depth studies teams are organized in the cities to be studied. These include a local social scientist and an urban administrator.

One strategic aim in all of these studies is to generate closer cooperation between social scientists and urban administrators. This is designed to bring a more powerful scientific base to urban planning and a more practical orientation to social sciences. For the five city studies reported in Part II of this book, teams of local social scientists and urban administrators were used. These local 'study directors' met to devise an overall research design, so that the individual studies could provide for useful comparisons across cities. In addition, the meeting allowed for tailoring the general research design to the distinctive conditions of each city.

The continued activity of AUICK represents a distinct success in a strategic aim of the UNFPA. During the 1980s, UNFPA convened four international conferences to deal with what was seen as an important emerging population issue: urbanization and its relationship to population dynamics. Each conference was to be followed by the creation of an institution to continue to study urban issues. Only in Kobe was this strategy successful. Some conferences were followed by the creation of centres that did not last for more than a year or two; in other cases there was no follow-up activity at all. In large part, the reason for the Kobe success lies in the visionary leadership of the Kobe City government officials, especially Mayor Miyazaki, and the long-term tenure of Kobe City government officers. Later studies reinforced the view that long tenure and low turnover rates for city administrators provide certain distinct advantages for urban administration.

Lessons Learned

The lessons learned from a decade of surveys and in-depth studies can be summarized under three main headings: urban administration, urban conditions and methodological issues. Much could be said on each issue, but here it is useful to cover a broader range of lessons by summarizing them briefly.

Urban Administration

Good information can be obtained from administrators. These front line managers, as AUICK has come to call them, deserve to be heard. Data were available to test the validity of administrators' responses in a number of cases. These generally showed close correspondence between responses and objective conditions. If objective data showed high traffic volume, overcrowded schools or heavy air pollution, the respondents tended to rate these problems as serious. On the other hand, where fertility and death rates had declined dramatically, the administrators reported that health and high fertility were not serious problems.

Stable administrative staffing, with personnel committing long periods of time or even a lifetime to one city, makes for more effective problem solving. Low turnover, especially among top administrators, increases both the knowledge and commitment of urban administrators, leading to better urban leadership.

Effective urban planning requires control over a relatively large area, over which consolidated authority can be exercised. Cross-cutting authorities in one territory were found to impede effective urban administration. This was an unanticipated finding, but it arose clearly. In Singapore and Kobe, urban boundaries were expanded to provide a larger area for coordinated planning. In both cases this increase in administrative area was a major contributor to effective urban planning. The reverse has also been observed; many problems of weak urban administration in Pakistan were traced directly to cross-cutting authorities in a single urban area.

Combining population dynamics *and* development activities works most effectively to raise the quality of life. Too often, programmes of urban development fail to take note of the movements or composition of the city's population. On the other hand, urban population programmes often fail to take account of other dynamics, such as production and consumption patterns or the environmental impacts. AUICK's experience shows that where administrators were able to link population planning to overall development planning, they could play a critical role in improving the quality of life and protecting the urban environment.

Devolution of authority makes sense. Giving local administrators greater authority over resources and greater initiative in decision making makes for more effective local problem solving. AUICK's 1992 study of population and port development in five countries, for example, found that Kobe's traffic flowed far more efficiently than did that of Pusan. One apparent reason was that Kobe has greater local authority for urban planning than does Pusan, where the central government in Seoul assumes far greater authority. The importance of devolution was one of the unexpected findings, which was confirmed in a partial failure in the first round of surveys.

In the first round, administrators were asked about the quantity and quality of their urban personnel, and about their direct control over financial resources for the city. In the LDRs, the results were quite striking. Administrators tended to rate the quality of their personnel quite high, but they also saw a serious problem in their lack of control over resources. In effect, administrators were saying that they had the personnel needed to achieve desired results, and would like more control over the resources needed to proceed. This reflects a common problem of central control and the need to devolve resources, authority and responsibility, which emerged in the 1987 Medium-Sized Cities Conferences. It is also a problem that has been recognized by urban scholars for some time (Shills, 1959–60).

An error in this first round of the inquiry in Nepal provided interesting confirmation of this interpretation. Although all *access persons* were asked to send the questionnaires to local urban administrators for completion, in Nepal a single official of the central government in Kathmandu completed the questionnaires for all five towns. Nepal also showed the reverse of the other countries on judgements of personnel quality and resource control. This central official tended to see low quality urban administrative personnel as a major problem. On the other hand, he did not see a problem in the control of resources. The reversal in the score was pronounced and dramatic, lending support to the views of other local urban administrators, who believed they had the quality of personnel needed to be effective, but needed more control over the financial resources that were in the far-off hands of the central government.

Urban Conditions

One of the early findings reflected the major progress most of Asia has experienced in the social sector. Most, but not all, Asian countries have been successful in expanding education and promoting family planning (Ness & Ando, 1984). This has raised levels of health and education, and has helped to reduce fertility and population growth. Where this support has been steady and programmes have been successful, urban administrators recognize the progress that has been made. Where there has been neither government support nor success, as in Pakistan, urban administrators recognize that both population growth and the lack of education constitute major problems.

Most urban problems are clearly tied to national wealth. Administrators in Japan, Korea, Singapore, and to a lesser extent, Malaysia, note fewer urban problems than administrators from other, poorer, countries. In such poorer countries, major problems centre on inadequate infrastructure. Rapid population growth from in-migration and natural increase together with rapid economic development have produced great strains on the inadequate infrastructure of most cities. There is need for more water supplies, better roads and sewers, more reliable energy sources, and more effective management of solid wastes. All these things require money.

Population growth causes major problems for cities in the poorer countries, but urban administrators in these towns also see people as a resource. Thus the increase of people can also imply more resources, and greater attention from the central government. This, too, was an unexpected finding. Administrators in smaller cities recognized that a larger city would give them greater influence with the central government, allowing them to obtain more resources, especially for the infrastructure construction they all recognized as a major need.

National levels of population growth also affect administrators' perceptions of the problem. In Thailand, where overall population growth has slowed dramatically due to a very successful family-planning programme, urban centres are not overwhelmed with rural in-migrants. In the Philippines or Pakistan, on the other hand, continued high levels of national population growth translate into heavier pressure of the cities from in-migration.

Air pollution is a problem that is also closely tied to wealth. Kobe's wealth means the use of more efficient transportation technologies, and effective emission control in factories. Moreover, like many wealthy cities and countries, it has seen the relocation of heavy, more polluting industries out of the city and even out of the country. Poorer countries suffer lower air quality, though it also is tied to geographic factors in complex ways. Frequent rains and steady wind currents can remove much air pollution. But air pollution does not vary in source; most administrators see the rapid rise of vehicles as the major cause. Creating a more efficient public transportation system, as, for example, Kobe has done, requires wealth that the poorer cities do not have. Moreover, poorer countries do not have well-developed environmental protection legislation. Even where they do, cities have little administrative capacity to monitor or control emissions.

Housing is also tied to wealth, but again, in somewhat complex ways. Poorer cities report more serious problems than do richer cities. But even in poorer cities, the main problems are those of the homeless, or lack of low cost housing. Few administrators, even in poorer cities, see middle- and upper-class housing as a problem.

Finally, poverty and gender inequality present more complex issues. In the poorer cities, urban administrators see poverty as a clear and urgent problem. They feel the problem would be alleviated by more jobs, making employment a serious and urgent problem in most poorer cities. Gender inequality is also recognized, but again the picture is a complex one. Women have made great progress everywhere in health, life expectancy and education. In life expectancy, women have a clear advantage and that has been increasing over the past four decades. However, urban administrators recognize that women are still disadvantaged in employment and positions of power and influence.

Methodological Issues

There were a number of methodological issues raised by the surveys and in-depth studies, but two are considered most important at present: the issue of city size and the measurement of migration.

Cities grow from three different sets of forces, but only two are systematically recorded. In-migration and natural increase are recognized and recorded when data are available. But cities also grow by extending their administrative boundaries. This latter source is seldom recognized and not systematically recorded though it has different policy implications for the city. For example, cities that grow by natural increase will experience heavy demand for maternal and child health care, and for primary education. Cities that grow by heavy in-migration, on the other hand, will experience new demands for jobs, housing and recreational activities, especially for young males, who tend to dominate the in-migrant stream. But cities that grow by extending their boundaries often benefit by expanding tax rolls or by gaining control over a larger area for planning. The problems that arise, such as integrating the transportation system, tend to be less demanding than problems that arise from heavy in-migration. Yet seldom is urban growth through a real expansion assessed. AUICK recommends that this source of growth be more systematically tracked.

Even though migration is well recognized as a source of urban growth, data on urban migration are sadly deficient. Japan and South Korea are exceptions. Both have population registers. All citizens have registration numbers, which record place of residence. When a residence changes, the citizen reports both to the old and new registration offices. This basic registration provides a wealth of data for analysis. For Japan and South Korea, the quantity and quality of data are truly remarkable. Cities know how many in- and out-migrants there are each year, where they come from and where they are going. Moreover, with both residence and place of work recorded, cities know the differences between daytime and night-time populations.

This is both remarkable and rare. The other cities in the following studies have little solid information on migration. Administrators do have a sense of how large their city's migrant stream is, and the direction in which it flows, but detailed information and precise figures are rare. Thus a major methodological problem faces the administrator and the urban social scientist: how to find ways to estimate accurately the flows of in- and out-migration in the absence of good data.

With these lessons learned, AUICK's experience can provide an informed basis for examining the problem of urban population-environment dynamics in some detail. They help to identify the areas in which observation, monitoring and measurement can be most helpful. From these lessons, we can begin to construct a simplified model of urban population-environment dynamics to guide research or the process of recognizing and understanding population-environment problems. To do this, however, it is necessary to turn to a consideration of models and modelling.

MODELLING AND DYNAMIC MODELS[3]

Repeat Warning: Dynamic Modelling Ahead

It is useful to repeat the warning posted in Chapter 1. Dynamic modelling is the analytical technology used in the five city studies that follow in Part II. Again, for those who adhere to, or detest, dynamic modelling, this section will be either unnecessary or unconvincing. Those who have had little experience with and no prejudices of dynamic modelling, however, are invited to follow this discussion carefully.

Models are simplified versions of objects, conditions or processes. They are useful tools for understanding because they allow us to cut through the immense complexity of any reality to identify and understand that reality's critical conditions and relationships. The world of modelling, especially in environmental studies, has become rich, complex and highly productive. It can often appear complicated, technical and inaccessible. The Global Circulation Models, for example, on which studies of future possible climate change are based, involve hundreds of pages containing thousands of equations with millions of measurements. They are quite beyond the comprehension of lay persons, and few technical experts can claim to have a full grasp of an entire model. Nor would such models be possible without the massive computational power found in modern computer technology.

Even the much simpler WORLD3 Model, with which Meadows, Meadows & Randers (1991) ran simulations of the entire world system for the period 1900 through the year 2100, contains over 250 equations. These equations tell of a possible collapse of the world system in the middle of the next century *if* the world continues to grow and produce as it does now. But who can comprehend the meaning of such a 'collapse'? And what is in those over 250 equations that can possibly predict such an unthinkable event?

The world of modelling may appear complicated and inaccessible, but it need not actually be so. Although the data collection and computations can be highly complex, the basic ideas in modelling are quite simple, and their use can be extremely productive. Since four of the five urban studies presented in Part II use modelling techniques, it is useful here to discuss the modelling process to identify both its strengths and its limitations.

The simplification implicit in all modelling is both a strength and a limitation. The visibility of assumptions, on the other hand, is a constant source of great strength.

For modelling, simplification is both necessary and useful. In modelling air quality, for example, it can be assumed that pollution is related to the number of cars on the road. As the number of cars increases, air quality will decline; as cars decrease in number, air quality will increase. This is a useful, but highly simplified model. It leaves out, for example, wind currents and rain, which can clean the air. Nor does it consider changing technology that might reduce, or increase, the emission from cars or industry. Although this simplification leaves out many important conditions, it is useful to show how air quality can be related to the number of cars, which are known to be its major determinants. If that number can be tracked from the past and a *guess* can be made about its growth in the future, it would be possible to *suggest* how air quality might change in the future. From that it would be possible to *suggest* how human health, in particular respiratory diseases, might be affected. Constructing such a view of a possible future would not be possible if one attempted to include every condition that affects air quality. Thus, although it distorts reality, simplification offers opportunities to examine things that otherwise would be fully beyond comprehension.

Models are often called 'dynamic models' (Hannon, 1994), and the process is often referred to as 'simulation modelling'. 'Dynamic' simply means that changes in one part of a model are linked to changes in another part. For example, births and deaths can be linked to population growth or decline, which would be related to increases or decreases in human wastes, the demand for sewage, and potential health effects. A change in the number of cars on the road is linked to changes air quality, or the amount of nitrogen oxides in the air. This simple relationship can be complicated considerably by adding levels or changes in emission technology, production and cost of cars, changes in household income, propensities to save or consume, costs of credit, and even conditions of the world economy and international trade. Each set of these relationships can be specified, and simulations, or future projections, can be done to *suggest* what the future might be like, under *identifiable assumptions*.

Simulation basically means pretending, assuming or representing the similarity in things. In the paragraphs above, the terms 'guess' and 'suggest' are italicized to bring attention to the tentative nature of statements that come from simulation modelling. If the relationship between numbers of automobiles and amount of nitrogen oxide in the air is known, for example, it is possible to *pretend* that the number of cars will increase in the future, and from this to calculate what the air quality will be like. Simulations simply calculate future scenarios or processes under given and identifiable assumptions. They produce *projections*, not predictions, of what the future might look like if the stated assumptions prove to be correct.

The identifiable character of these assumptions says something very important about the explicit process of modelling. In effect, all people carry around in their heads models of how things work. These models are unstated maps of relationships. Often they are not even recognized as models, but are taken as 'the way things really work'. On the basis of these models, people look forward and make predictions about the future. The important, and unique, characteristic of the explicit modelling discussed here is that the assumptions in the model are clearly stated and made visible. Thus they can be questioned, and changed. It is the 'visible' and 'challengeable' nature of assumptions in formal modelling, not its speed and certainty, that makes modelling so useful. Any assumption used in a model can be examined and criticized by people technically expert on the issue. Alternate assumptions can be proposed, and calculations of future scenarios done with those alternate assumptions can be pursued and examined.

A Simple Model of Urban Population-Environment Dynamics

For the five city studies in Part II, a simple model of urban population environment dynamics was constructed. The construction began with two sets of questions. First, how is 'the environment' to be conceived? What is it and what about it should be measured? Second, what urban conditions should be included as linked to the environment? What causes changes in environmental conditions, and what is the effect of environmental change on the human population?

To answer the first question, the work of Wolfgang Lutz (1994) and the IIASA team provides a practical and powerful answer. For a useful definition of 'the environment', Lutz turned to the sixth-century BC Greek Philosopher,

Anaximander, who defined the world as made up of earth, air, water and fire. If energy is substituted for fire, a useful definition of the environment is provided. *Air* quality, and *water* quality and quantity, are certainly two of the most commonly examined environmental conditions today. They are also closely related to one of the most common concerns of environmental organizations today: *land* use and conservation. The protection of forests, wetlands, savannahs, arctic regions, coastlines and marine systems dominates the work of worldwide environmental organizations. Moreover, classifications of land use are well developed, and a good part of the world is mapped with such classifications (UNFPA, 1982). Finally, as noted in Chapter 2, it was the *energy* revolution in the 18th to 19th centuries that produced our current distinctive era of rapid population growth, urbanization and environmental threat. It is also the prospect of another energy revolution, to clean and environmentally benign forms of energy, which makes it possible to envision a new and healthier future for the planet and its inhabitants. In addition, one can measure energy output and use to show how different forms of energy carry different environmental impacts. Thus air, water, land use and energy do well to represent 'the environment' in a manner that is both simple and comprehensive. This also gives us a set of conditions for which we can develop operational definitions and find empirical measures, often in the statistics that governments normally collect.

To decide what institutional conditions should be included in a model of urban population environment dynamics, the extensive studies of AUICK are most useful. Asian urban administrators have told us, for example, that one of the most important systems affecting the urban environment is the transportation system, particularly the increase of vehicular traffic. A second is the economic or productive system that produces jobs as well as material goods and services. The administrators have also told us that the social sector – including health, education and family planning – is one of the most important sets of institutions affecting the human population.

Put together, these four environmental and three institutional sectors produce the model shown in Figure 3.1. It is important to note that this model was developed from concrete experiences with Asian cities and their administrators. Moreover, the model was reviewed and developed collectively by local study directors of the five cities. It is designed to be both simple enough to grasp readily and comprehensive enough to include the most important population-environment conditions. It is also designed to focus on conditions over which the urban administrators might have some direct control.

Figure 3.1
Model of Urban Population-Environment Dynamics

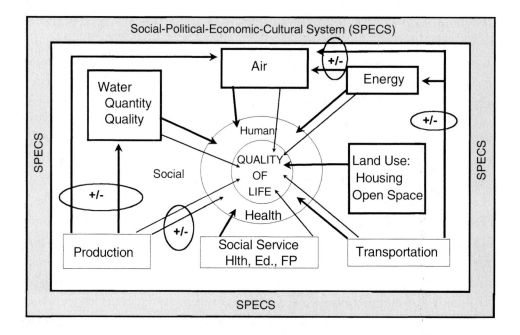

Figure 3.1 was adapted from an earlier diagram of Urban Metabolism (Ness & Golay, 1997), which was also the subject of a Kobe conference in 1993[4]. The term 'metabolism' is used as a metaphor. The city is seen as a living organism, driven by what is essentially a metabolic process. The outcome of any metabolic process is life itself. This can be viewed as a dichotomous attribute: life or death, or as a variable: the quality of life. As in a human or other living organism, a well functioning metabolic process means a high quality of life. When the metabolic process is less than optimal, the quality of life is reduced. Thus the inner circle, quality of life, is considered the output or outcome of the urban metabolic process.

The central circle, **Quality of Life**, represents the final outcome of the dynamic process. It is a variable, concerning human life, in both current and future generations. A high quality of life in the present is desirable, but the essence of the more desired goal of sustainable development is that the current quality of life not be purchased at the expense of future generations. For the present, however, this exercise is concerned only with the current generation, as it exists under the most directly observable and measurable condition. No specific measures are proposed for the quality of life, since the latter is deemed primarily subjective. Nonetheless, it will be possible in the overall comparison of the five cities to provide a general assessment that brings together a variety of conditions.

Beyond the central circle is one labelled 'Hu. Health', or the human health system or the basic demographic conditions that affect the quality of life: births, deaths, illness and causes of death. Separating these two circles is a tacit assumption that quality of life has both subjective and objective dimensions. The inner circle refers to the more subjective aspect of life quality, which is less easy to measure with objective indicators. The outer circle can be conceived as the more objective character, for which a series of objective measures are available. Arrows indicate the *assumed* impact of various sectors either directly on the more subjective quality of life, or indirectly, affecting the objective quality of life through their impact on births and deaths, illness or more generally on what we shall call human system health. To anticipate the discussion below, death is generally a negative value, and birth a positive one, but we shall propose that the highest quality of life comes from a TFR of 2.1, and that TFRs of higher or lower levels imply a lower quality of life.

The arrows are of two types: heavy and light. The light arrows suggest a lesser impact; the heavy arrows suggest a stronger impact. Where valences are not indicated, a positive impact is implied. Most critical, in part because they are the most subject to policies and technology, are those arrows marked +/– in a circle. For these arrows, it is specific technologies (e.g. leaded or unleaded gasoline) or policies (e.g. water pricing and treatment, pollution control legislation and enforcement) that determine whether the impact will be a negative or positive one.

In addition to the central circles that represent the quality of life, the model uses seven sectors to identify environmental and institutional conditions. We briefly discuss these sectors below.

Environment

Water is essential to life itself, but its direct impact on the subjective quality of life is here assumed to be minor. The most important impact of water is through its impact on human health and mortality. Both the quantity and the quality of water are important, and both can be measured and modelled. Humans, as indeed all forms of life, need a certain minimum of water and are subject to extreme stress under water shortages. Various chemical pollutants, human waste materials and 'biological oxygen demand' (BOD) can be relatively easily measured, and their impacts of various aspects of human health are generally well established.

Air quality is assumed to have a minor direct impact on the quality of life, in that clean air and blue skies are thought to be more pleasant than dirty, smoke-filled ones. More importantly, air quality, like water, has its major impact on the quality of life through its impact on human health. This, too, can be readily measured and modelled. For example, lead emissions or amounts of lead in the air can be measured, and some safe assumptions can be made about the relationship between air lead levels and human health, especially that of children. Particulate matter can also be readily measured, and its relationship to respiratory diseases and death rates is relatively well established. Figure 3.1 posits that production, energy use and transportation are the major conditions that affect air quality. Emissions from these three sectors can be measured, and their impact on air quality can be modelled.

Energy, too, is assumed to have a small direct impact on the quality of life and is assumed to have a greater impact indirectly through human health. Energy provides protection against the weather, through heat and light, and also implies better capacities to prepare healthy food. Energy also has a problematic impact on quality of life through its impact on air quality. Heating and cooking with wood or high sulphur content coal, and electricity generation with inefficient coal-burning generators, produce unhealthy air. Natural gas, hydroelectric power or solar and wind power produce cleaner and healthier air.

Land Use has many dimensions, many of which have well-developed classifications and measures. To simplify the system, however, this model uses just two measures: available housing space and available open space. The urban administrators have consistently placed housing, especially low cost housing, on the list of major conditions affecting the quality of life. Both housing and open spaces are assumed to have a direct impact on the more subjective quality of life. As yet there is no clear evidence of a linear impact of either measure on birth or death rates; thus this relationship is not posited as an indirect measure.

Human Institutions and Technology

Production is assumed to affect the subjective quality of life in a minor way. More goods and services produced make for a better quality of life. But production has a problematic impact (+/–) on births and deaths. Heavy industrial production may directly cause illness and death through toxic emissions. On the other hand, agricultural production directly increases food supply, thus reducing death rates. Production is assumed to have its major impacts through the way that it affects water and air quality, which in turn directly affect death and illness rates. The impact on water and air can be measured and modelled relatively easily.

Transportation is assumed to have a minor direct impact on Quality of Life. It is simply more pleasant to be able to move about easily and quickly than to spend hours in traffic jams. Like energy, transportation has its major, and problematic, impacts on energy and air quality. Inefficient automobiles are a major source of serious air pollution, producing deadly particulate mater, nitrogen oxides and lead. A transportation system marked by extensive public services fuelled by LPG or hydro-electrical power produces much cleaner air. Moreover, transportation systems vary considerably in their direct impact on death rates. Traffic patterns can be designed to reduce deaths; the lack of such design increases traffic deaths.

Social Services here include health care, especially primary health care, family planning (private or public, whose outcome is contraceptive prevalence and fertility decline), and education. All are assumed to have a minor direct effect on the subjective quality of life, since it is more pleasant to be educated, healthy and able to choose the number and spacing of children. The major impact, however, comes through the human system health.

Social-Political-Economic-Cultural System (SPECS). This label is long and cumbersome, but it is difficult to find an alternative. Sociologists would call this the 'social organization' of the city, but this would probably produce just as much confusion and resistance from the other social sciences. The more cumbersome term is used to include the urban political system and administration. This involves both the structure of authority and the culture that affects how that authority is defined, enforced, and followed. It also includes the economics of the city, the processes of trade and production, and the distribution of wealth and income. Overall, this is the arena where policy decisions that affect the seven sectors are made and implemented. These policies also affect the flow of physical, human and symbolic resources – information and knowledge – into and out of the city. Finally, this is the arena in which quantitative analyses are most problematic. This portion of the model's analysis will therefore rely on narrative, qualitative analyses.

The diagram can indicate that the various sectors of the model are linked to one another in specific ways. To make these linkages specific and precise, however, we need a specialized tool. The tool used for these five city studies was STELLA.

MODELLING WITH STELLA[5]

The studies of the five cities used the computer program, STELLA, to model aspects of the population-environment relationship identified in Figure 3.1[6]. The attempt was made in each city to encompass the period 1970 to 2020. Using 1995 as the base point, the program provides 25 years of data with which to build various parts of the model, and 25 years for the development of future scenarios.

STELLA was originally developed for the well-known and highly controversial 1972 Club of Rome Study, *The Limits of Growth* (Meadows et al., 1972). That study was controversial because it was taken to propose that the LDRs could not become more developed and wealthy without bringing the world system to the point of collapse. In their 1991 revisit, *Beyond the Limits*, the authors clarified this misconception by reiterating the basic point they had made in 1972. The model that they developed and have continued to use suggests that the world's current pattern of reproduction, production and consumption are unsustainable. The model pointed out that continued population growth and continued growth of the kind of wasteful and often toxic production processes being used cannot continue. At the same time, both the 1972 and 1991 studies have shown that a more sustainable future is possible. This was especially explicit in the 1991 publication, which showed scenarios by which the earth could sustain a population of 7.5 billion, with the standard of living for the entire world equal to that now found in Western Europe.

STELLA provides a simple tool for thinking through a series of connections, and projecting into the future a variety of scenarios. It leads one to think about stocks, flows, converters and connectors.

Stocks are the actual numbers at a specified time of whatever it is that is being analysed: people, cars, or water, for example. *Flows* are the processes by which the stock is increased or depleted. A city's population is a stock, increased by the flow of births and in-migration and decreased by the flow of deaths and out-migration. The number of cars in a city is a stock, increased by the purchase of cars, and depleted by disposing of or 'junking' old cars. The amount of nitrogen oxides in the air is a stock, increased by emissions from vehicles and other fuel consuming engines and decreased by wind currents or rain.

Converters are bits of quantitative information about the connection between stocks and flows. For example, the number of births by which the stock of population increased is determined by the *birth rate*. The birth rate *converts* the flow of births to the stock by adding specific numbers of births. Similarly, *rates* of death or migration determine the specific amount by which the population will be increased or decreased by deaths and migration.

Connectors are the mechanisms by which converters are specifically linked to flows or converters. Thus a flow of births, for example, is connected to the birth rate converter, and the stock of population is connected to the flow of births to allow for a calculation of how population will increase or decrease over time with specific rates of births and deaths.

These various elements and their interconnections can be seen in the following diagram, which produces a model of population affected by migration, and birth and death rates.

STELLA permits the analyst to draw these simple and highly understandable diagrams to represent a dynamic system, such as a city, then to indicate the beginning values of stocks and the values of converters. When these elements are included and connected, the computer generates a set of simultaneous equations whose solution will provide an outcome. For example, to model a city's population, a stock would be created, designating the value of the population at the time the analysis was to begin. Then flows of births, deaths and migration would be entered, and in each case rates would be created as converters. The rates can be listed either as a single constant, or as values that would change over time. Thus, actual past rates of births, deaths and migration can be entered, and future rates can be assumed. With these elements and data, the program can be run to determine a number for the total population at some future time. It can also show the numbers of birth, deaths and migrants that would have produced that specific population. If the past (assumed or actual) rates are correct, the model will provide a calculated total population for the current year equal to the actual present population. If it does, the model could be said to be validated. Figure 3.2 illustrates a STELLA model of a population.

One cannot know, of course, what future birth, death and migration rates will be, but one can make educated guesses. The better the past data, the closer one can come to good assumptions about the future. In addition, the more

Figure 3.2[7]
STELLA Model of Population

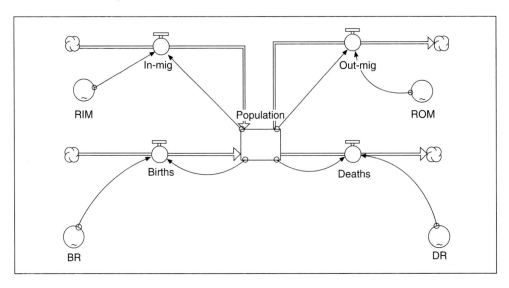

expert the knowledge used to make assumptions about the future, the more likely it is that they will be correct. In the five city studies that follow, AUICK sought to enlist the work of knowledgeable local social scientists, and to have them work closely with experienced urban administrators. This increases the probability that assumptions made about the future will be close to reality.

More important, the assumptions made about future rates and relationships are explicit and visible. These assumptions can also be changed easily, to examine the outcome of such things as higher or lower rates. As noted earlier, this constitutes one of the most important aspects of explicit modelling. On the basis of their models-in-the-head, people make predictions about the future, but the problem with these informal predictions is that we do not know the assumptions on which they are based. The kind of modelling exercise used here **makes those assumptions open, visible and explicit**. As such, they can be challenged by knowledgeable people. If the outcome of a model run is considered highly unlikely, for example, the assumed rates can easily be examined and changed to produce something assumed to be more likely. On the other hand, if the assumed rates seem quite reasonable, the modelling exercise shows explicitly what outcome can be expected from those rates.

In adopting this modelling technique for the in-depth studies, AUICK sought to bring social scientists and urban administrators closer together to promote better understanding of urban processes, and better urban planning. Using a 25-year period for the past provides a time span that both administrators and scientists have experienced directly. Looking 25 years into the future provides a time span that many people can expect to experience themselves. Thus, in looking at the likely outcome of current conditions, urban administrators have tools to help them make better plans for their own near future.

LIMITATIONS

This set of studies of urban population-environment dynamics is presented as an important first step. Population-environment relations are, in any event, highly complex and location specific. They have been studied in a number of situations, but not in urban scenes. Since the world is moving rapidly toward full urbanization, examining the relationship in this inevitable future is especially important.

For the set of studies here, the city is treated more or less as a closed system. It is true that, for population, in- and out-migration are considered. But even here, there is at best only a cursory thought given to the external conditions that push people into the city or pull them out to other areas. All the other conditions considered – health and social services, transportation, production, or the four elements of the environment – deal with the city alone. The model is a closed-system model.

This strategic decision was made for two reasons: simplification and administrative practicality. The exclusion of external forces greatly simplified the conceptual development, data collection and analysis required. In effect, simplification made the studies feasible.

In addition, this design has a practical administrative base. That is, focusing on the city itself provides the urban administrators with the arena in which their actions are most important. These conditions are, for the most part, things over which they might have some control.

This decision follows from the basic strategy of AUICK. It aims to assist the urban administrators with the technical and organizational issues of urban administration in their own locations. The research is designed to help them do what they can to deal with their problems.

In addition to focusing on local problems in a city as a closed system, the studies are also limited to working with data that the cities now have at their command. The local teams did not collect any new data through surveys or other forms of data collection[8]. This was largely due to the lack of resources for more extensive data collection, but it does have a useful advantage. The local teams were able to show what the city administrators can learn from the data they do have, and also how much more they could learn from some simple additions to current routine data collection.

But the limitation, especially of the closed system model, is equally important, and must lead to future developments to include greater complexity (see Chapter 10 for proposed future steps). For example, various pollutants may be found to be taken away by wind currents or water flows. But they do not, therefore, just disappear without an effect on other environments and populations. When people move, they have an impact on the areas they leave as well as on those they enter. The energy a city uses comes from somewhere. Even if it is a clean form of energy, such as electricity, produced outside the city, it may still create other forms of environmental strain or pollution where it is produced. For example, in Kobe, an efficient and environmentally benign electrical rail public transportation system may involve some pollution or environmental degradation where the electricity is produced.

The list could go on and on. The simplification of a closed system model will have a high cost in analytical reality. What is to be done? What units of analysis should be adopted to provide a better understanding of how urban population environment dynamics work, and how they affect the larger population, first of a nation, but ultimately of the entire world? These are only questions to be raised at this time; no real answers will be given. Cities can still be important units of analysis, even if it is found that they vary considerably in their geography or in the impact of their administration on their functioning. But ultimately, it will be necessary to examine systems of cities, and the way a set of cities functions in the larger arena of the nation state, where important policy decisions are made. It will also be necessary to carry this kind of analysis beyond the confines of the nation state, to examine how urbanization itself varies and what the causes and consequences are of that variation for long term sustainability. We shall return to these issues in the final chapter with some suggestions for further research.

For the moment, however, the simplification employed in these studies is considered necessary and important. But it is also considered necessary and important to call attention to the limitations such simplification inevitably entails.

Notes

1. The work of AUICK is summarized in AUICK 1997.
2. In 1997 AUICK decided to carry out the surveys once every three years, leaving two intervening years for the in-depth studies.
3. This section owes much to the work of Wolfgang Lutz (1994) and his colleagues at the International Institute for Applied Systems Analysis (IIASA) in Laxemburg, Austria. See also Ness & Golay (1997) for a general review of modelling in population-environment analyses.
4. In the discussion of urban metabolism, however, the city was treated not as a closed system. There was provision for dealing with both inputs into and outputs flowing from the city. In the current model, the city is treated as more or less a closed entity, with no inputs and no outputs to the city. This was considered necessary as a first step, but its limitations are important and will be considered in Chapter 10.
5. STELLA is a dynamic-modelling computer program produced by High Performance Systems, Inc. of Hanover, New Hampshire. See Hannon & Ruth (1994) for an extensive discussion with accompanying demonstration disks.
6. As will be seen shortly, not all cities used the STELLA program. In Cebu City, data limitations were such that it did not appear useful to employ STELLA. This, however, provides an opportunity to consider the impact of data availability on analyses of population-environment dynamics. It also provides an opportunity to demonstrate what could be done if appropriate data were collected by the city. These issues will be dealt with in Chapter 9.
7. This figure is a simulation, prepared on Harvard Graphics. The STELLA version will be slightly different, but fully recognizable.
8. Cebu presents a slight exception, where the local study director used hospital records to construct a life table, from which he could estimate life expectancy and infant mortality for the city alone.

Part II

Five Cities:
Individual City Studies

EDITORS' NOTE

We began the book with the following ten-part list of issues:

1. The Urban Setting
2. Population Change
3. Social Services: Health, Family Planning and Education
4. Water Quantity and Quality
5. Air Quality
6. Energy
7. Transportation
8. Land Use
9. The Economy
10. The Quality of Life

In Part II, each of the five city studies attempts to deal with the same issues, in the same order. However, not all issues are dealt with in all cities, and the amount of detail differs considerably. This was the result of data availability and the salience of issues for individual cities: data were either not available or insufficient. Thus, in some studies, two or more issues may be discussed together in one section. In other cases, such as energy in Kobe, the issue was not a salient one for the city itself. In Kobe, energy was not an issue the city government could deal with directly, and there were no prospective shortages or problems on the horizon. Thus the issue was omitted.

Chapter 4

Faisalabad City:
A City Under Double Pressures

Prof Kishwar Ejaz
Dr Kareem Ikbal
Mr Ali Ejaz

THE URBAN SETTING

Faisalabad lies on the broad plain of the Indus River-system, roughly 550 miles north-east of Karachi. The rivers of this great system rise in the western Himalayas and flow some 1800 miles through the flat Punjab Plain, debauching into the Arabian Sea near Karachi. The waters derive almost completely from Himalayan snowmelt, bringing life to an essentially arid plain. The entire basin receives ten inches of rainfall or less per year. The development of dams and canals from this great river system has made Pakistan the most irrigated national agricultural systems in the world.

This broad plain once knew a rich and flourishing empire. Not far to the south of Faisalabad, in the middle of what is now the Cholistan desert, lies Mohenjo-daro, centre of a great civilization dating back 3000 years. This is also the flat plain across which invading armies have marched since the days of Darius and Alexander the Great.

Faisalabad itself, however, is a new city, established by deliberate plan only at the end of the last century. Here British colonialism worked its transformations, turning unproductive wilderness into land that bears goods for the market. A Lieutenant Governor of the Punjab, Sir James Layall, conceived the idea of digging a canal from the Chenab River to bring life-giving waters to a new colony. This canal was opened in 1892. Faisalabad, then named Lyallpur in Sir James' honour, was established as a market town in 1895. It was laid out 'rationally' on 110 acres, with eight bazaars, or market areas, on roads radiating like spokes on a wheel from a central clock tower. The design of the town was prepared by a Mr Young, and was further improved by Sir Ganga Ram, a renowned town-planner of the time.

Geography of Faisalabad

Faisalabad district lies between 30°35′ and 31°50′ north latitudes and 72°66′ and 73°40′ east longitudes. It consists of a flat alluvial plain of recent formation. With a fall of only 181 feet from the north-east to the south-west, it is exceptionally well suited for canal irrigation. The Ravi River flows on the eastern and the Chenab River on the western boundaries of the district. The climate of the district is hot and dry, though the temperature varies considerably from season to season. The maximum and minimum mean temperatures in summer are 37 and 24 degree Celcius respectively, while in winter the range is between 24 and eight degree Celcius. The highest temperature in summer may hit 50 degree Celcius, and the lowest in winter may fall below freezing point. Summer dust-storms are frequent, characterized by choking wind-blown dust capable of up-rooting trees and tearing thatched roofs from houses. With the extensive cultivation brought by the canal, rainfall in the district has increased slightly, but still averages only about 27.5 centimetres per year.

City Background

With its rich agricultural hinterland made possible by the canal, Faisalabad became a major textile centre. Fully planned from its beginning, the town has been overwhelmed by population growth from both natural increase and in-migration, which seem always to remain ahead of the development of urban infrastructure.

The first prominent building in the area was the Deputy Commissioner's house, which was built after the town became headquarters of newly founded District. It was followed by the Qaisri Gate in 1898, a prominent Clock Tower in 1905, and a District Board and Town Hall Building. A Railway Line was developed in 1910, connecting Faisalabad with Lahore via Sangla Hill. The first neighbourhood settlement of the Town was Douglas Pura, established in 1920. The era of industrialization began as the Lyallpur Cotton Mill was completed in 1934. Three other industrial plants, two flour-mills, and a cotton mill were established during the period between 1930 and 1940. New settlement areas were laid out as the city expanded to three square miles.

Independence in 1947 with the partition of Pakistan from India saw a major influx of Indian-Muslim refugees. In 1951 the Government of Pakistan developed a plan to promote industrial activities. Faisalabad was declared an Industrial Zone, thus providing many incentives for investors. This led to the creation

of five major textile mills in addition to other factories. Industrialization continued to expand rapidly, making Faisalabad the second largest industrial town in
Pakistan, with over 235 industrial enterprises of various types and sizes. To
accommodate the growth, the town limits were extended to 29 square miles. At
present the Municipal area is about 35 square miles. Although industrialization
has moved ahead rapidly, housing and urban infrastructure have lagged behind.
With its current estimated population of 2,012,000, Faisalabad ranks as the third
largest city in Pakistan.

Urban Administration[1]

The city is governed by a Deputy Commissioner under the supervision of the
Commissioner of Faisalabad Division; both administrative officers are appointed
by the central government. The Deputy Commissioner combines the functions
of District Magistrate and Collector of Revenues. He is also responsible for the
coordination of the functions of all 'nation-building' departments in the district.
On the judicial side, an Additional Deputy Commissioner General and Assistant Commissioners assist him. For revenue administration, the district is divided
into three sub-divisions. There is also an elected town council. As Pakistan has
shifted between democratic and military forms of government, there has sometimes also been an elected Mayor.

Monitoring and Management of Environmental Hazards

In an effort to address problem of environmental degradation, the Government
of Pakistan promulgated the Environmental Protection Ordinance of 1983. This
called for the establishment of Environmental Protection Agencies (EPAs) for
each of the country's provinces. The Punjab EPA was established in 1987. The
ordinance created by this Agency established standards for 32 parameters, from
temperature and PH to fluorides and toxic metals, and 16 gases, from smoke and
particulate matter to nitrogen oxides and zinc. Unfortunately, implementation
has been exceptionally weak. The city lacks legislative authority to enforce
emission standards, and there is as yet no monitoring of air quality in the city,
nor is there a local facility for chemical analysis of effluent samples taken from
the industrial plants. Water is monitored at the source, but not at the users' end.

As might be expected, the textile and grain mills are a major source of air,
water and land pollution. Local studies (Ahmad et al., 1989; Ahmad, 1990)

have shown significant impacts of textile industry chemicals on the heart and liver. Dying processes in the textile industries are major sources of pollution that go unchecked. Noise and offensive industrial odours are generally recognized as serious problems, but neither is monitored nor controlled. Untreated industrial water is the main source of pollution and it has become dangerous to both human and marine life.

In an attempt to deal with these environmental problems, the Chief Minister of Punjab announced the creation of a new water treatment plant. This plant will treat one third of Faisalabad's total industrial effluent, or about 100 cubic metres per second (cusecs), and turn the collected wastes of the store ponds into fertilizer. In addition, a 1997 law has been passed envisioning the creation of Environmental Protection Courts to deal with violations of minimum standards.

The impact of these moves lies in the future, however. Overall, the industrial development of Faisalabad has brought about wealth and jobs, but it has also caused major environmental degradation, reducing the quality of life in the city.

Culture, Customs and Traditions

As in all of Pakistan, the family constitutes the major unit of social organization in Faisalabad. Family ties remain strong despite rapid urbanization. Marriages are generally arranged by parents. The initiative usually comes from the boy's parents, who are generally on the lookout for a good match for their son. The birth of a male child is celebrated with great enthusiasm, while the birth of a female child is received with considerably less.

This disparity in gender roles can be seen in the country's school system. While the national primary school enrolment rate for boys grew from 51 percent in 1980 to 80 percent in 1993, that for girls grew only from 27 to 49 percent (World Bank, 1997). As we shall see later, however, Faisalabad has achieved more progress in educating girls than has the country as a whole.

POPULATION

Overall, Pakistan appears to be stalled in the middle of the demographic transition. Death rates have fallen from 28.5 per 1000 in 1950 to less than ten today. They were halved in the first 25 years, but have declined more slowly since then. At the same time, the birth rate has remained high. The crude birth rate was about 40 per 1000 through the 1970s, and the total fertility rate remained at seven in the same period. Since 1975, there has been a slight decline in the crude birth rate to 39, and a more substantial decline in the total fertility rate to 5.5. UN projections foresee a further decline in fertility, but it is not expected that the total fertility rate will reach replacement level until about 2025.

All of this means that Pakistan's population has exploded, growing from about 35 million at independence in 1947 to 146 million in 1995. The (median variant) projection suggests the population could reach 357 million by the year 2050. This prospective ten-fold growth in one century poses great challenges for the country as a whole. The situation in Faisalabad reflects the national trend, with both advantages and disadvantages over the national scene.

Faisalabad's Population: The Past

Faisalabad recorded its first population count in 1931, when the number stood at 43,000. The census of 1931 and 1941 were conducted under the British government for both of what are now Pakistan and India. The 1951 and 1961 censuses were conducted by the Government of Pakistan, using the framework and organization established under British rule. From that point, census work began to deteriorate. Reports have still been provided, but their coverage and accuracy have been questioned. Thus the actual population of Faisalabad remains in question. The Faisalabad Development Authority (FDA) has undertaken its own sample surveys, which seem to indicate that the national Population Census Organization (PCO) underestimates the city's actual population. The FDA estimates, which we use here, show a city population of 2,014,000 in 1997.

Table 4.1 provides a summary of both this past growth and our projections for the future.

Faisalabad's Future Population Projections

We begin with just two relatively firm data points: 1970 with a population of 770,000, and 1997 with a population of 2,014,000. From this point, we develop a model of the population using STELLA. Since the official census data are incomplete and somewhat suspect, we began with the UN estimates of Pakistan's population in the five-year period, 1970 to 1995. We assumed that the crude birth rate for Faisalabad would be slightly lower than that for the country as a whole. Thus, in our model, crude birth rates are four to five per 1000 lower than for the country as a whole. We also assumed that the crude death rate would be slightly lower than for the country as a whole, or two to three per 1000 lower than the national average. Using these vital rates, our model provide a popula-

Table 4.1
Population Growth of Faisalabad City

Year	Population
1931	43,000
1941	70,000
1951	179,000
1961	425,000
1970	770,000
1971	823,000
1981	1,104,000
1991	1,582,000 a
1997	2,014,000 b
2020	5,164,264 c 4,123,759 d 3,391,080 e

Source: Government of Pakistan, Population Census Organization, Statistics Division, *Hand Book of Population Census Data*, 1985.
a. Government of Punjab, Punjab Development Statistics Bureau of Statistics, Lahore, 1994.
b. Faisalabad Development Authority, Directorate of Environmental Control Structural Plan of Faisalabad (up to 2000), Faisalabad.
c. High population growth STELLA scenario
d. Medium population growth STELLA scenario
e. Low population growth STELLA scenario

tion growth by natural increase alone that took the city from 770,000 in 1970 to 1,596,300 in 1997, or 418,700 less than the accepted 1997 figure.

This deficit was made up for by migration. Effectively we used the FDA estimate of 1.2 to 1.3 percent in-migration and 0.5 percent out-migration for the period 1970 to 1997. This gave us a modelled estimate for 1997 of 1,996,600, or just 17,400 less than the accepted 1997 figure. We accepted this small difference as indicating the validity of our model. An important caveat must be recorded: we really do not know what the birth, death and migration rates have been for Faisalabad for the past 25 years. Our assumptions could be inaccurate on any of the rates. Nonetheless, these estimated rates seem reasonable to informed observers in the city government and to researchers. Thus we feel some confidence in using them as the base for make future projections.

For the future, we must consider births, deaths, in- and out-migration. We have constructed a set of estimates, with high-medium-low variants, which we feel are justified on grounds of possible population and environmental changes. We lay these changes out here in detail, and invite informed observers to challenge them, to disagree, and to present alternatives. In all cases, we begin with the UN projections of high-medium-low variants for the country as a whole (UN, 1996).

High Variant (Agricultural Collapse)

We first assume that the crude birth rate will be slightly lower, i.e. four to five per 1000, than the UN high estimates for the country as a whole. We further assume that the crude death rate will be the same as the UN estimate. The UN crude birth rate estimates do not vary for the high-medium-low estimates; all decline from seven to five per 1000 over the period 1995 to 2020. As these rates are already so low, it is difficult for them to decline further. Indeed, they result in part from the very young age of the population, and while they are expected to rise as the population ages, this will not be until after our period of consideration, which ends in 2020.

The migration estimates are more critical. For the high variant, we assume that two forces act in tandem. First, we consider the possibility of a major agricultural decline from soil salinization, which will drive many people from the rural areas into the city. In addition, the large rural families and the increasing fragmentation of holdings will be incapable of providing a livelihood for all children, driving many younger sons and daughters into the city. Thus we assume that in migration rates will rise steadily from 13 to 35 per 1000 over the period. Out-migration rates will remain below five per 1000, and will actually decline. This will occur since we assume that the agricultural collapse will not be localized, but will be generally felt, thus people pushed off the land into Faisalabad will have nowhere else to go.

Medium Variant (Continuing Current Conditions)

Here, we again assume slightly lower crude birth rates than for the country as a whole and the same crude death rates. For migration, we assume no major agricultural decline from salinization of soils. Progress in developing new crops could avert a major disaster. But there will still be increasing dislocation from large families, and farm fragmentation, which will drive young people off the land. Thus we assume in-migration rates will rise from 13 to only 20 per 1000. The out-migration rates are still assumed to be less than five per 1000.

Low Variant (Improving Conditions)

Again we assume lower crude birth rates, four to five per 1000, less than the UN low variant estimate. Crude death rates, as for the other variants, are assumed to be the same as the UN estimates. For migration, we assume some major developments in agriculture that will avert a major decline and provide opportunities for many young people to stay on the land. In addition, we assume that better health and family planning services in the rural areas will reduce the pressure on rural out-migration. Thus the city's in-migration rates will actually decline from 13 to ten per 1000, while out-migration rates remain less than five per 1000.

As discussed in detail in Chapter 3, we cannot know what future rates of births, deaths and migration will be. We can, however, make some educated

Figure 4.1
Population Growth, 1931–2020
(Showing High, Medium and Low STELLA Projection Variants)

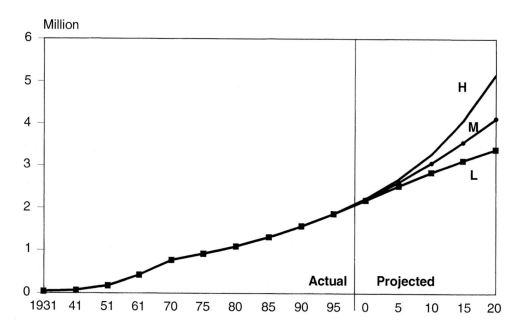

guesses. Even more important, we can state clearly the assumptions behind those guesses. Thus, knowledgeable people can question those assumptions; change them and run scenarios to specify the outcome of those assumptions. With the assumptions we have specified here, Figure 4.1 shows the outcomes.

Table 4.2 shows the birth, death and migration rates we have assumed for the future.

Table 4.2
Crude Birth Rate, Crude Death Rate, Out-Migration and In-Migration

Years	CBR (%)			CDR (%)			Out-Migration (%)			In-Migration (%)		
	H	M	L	H	M	L	H	M	L	H	M	L
1997	3.2	3.2	3.2	0.7	0.7	0.7	0.5	0.5	0.5	1.3	1.3	1.3
2000	3.2	3.1	3.1	0.7	0.7	0.7	0.5	0.5	0.5	1.8	1.5	1.2
2005	3.0	2.8	2.7	0.6	0.6	0.6	0.4	0.5	0.5	2.0	1.7	1.1
2010	2.7	2.3	2.1	0.6	0.6	0.6	0.4	0.4	0.5	2.5	1.8	1.0
2015	2.5	2.0	1.8	0.5	0.5	0.5	0.3	0.4	0.5	3.0	1.9	1.0
2020	2.0	1.7	1.4	0.5	0.5	0.5	0.1	0.3	0.5	3.5	2.0	1.0

H = High variant; M = Medium variant; L = Low variant

Maternal and Infant Mortality Rates

Infant and maternal mortality rates provide good indicators of a population's general welfare. The infant mortality also contributes greatly to both the crude birth rate and life expectancy. In all developing countries, the maternal mortality rate has remained rather high in the past. Maternal mortality increases chances of family disintegration, coupled with subsequent survival problems for the stranded infants. Infant mortality in Pakistan has remained relatively high. The UNDP estimates Pakistan's IMR to be 95 in 1996, and the MMR to be 340 (UNDP, 1998). World Bank and United Nations estimates are roughly similar. These high maternal and infant mortality rates have been attributed to many factors, including poverty, ignorance, poor health care and cultural pressures.

As reported by the officials of health institutions in Faisalabad City, there has been significant reduction in maternal and infant mortality rates over the recent past. It was estimated at 90 per 1000 live births in 1970, when the national figure for Pakistan stood at 140. Even the lower city rate is considered high, however, especially compared with other developing countries of the region[2]. In the view of Faisalabad Municipal Corporation (FMC) health officials, greater financial support from the government will help to reduce these mortality rates further in the future. Both rates are expected to decline considerably over the next few decades. Table 4.3 shows the infant and maternal mortality rates in Faisalabad City.

Table 4.3
Infant and Maternal Mortality Rates in Faisalabad City over Time

Item	Year		
	1970	1997	2020
Maternal mortality/100,000 live births	90	62	18
Infant mortality/1000 live births	109	91	30

The Status of Women

The present sex ratio in Faisalabad city is 108 (i.e. 108 men for 100 women)[3]. This is not considered unusual for a city with many male in-migrants who left families behind in the agricultural hinterland in search of urban work. But the ratio also indicates a general condition of female disadvantage that is found throughout South and West Asia (with the notable exception of Sri Lanka, where the sex ratio of 99 is similar to that of the MDRs). While female seclusion and low rates of female labour force participation have existed in the past, our studies indicate considerable change taking place in Faisalabad at present.

We still find over 95 percent of women who are housewives; only five percent are employed. Among the employed, most women are engaged in education and health services. There is, however, a noticeable trend of trained women entering other jobs, such as banking and the private industry. Discussion with academic researchers and other social scientists reveals that induction of woman-power is likely to pick up in future, and that by the year 2020, a sizeable proportion of educated women will have entered the job market.

Our findings of the trends of female employment in public and private institutions of Faisalabad City are shown in Table 4.4.

Table 4.4
Female Employment Trends (Numbers)

Institution	Year		
	1970	1997	2020*
Educational institutions			
Primary level	535	1645	5685
Secondary level	406	1526	7203
Tertiary level	100	350	2500
Medical institutions			
Doctors	30	152	1075
Paramedical staff	125	1325	6058
Financial institutions	10	60	1000
Police	5	32	500
Communication and telegraph	10	30	200
Insurance	–	3	50
Telecommunication	4	45	375
Social Welfare	1	5	130
Others	6	30	200

Source: Research team estimates

SOCIAL SERVICES

Health

Data on the health of Faisalabad's population are not readily available. The health department reports three major diseases, however, and these have changed only slightly over the past 27 years. In 1970, the major illnesses were tuberculosis, malaria and typhoid. By 1997, malaria had been brought under control, and the three main diseases were typhoid, dysentery and liver diseases. We do not have data on the incidence of other diseases, but these few observations indicate that infectious diseases are still prominent. Moreover, they derive from environmental conditions that could be controlled by more adequate urban infrastructure, in particular the provision of clean water and more effective management of human wastes.

Facilities

Data on health facilities and practitioners are readily available, and we were able to model both for the period 1970 to 2020. Discussion with the medical officer of Faisalabad has revealed that there are at present 43 hospitals in the city (4 Government, 39 Private) with 3000 beds overall. There are also 55 dispensaries, 388 general clinics, 25 dental clinics and 102 primary health care units. An analysis of the existing health facilities showed that these institutions are working under the great pressure from Faisalabad's increasing population, as can be seen from the number of individuals being served. Overtime changes in health institutions in Faisalabad based on the above assumptions are shown in Tables 4.5 and 4.6.

Table 4.5
Number of Health Institutions

Status of Institution	1970	1997	2020 Population Variants		
			High	Medium	Low
Hospitals					
a) Government	1	4	19	16	13
b) Private	2	39	266	231	185
General clinics	50	388	2331	2020	1613
Dental clinics	3	25	186	162	129
Primary health care units	10	102	583	505	404
Number of dispensaries	10	55	311	269	215

Table 4.6
Population Served Per Unit of Health Facility

Institution	Population served/Unit	
	1997	2020
Hospitals		
a) Government	503,500	500,000
b) Private	51,641	35,000
General clinics	5191	4000
Dental clinics	80,560	50,000
Primary health care units	19,745	16,000
Number of dispensaries	36,618	30,000

Here we see a major problem for the country as a whole, which is clearly reflected in Faisalabad as well. Government plans for the provision of health services have been quite inadequate, and the private sector is increasingly taking up the provision of service.

Medical Practitioners

At present, there are 1080 doctors (324 Government and 756 Private), along with 2650 paramedical staff (1760 Government and 890 Private). Tables 4.7 and 4.8 show the numbers for staff, beds and people served, with estimates for the future.

Table 4.7
Medical Practitioners

Particulars	1970	1997	2020 Population Variants		
			High	Medium	Low
Doctors	100	1080	6670	5300	4615
a) Private practitioners	50	756	5180	4429	3589
b) Government doctors	50	324	1695	1449	1175
Doctors/1000 population	0.13	0.51	0.66	0.66	0.66
Beds	800	3000	18,648	15,094	12,921
a) Government	650	1651	7770	6735	5384
b) Private	150	1349	8108	7028	5618
Beds/1000 population	1.04	1.49	1.87	1.87	1.87
Paramedical staff	250	2650	13,979	12,116	9,686
a) Government	150	1760	8476	7347	5873
b) Private	100	890	5180	4490	3589
Paramedical staff /1000 population	0.32	1.26	1.50	1.50	1.50
Pharmacists	50	599	4662	4041	3230

Table 4.8
Parameters Assumed for Projecting Health Facilities

No.	Particulars	Population Served Per Unit	
		1997	2020
1	Doctors	1865	1400
	a) Private practitioners	2664	1800
	b) Government doctors	6216	5500
	Doctors/1000 population	0.51	0.66
2	Beds	671	500
	a) Government	1220	1200
	b) Private	1493	1150
	Beds/1000 population	1.49	1.87
3	Paramedical staff	760	667
	a) Government	1144	1100
	b) Private	2263	1800
	Paramedical staff /1000 population	1.26	1.50
4	Pharmacists	3362	2000

Family Planning

Pakistan was one of the first countries after India to proclaim an official policy to reduce population growth by reducing fertility in marriage. This new policy and the creation of a national family planning programme were announced in 1960, along with plans for promoting economic development. After what appeared to be a promising start, however, the programme became almost inoperative (Ness & Ando, 1984). In Faisalabad, only four percent of eligible couples were using contraceptives in 1970. This did not change for the country as a whole until about 1980, when the national family planning programme's supervision was moved from the Ministry of Health to the Ministry of Planning. Considerable improvement followed, as was seen in the rise of the contraceptive prevalence rate to 42 percent in Faisalabad. This was much higher than the national average of 14 percent, indicating the more advanced condition of the city with regard to views of reproductive behaviour.

Family planning officials in Faisalabad recognize the advances made over the past decade, and look forward to continued progress. They anticipate that contraceptive use will rise to about 70 percent by 2020.

Today, there are 55 family planning clinics in the city, with 180 trained medical staff and 275 trained birth attendants (TBA). Based on alternative assumptions of high, medium and low population scenarios, the estimated family planning facilities in the future are given in Table 4.9.

Table 4.9
Family Planning Facilities and Personnel

Facilities/Personnel	1970	1997	2020 Population Variant		
			High	Medium	Low
Family-planning clinics	10	55	300	260	208
Family-planning staff	22	180	1154	1000	799
Trained traditional-birth attendants	60	275	1385	1200	959
Contraceptive prevalence rate (CPR) %	4	42	70	70	70
Primary health-care staff	–	122	519	450	360

Non-Allopathic Systems

In addition to the 'western' professional medical staff, there are also homeopathic practitioners in Faisalabad city. Our survey found the numbers reported in Table 4.10.

Table 4.10
Homeopath Practitioners, Hakims and Quacks

Category	Year		
	1970	1997	2020
Homeopath practitioners	25	400	1600
Hakim	125	281	700
Quacks and others	150	350	800

This indicates that besides allopathic services, a significant contribution to the health needs of the population will continue to be made by other methods of healing in years to come.

Education

Education is widely recognized as an important component of a city's quality of life. The national government has put forth ambitious plans to expand education, but it has not produced much success. Educational resources and achievements in Faisalabad are more extensive than in the rest of the country, but our observations and discussions with educational officials in the city still reveal considerable problems.

The physical facilities of the schools are of low quality, supplies are inadequate, teachers are often untrained, and there is a general shortage of funds. Nonetheless, Faisalabad officials note progress in the past and predict greater advances in the future. The actual number of schools has near doubled from 1970 to 1997, and enrolment has increased substantially for both girls and boys. At present, out of children between five and nine years old, 97 percent of boys and 77 percent of girls are enrolled in school. These figures are substantially higher than the overall national average of 80 percent for boys and 49 percent for girls.

With the assistance of Faisalabad educational officials, the number of school buildings and enrolments for the period 1970 to 2020 have been modelled. As before, we have actual data for only two points in the past: 1970 and 1997, and we assume that rates of building and enrolment will increase for the future. For example, we assume that enrolment rates will rise to 98 percent and 91 percent respectively for boys and girls in primary school. For secondary schools, we assume enrolment rates of 83 percent for boys and 80 percent for girls. These assumptions give the data in Tables 4.11 through 4.13.

Table 4.11
Educational Facilities

Status of Institution	1970	1997	2020 Population Variant		
			High	Medium	Low
Primary					
Boys	225	518	1456	1263	1010
Girls	107	328	1311	1137	909
Secondary					
Boys	96	176	1289	1118	893
Girls	58	218	1188	1029	823
Tertiary (College & University)					
Boys	5	10	62	54	43
Girls	2	7	57	50	40

Figures given in the above table clearly show that a distinct change has come about in the education sector, especially in female education. There has been a significant change in the attitudes towards female education, which can be considered a very healthy sign of the rising status of women in Faisalabad society.

Table 4.12
Enrolment of Students

Level/Sex of Student	1970	1997	2020 Population Projections		
			High	Medium	Low
Primary					
Boys	55,620	156,719	263,894	210,724	173,284
Girls	25,150	115,060	252,533	201,652	165,824
Secondary & High					
Boys	51,000	151,038	292,283	231,797	190,613
Girls	23,606	119,635	277,786	221,817	182,406
Tertiary					
Boys	4774	19,196	203,198	162,258	133,429
Girls	2127	12,516	194,450	155,271	127,684

Table 4.13
Projected School-Aged Population Enrolled in 2020

Level of Education	Actual school-aged population at medium population scenario	School-aged population expected to enrol at medium level of population	Proportion of enrolment to school aged population (%)*
Primary			
Boys	210,724	206,509	98
Girls	201,652	183,503	91
Secondary			
Boys	231,797	192,392	83
Girls	221,817	177,434	80

* It is assumed that the proportion of population actually enrolled at the primary and secondary school level to the total young school-aged population will remain the same under all three population scenarios.

WATER

Quantity

Originally, Faisalabad's water came from the canals and wells. Over the years, the FMC has led a haphazard expansion of water sources, relying much on canals and wells. In 1978, a major turning point was reached with the creation of the Water and Sanitation Agency (WASA), which took over responsibility for water and sewage. At that time, 50 percent of the population was being served with municipal potable water at the rate of seven gallons per capita per day (FDA, 1994). The system of potable water was mainly dependent on the canal water supply, which was being treated at two water treatment plants. The first breakthrough in water supply came in 1978, when WASA installed 40 tube wells – each of one cubic metre per second (cusec) capacity – along the Rakh Canal Branch, which passes through the city. The water of these tube wells, however, has gone brackish with time due to increased withdrawals, and at present only eight tube wells are in working condition. The next advance in water supply came in 1992 when 25 tube wells, each of four-cusec capacity, were installed in the Chenab well field. This project increased supply to 55 million gallons per day (mg/d). The quality of this water at the source is very good, meeting WHO standards. There are problems in the distribution system, however, and the water at end use is often contaminated due to the poor quality of the pipes.

The major consumer of water supplied by WASA has been the residential sector, which accounts for 90 percent of withdrawals. Although Faisalabad has over the years become an industrial giant, the nature of this industrial complex is such that it does not consume a significant portion of WASA water supplies. This is not likely to change in the future. Water for agricultural purposes has been coming through a well-spread perennial canal-system in and around Faisalabad. Therefore, agriculture makes no major demand on WASA water supplies.

By 1997, water distribution had been increased, and it is estimated that 60 percent of the population now has access to piped water. Unfortunately, however, 40 percent of Faisalabad households still get drinking water from hand pumps. WASA officials plan to provide piped water to an additional 136,000 households by the year 2020. This will still leave an estimated 20 percent of households without a safe water supply. Moreover, it is estimated that by the year 2000, 92 mg/d of water will be required, whereas present resources can supply only 58 mg/d.

Table 4.14
Water Supply

No.	Item	Year		
		1970	1997	2020
1	Household served (%)	44	60	80
2	Population served (in 000)	339	1208	3299

Source: WASA, Faisalabad

Quality

The roughly 40 percent of the population dependent on underground water faces another problem: salts. The underground water of Faisalabad city is saline, with a TDS (Total Dissolved Salts) ranging between 2500 and 10,000 PPM. Piped water, as was noted, is of high quality at the sources, but is often contaminated by inadequate distribution facilities. To address this problem, WASA has initiated chlorination processes. WASA officials believe their short and long run projects will definitely improve water quality by the year 2020, but statistical estimates are not available.

Sewage and Drainage

The existing sewage situation in Faisalabad is far below acceptable standards. During the last 40 years, the city has grown considerably, but the necessary extensions to the sewage system have not followed suit. The result has been that the inefficient sewage system affects the living conditions and health of all the city's population.

Due to the flat topography of the region, several sewage-pumping stations are required. Raw sewage is discharged from disposal channels into two main seepage drains. The estimated sewage generation for Faisalabad city is 250 to 260 cusecs, of which 150 to 160 cusecs come from households, and the remaining 100 cusecs are produced by industrial establishments. Effective disposal is about 95 percent.

WASA surveys indicate that only about two-thirds (61 percent) of all households are connected to street sewers. Another 30 percent discharge into open, improved drains, leaving only about ten percent with no controlled discharge. The conveyance systems of sewers and drains are, however, in poor condition.

Due to the widespread use of private tube wells, sewage flows are higher than the volumes of water supplied by WASA. The sewage system has been particularly under-funded, and consequently pump stations are not working, sewers are blocked, and raw sewage frequently spills onto streets.

Solid Wastes

Faisalabad generates almost 1700 tons of solid waste per day from both private and public sources: an average of about 0.8 kg per person. Household wastes constitute some 35 percent; wastes delivered to a transfer point represent 42 percent; street sweepings and animal wastes constitute 12 percent; and recycled household waste make up another 10 percent. Data are not available on the growth of solid wastes over time, making the projection for the future quite uncertain. FDA surveys, however, suggest that only about 50 percent of generated wastes are actually collected and disposed of by the FMC.

There are four landfill sites where solid wastes are disposed of without any precautionary measures. No treatment of wastes is carried out except for incidental recycling by scavengers. No system exists for the separate disposal of hazardous waste. Measures are not being taken to negate adverse environmental effects. Surveys also indicate that the city's population is dissatisfied with the waste disposal system, which is judged inefficient and ineffective.

ENERGY

Energy Use

Traditional sources of energy for household use historically consisted of wood and cow dung. Over the past few decades, kerosene has been added and become fairly common, especially for lighting. It is estimated that about 30 percent of households used kerosene for lighting in 1970, compared to eight percent today, but there are no estimates of wood and cow dung use for cooking at present. It is further estimated that the proportion using kerosene for lighting will fall to only one percent.

Modern forms of energy for domestic, agricultural and industrial use include natural gas and electricity. At present about 80 percent of the population has access to electricity and this is expected to rise to 99 percent by 2020. The largest consuming sector is industry. At present, the total amount of electricity consumed by all sectors is 800 megawatts. To accommodate future industrial and population growth, this will have to increase to 1600 to 2300 megawatts by 2020. Electricity is supplied by a public authority, the Water and Power Development Authority (WAPDA).

Private companies supply natural gas. About 65 percent of the population now have access to natural gas, and this proportion is expected to rise to 95 percent by 2020. There is now no fear that supplies or distribution will be inadequate in the future. If this becomes an actuality, it will have a positive impact on air quality, and also on the general quality of life.

Communication Services

As in many developing regions, modern communications have been growing rapidly in Faisalabad. The number of radio sets has actually declined slightly, but television sets have increased dramatically. The 32,000 radio sets counted in 1970 implied one for every 25 persons, declining to 25,000 sets in 1997, or one for every 83 persons. The number is expected to decline further to 15,000 by 2020. By contrast, in 1970 there were only 5500 television sets, or one for every 145 persons. By 1997, this had risen to 225,000, or about one for every ten persons. By 2020, the city expects to have 1.17 million television sets, or one per every 4.4, 3.5, or 2.9 persons, depending on the population projection variant used.

Telephone service has increased as well, and with the burgeoning new technology, it will certainly increase more rapidly in the future. In 1970, there was only one telephone exchange, with 15,000 connections, or about 20 phones per 1000 people. Today there are 28 exchanges with 115,000 connections, or 57 phones per 1000 people. By 2020, the conservative estimate is for 545,000 connections, or 105 to 160 phones per 1000 people.

TRANSPORTATION

Road Development over Time

The city was originally laid out in a square, with eight bazaars radiating from the Central Clock Tower, which acted as a focal point for traffic flow. These radiating roads merge with the fringes of an outer road, which runs along the perimeter of the square, called the 'circular road'. Another road rings the eight bazaars. Commercial activities were in front of each bazaar, while other activities such as residential, religious and educational ones were sited between the bazaars. Urban sprawl caused by the influx of people after independence necessitated a piece-meal development, resulting in the choking of the central business district. Increased commercial activities began to invade the residential areas, resulting in heavy traffic congestion on streets meant to serve residential developments. The central business district is now overcrowded with structures, and parking space is very limited. Long queues of bicycles are a common scene in all of the bazaars. The uncontrolled physical growth of the city, the lack of a ring road linking the different spokes radiating from the centre, and the spread of industrial activities into residential zones has destroyed any capacity for a smooth and safe flow of traffic. Moreover, the surrounding settlements are now being served by an inadequate and irregular pattern of roads.

Inner-City Traffic Flow

Traffic is highly congested on most roads. The general pattern of traffic beyond the main circular road is radial in nature, and traffic volumes decrease with the distance from it.

The increase of automobiles, motorcycles, bicycles and animal-drawn vehicles is causing a series of problems. High congestion is exacerbated by large differences in vehicle speed and lack of driving discipline. Traffic in Faisalabad can be accurately described as chaotic and undisciplined. No one pays attention to traffic safety rules; everyone drives in any manner they like. There is a complete lack of road courtesy, as everyone tries to outdo each other. No one obeys traffic signs and signals. There is near total absence of lane discipline. It is common to see vehicles overtaking others in the face of oncoming vehicles, on curves, and in other no-passing zones. All this creates a driving situation that necessitates a very high use of the horn, even in designated silence zones. When the undisciplined character of drivers is added to the great difference in vehicle speeds (marked by animal-drawn carts competing with speeding taxis or three-wheeled motor rickshaws), the combination becomes devastating.

There is also a great difference in road surfaces. Some broad, well-paved avenues permit rapid movement of motorized vehicles. In other areas, unpaved roads with many holes turn the multi-speed traffic into a twisting mass of moving vehicles and animals.

Vehicle Growth

There is a great variety of vehicles in common use on Faisalabad's streets. These include motorized or man-powered rickshaws, bicycles, motorcycles, large trucks, small vans and buses. In addition, there are carts drawn by donkeys, horses, camels and oxen. Tables 4.15 and 4.16 show the numbers of these vehicles in 1970 and 1997, and the STELLA projections up to 2020.

The actual numbers for 1970 and 1997 are from registration records. The projections for the future require explanation. Recall that the population projections presented in Figure 4.1 were based on assumptions about future conditions in agriculture and in government provision of social services. These assumptions also have implications for the projected numbers of vehicles. We assumed that, for small vehicles (including motorcycles) and cars, these projections would be reflected in the ratio of vehicles to population. They would increase only very slowly under the poverty expected in the high variant projection. Under the median variant, which is based on the assumption of a rough continuation of current social and economic conditions, they would about double from current levels. Under the very favourable social and economic assumptions of the low variant, these ratios would grow to roughly four times their current level. For trucks and buses, we simply assumed a very modest growth for the high variant, a slightly larger growth for the median variant and a 50 percent to 100 percent growth under the low variant. The projected growth is shown in Table 4.15 and in Figure 4.12.

This produces an unusual scenario, where slower population growth translates into larger growth in vehicles. We believe this is a reasonable projection, however, because the population variants also indicate assumptions about poverty: the more rapid population growth is associated with increasing poverty for the city and the surrounding area.

Table 4.15
Actual and Projected Number of Vehicles by Type

Vehicle Type	Actual	Actual	Projected by 2020 Population Variants		
	1970	1997	High	Medium	Low
Small vehicles	12,200	87,572	103,208	164,950	271,128
Cars	5409	34,421	51,642	61,865	101,730
Trucks	1430	6257	7000	8000	10,000
Buses	804	2681	3000	4000	6000
Total	11,669	70,203	164,851	238,806	388,858

Figure 4.2
Faisalabad Vehicles, Actual and Projected
(Based in Three Population Variants)

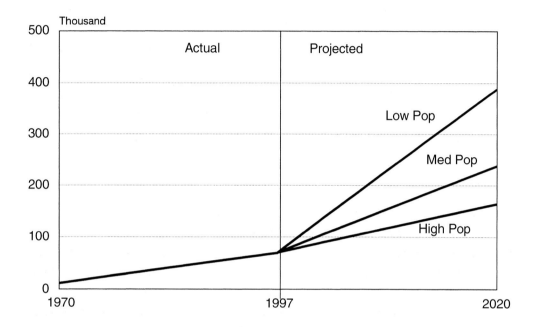

There are also many animal- and hand-powered vehicles that ply the roads in Faisalabad, slowing traffic and making road travel more dangerous. The numbers from the past are estimates from records of vehicle registration. Future projections are more difficult, but we believe they will also be linked to the social and economic changes that we have proposed will be related to different population variants. The increased poverty we expect from the high population variant implies an increased used of these vehicles. The continuation of current conditions assumed for the medium variant implies only a modest growth. The greater social and economic progress expected with the low variant should see many of these vehicles phased out, to be replaced by various motor-powered vehicles. These projections are really only guesses, but we believe they are at least educated guesses. In any event, they are made explicit, for others to disagree with, or to be tested by future conditions. Table 4.16 shows the number of these vehicles in the past and our projections for the future.

Table 4.16
Animal- and Hand-Powered Vehicles

Vehicle Type	Actual	Actual	2020 Population Variants		
	1970	1997	High	Medium	Low
Horse carriages	2550	1950	2500	1800	1000
Donkey carts	3600	5000	6000	4000	2000
Camel carts	405	405	500	400	200
Hand carts	273	300	350	300	200
Hand vans	185	185	200	180	100

Passenger Travel Pattern

Although detailed data are not available, estimates are that the city's public transportation system now carries about 40 percent of the daily traffic. This represents an increase from 25 percent in 1970, and the percentage is expected to grow further to 45 percent by 2020. About a third of daily commuting is done by bicycle, 15 percent by foot and ten percent by private automobile. The high uncertainty associated with future projections leads us to use a simple projection of recent trends for the medium variant 2020 population. These figures, the past growth and future projections, are shown in table 4.17.

Table 4.17
Pattern of Passenger Travel

Mode of Travel	Percentage		
	1970	1997	2020
Foot	40	15	5
Bicycle	25	32	35
Public transport	25	40	45
Private transport	10	13	15
Total	100	100	100

Faisalabad is served by bus, trains and a rail system that link it to its hinterland, other cities in Pakistan, and to the outside world.

Road Accidents

The number of road accidents in Faisalabad remains small, but is growing. Fatal accidents increased from 70 in 1970, to 122 in 1997. Our projections, based on discussions with traffic police, anticipate a rise to 235 by 2020. Non-fatal accidents numbered 35 in 1970, growing to 58 in 1997, and are expected to rise to about 370 by 2020 for the medium variant projection.

Environmental Hazards through Transport Vehicles

There is currently no monitoring of air quality in Faisalabad. Personal assessments note that vehicle exhaust pollution containing particulate matter, nitrogen oxides and lead is high. One study by scientists at the University of Agriculture (Rehman et al., 1988) showed plasma levels varying from 0.14 to 0.4 ppm in clean areas, contrasted with levels of 0.64 to 1.6 ppm in highly congested areas. It seems certain that growth of vehicles has brought more air pollution. There is need both for more empirical studies and for better emission control.

LAND USE

The Land Use Pattern

Faisalabad City has, over the years, become an industrial giant of Pakistan. The old city was planned for mixed residential and commercial uses, with shops lining the major bazaars and their attached residences facing the streets at the back. Other major functions, such as Administration, Education, Industry and Transportation, were situated around the commercial and residential part of the Old Town. After independence, however, the town emerged as a major industrial and commercial centre. Since there was no comprehensive plan for an industrial city, land for industrial use was allocated in a rather haphazard fashion. As a result, except for the new planned residential areas the city presents a picture of mixed land uses. There are four major land use zones in the city:

1. Central Business and Commercial
2. Administrative and Educational
3. Mixed Land use
4. Planned Residential Colonies

The 'Circular Road' surrounds the Central Business and Commercial zone of the Old City. The development of this commercial area was planned along with residences. This area contains a concentration of wholesale, specialized trades, banking and other commercial activities. The Administration and Educational zone encompasses the area of the Civil lines and College Road. The area along Satiana Road, Maqbool Road, Abdullahpur and Ghulam Muhammad Abad has small-scale industries along with residences, resulting in a very mixed-use zone. This composition is due to the large influx of people that took place immediately after independence. The zone of planned residential colonies is now the only really planned area in the city. The FDA is developing a few new colonies, in which the land use pattern is entirely different. The residential density in these colonies and in single-use areas is very low.

The FDA and MCF conducted two surveys of land use in 1981 and 1985. Table 4.18 gives data on changing Municipal area land use since 1970 and projections for the 2020 medium population variant.

Table 4.18
Changes in Land Use Pattern in Faisalabad City over Time

Land Use	Acres (%)		
	1970	**1997**	**2020**
Residential	5110 (25)	14,469 (43)	50,183 (62)
Agriculture land	6728 (33)	1895 (6)	715 (1)
Public building	918 (4)	930 (3)	947 (1)
Education	1700 (8)	2201 (7)	2800 (4)
Graveyards	100 (1)	580 (2)	1000 (1)
Industrial	1100 (5)	1800 (5)	2200 (3)
Commercial	600 (3)	1850 (5)	3400 (4)
Roads	3500 (17)	9000 (27)	17,500 (22)
Miscellaneous	750 (4)	1300 (4)	2200 (3)
Total	20,506 (100)	34,025 (100)	80,945 (100)

It can be seen that of the total area, the largest portion, 43 percent, is now under residential use. This is an increase from the last survey in 1985, which showed 37 percent residential use. Residential areas are expected to continue to grow. Next, roads, which now take up about a quarter of the land, are up from 17 percent in 1970, and are expected to decline slightly in the next two decades. Agriculture was the second largest land use in 1970, taking up a third of municipality land; it has now dropped to only six percent and is expected to decline even further. The city has some large parks and natural areas, and the campus of the agricultural university has extensive open spaces. Finally, the area surrounding the city is open agricultural land. In all, residents are well provided with open spaces.

Housing

According to a survey conducted by the FDA, Faisalabad is facing an acute shortage of houses. The problem is twofold. First, many houses have out-lived their lifetimes and should be replaced; second, the construction rate of new buildings is not keeping pace with the population's rate of increase.

According to the survey, in 1985, there were 195,452 housing units in Faisalabad, out of which 2.25 percent were detached, 19.23 percent were semi-detached and 78.52 percent were row houses. Further, 49.11 percent of the houses were in good condition, 44.61 percent were fair, 6.27 percent were in bad condition and 0.98 percent were dangerous to live in and needing to be demol-ished immediately. The great majority of houses (78 percent) were resident-owned, while 19 percent and three percent were rented or on hire purchase, respectively. A large portion (70 percent) of the houses was well built, made of brick and cement.

Persons per household have remained high and even increased slightly, from seven to 7.4. At the same time, area per house has decreased from 120 to 100 square metres, though the number of rooms per house has increased from 2.5 to 3.5. All of this illustrates a crowding problem that FDA officials note as a major one. Moreover, FDA data also indicate that only about 80 percent of actual housing needs are being met. The basic data on housing are shown in Table 4.19.

Some development projects and future plans of the FDA show that there is very little effort on the part of the public sector to ease housing problems. On the other hand, the participation of the private sector in home construction during the last few years has signalled some improvement, through development of new residential colonies and other housing plans. On the whole, the housing situation in Faisalabad city will remain problematic in the future, though the

Table 4.19
Trends in Housing Units

Item	1970	1997	2020 Population Projection		
			High	Medium	Low
Number of housing units					
a) Required	110,000	272,000	727,361	580,811	477,616
b) Actual	110,000	215,000	–	–	–
Number of rooms per housing unit	2.5	3.5	4.5	4.5	4.5
Number of persons per housing unit	7.0	7.4	7.1	7.1	7.1
Space (sq. metre) per housing unit	120	100	80	80	80

population of homeless individuals is likely to remain small, at around 0.5 percent.

THE ECONOMY

Industrial Growth

Faisalabad began its life as a market town for a rapidly growing agricultural area. Three decades passed before it took on its present character as a major industrial centre. In 1932, the Lyallpur Cotton Mill was established, marking the beginning of a new era. When Pakistan came into existence in 1947, there were 20 industrial enterprises in Faisalabad, three of which were large establishments. In the following decade, the number of plants rose to 368, then to 1062 in the next decade, and to 4533 by 1977. The 1981 census found 11,588 industrial establishments. Of these 512 were classified as 'large establishments', i.e. having more than 50 workers. The dominance of textiles can be seen in the fact that 328 of the 'large establishments' were textile factories, dealing with cotton, jute or wool.

Faisalabad has become known worldwide for its textiles. Its cotton is prized for its whiteness and the excellent way in which it takes dyes. Today there are yarn and cloth markets where hundreds of thousands of metres of white cloth can be purchased from one of over 300 textile factories. There are also engineering, chemical and pharmaceutical firms, as well as woollen, lace and rug making industries that have spun off from or support the textile industry. The multi-faceted textile industry employs over 45,000 workers. Agricultural and food processing employ 7000, and scores of other plants employ thousands more. The city provides a large source of employment, and produces goods for export as well as local consumption.

Local officials and businessmen have reported a move of some of the larger firms out of the city. Smaller firms appear to remain and may become more common. It remains to be seen what impact this will have on the city. All are agreed, however, that the industrial sector will continue to grow, as the basic supportive infrastructure and manpower pool of the city will continue to attract investors and entrepreneurs.

Income

The industrial character of the city implies a high level of wage and salary workers, bringing a steady stream of income to the town. This creates a demand for all manner of services, multiplying the economic impact and producing income for many others outside the industrial core. Although detailed data are lacking, informed observers in the city have provided estimates of both the sources of income and its distribution. Tables 4.20 and 4.21 provide their estimates, again using the 2020 medium population variant.

Table 4.20
Changes in Sources of Income

Source of Income	Year		
	1970	1997	2020
	— Percent income originating from —		
Business/Commerce	63	75	80
Skilled labour	6	8	10
Daily wage earning	8	5	3
Private sector employees	9	8	5
Government employees	14	4	2
Total	100	100	100

Source: Estimates by research team, based on interviews with city officials

Table 4.21
Distribution of Population according to Income Strata

Income group (Rs/month/household)*	Year		
	1970	1997	2020
	— Percent Population —		
Up to 2000	50	37	30
2000 – 4000	20	23	25
4000 – 6000	12	15	20
6000 – 8000	6	10	13
8000 – 10000	5	7	7
10000 – 15000	4	5	4
15000 and above	2	3	1

* Note: The present rate of exchange is Rs.45 per US$1 (approximate) 1997.
Source: Interviews with city officials

Being an industrial and commercial centre, the citizens' major source of income eventually is business and commerce. Other sources, though important, contribute relatively less towards total income generation in Faisalabad. Table 4.20 shows the dominance of business and commerce, and their increasing importance. This pattern of growth is expected to continue in the near future.

The distribution of income shows a major proportion of the population concentrated in the low-income stratum, earning less than 2000 rupees per month. Currently this constitutes about one third of the wage earners. Note that this proportion has declined from 50 percent in 1970, and is expected to decline further to about 30 percent by 2020. The categories 2000 to 8000 rupees have all shown an increase and are expected to increase further in the future. This probably indicates some real increase in wages, but it also probably indicates mere increase in prices as well, since these figures are not corrected for inflation.

Another way to illustrate what this level of income means is to compare it with Pakistan's average per capita GNP. Although a direct comparison cannot be made, 2000 rupees per month amounts to approximately US$510 per year, which is slightly higher than Pakistan's estimated per capita GNP[4]. By another comparison, we can note that the World Bank's 'parity purchasing power' calculation gives Pakistan a 'real' per capita GNP five times that of the foreign exchange calculation (US$2460 vs. US$490). This would imply that a 2000-

rupee monthly income would be closer to US$2500 per year in comparable purchasing power.

QUALITY OF LIFE: FACTS AND PERCEPTIONS

Population-Environment Dynamics: Dilemmas

By comparison with other areas in Pakistan, Faisalabad enjoys a somewhat higher quality of life. The canal has turned a relatively unproductive wetland into a rich agricultural area. Past government investments have given the city a good basic plan, an excellent university, schools, health facilities, parks, good roads, and rail and air connections to the outside world. These public investments have attracted extensive private investments in factories, producing a rich textile industry. This large industrial base has provided wealth for the city and employment for thousands of people.

These are very real advantages, but they have also produced some massive and seemingly intractable problems. The first concerns population dynamics. If the canal brought life-giving waters that attracted many people, it also set in motion a problem in population-environmental dynamics that now challenges the city. Canal-irrigated agriculture in a basically arid climate ultimately leads to salinization of soils and loss of agricultural productivity. If the rich agriculture brought about population increase, the pattern of growth now threatens to overshoot the carrying capacity of the land. Large family sizes have led to extensive fragmentation of holdings to sizes that can no longer support a family. Thus, environmental degradation and population pressure have combined to produce an excess rural population that must migrate to find a source of living.

In addition, the government of Pakistan has displayed a high degree of instability and an exceptionally low capacity to provide good social services for its citizens, or to maintain the physical infrastructure it has built up in the past. Physical facilities and social services are deteriorating seriously.

The near future is very uncertain. An agricultural collapse is possible and would overwhelm the city and greatly increase poverty. Agriculture could continue to deteriorate only slowly, with no improvement in government services, implying simply a continuation of current conditions. Another more positive scenario is available, however, especially if government capacities would increase and provide greater social and economic services for the people. These possibilities have been explored through our use of three population variants for the future. The real future, however, remains uncertain.

If the public investment in the town attracted people from the rural areas, that same in-migration now threatens to outstrip the ability of public investment to keep up with population growth. The result is a continuing deterioration of an urban infrastructure that is already inadequate. Housing, sewage, waste collection, education, and health care now appear less than adequate, and there is little prospect for improvement. The internal movement of the population and an increase of motor vehicles threaten to produce heavier congestion and noxious air pollution.

Finally, if this city that is built with public investment attracted modern industry, the problems of industrial employment and environmental degradation may further reduce the quality of life. Global economic forces can have a devastating impact on the kind of urban industrial employment that gives Faisalabad a relatively good standard of living. Industrial pollution can also degrade the environment, reducing the quality of life through illness, and even cause death from toxic emissions.

All of these conditions will worsen if the decline of agriculture produces the heavy in-migration that this study has shown is a real possibility. If Faisalabad now strains under a population of two million, what will it be like under a population 1.5 to 2.5 times that much, which might come in the next two decades? These are all very real problems for city administrators and for business leaders in the private sector.

Perceptions of the Quality of Life

Our study also sought out a number of key leaders to obtain their assessments of the city's quality of life. First, on the positive side, most were optimistic about certain conditions and trends. They did not expect to face serious problems with water and energy. There are problems in these areas, to be sure. Water quality is threatened by a distribution system that needs upgrading, but for which funds seem lacking. Still, there should be no shortage of reasonably clean water. Energy supplies, especially under the private gas and electric systems, seem fairly well assured, even if there are problems with shortages and breakdowns.

Urban transportation and industry represent other problem areas in which some progress has been seen. Urban transportation is viewed as a serious problem, as it is now in most cities, but observers agree that since privatization, new bus companies have considerably relieved the situation. Although there can be some worry about the impact of global economic forces, observers are confident that the city will continue to grow as an industrial centre.

There is another, somewhat greyer, problem area in social services. It is well recognized that public schools and health facilities are highly over-taxed and inadequate. Nor does anyone foresee a large increase in public investment to deal with these problems. On the other hand, it is here that the private sector is emerging to meet people's needs. This is especially clear in the health sector, where we have seen a considerable increase in private facilities and practitioners. In schools, as well, we see the rise of private schools and tutorial arrangements as parents struggle to provide their children with the skills they will need for a good future.

Beyond this guarded or partial optimism, however, observers are cognizant of many intractable problems for which they see no quick or easy solutions. The pressures on an already inadequate urban infrastructure rank high on the list. Sewage, drainage and waste collection are now overwhelmed, and no real relief is in sight. Housing is barely adequate, and there is fear that it will not be able to keep up with increasing population growth. Attempts to deal with these problems are constantly frustrated by political interference. Elected representatives seem to have little vision of the city as a whole. Corruption is a serious problem. The use of public position for private gain constantly weakens the community's capacity to address its problems. No relief seems impending.

Our informants provided many insightful proposals to address these problems, though for the most part they recognized that shortage of funds and adverse political conditions would continue to frustrate efforts to find solutions. First, all agree that the government should do more to promote family planning. This move would provide immediate benefits in improved maternal and child health, and more long-term benefits in reduced population pressures. Many would like to see efforts to help reduce the pressure from in-migration, but there are few specific ideas on how this might be achieved. There are many good and specific ideas about relieving traffic congestion and providing a better transportation layout. Good ideas were presented for promoting public and private housing to relieve this shortage. Similar ideas were put forward to improve health and education. Most of these ideas, however, require two things that all agree are in short supply. One is public funds. Little help can be expected on this score from either the national or provincial governments. The second is a more political problem. The city needs elected leaders who can think about the city and its future more than they think about their immediate personal gain. However, this requires a kind of political change that observers are uncertain will come about.

Notes

1. This description applies to the period before the 1999 coup, which has changed political and administrative conditions considerably throughout Pakistan.
2. Bangladesh, India and Sri Lanka, show overall national infant mortality rates of 78, 72 and 15 respectively in 1995 (UN, 1996).
3. This is similar to the all Pakistan ratio of 107. It is also similar to the ratio throughout South (106) and Western Asia (105), but considerably higher than that in Southeast Asia (99), Africa (99), or all less developed regions together (103). The high sex ratio indicates considerable male dominance
4. By World Bank indicators, Pakistan's $490 GNP per capita makes it more wealthy than Bangladesh ($270), or India ($390), but less wealthy than Sri Lanka ($800) (World Bank, 1998).

Chapter 5

Khon Kaen: Heart of the North-East

Krasae Chanawongse
Peerasit Kamnuansilpa
Supawatanakorn Wongtanavasu
Yupin Techamanee

THE URBAN SETTING

Located some 450 kilometres from Bangkok, Khon Kaen is a small but rapidly growing city in the centre of Thailand's North-East region. It is the administrative seat of the Province and is fast becoming the major centre of education, finance, business and government activities for the entire region.

Khon Kaen province, of which the city is a part, extends for 10,866 square kilometres, and has a population (1996) of 1.67 million people. It is primarily agricultural, with farming accounting for 60 percent of its land and 70 percent of its population. As in most of Thailand, agriculture means rice, which makes up two-thirds of the province's farmland. The region is well watered, with three rivers flowing through it, and receives over 100 centimetres (about 40 inches) of rain per year. These rivers have been tapped for irrigation schemes, but they cover less than one percent of all farmland. Agriculture, especially rice, is primarily rain fed, and thus highly seasonal. The rains come from May to October with the south-west monsoon winds; the rest of the year is hot and dry. Although rice is the main crop in the area, the sandy soils are not well suited to it. Other crops, such as corn, tapioca, jute and vegetables have greater market value. Rice, however, remains the staple crop, as it feeds the population. Overall, the province is poor, and has for years been somewhat isolated from Thailand's main centre in Bangkok. A railroad built from Bangkok to the Laotian border at Nong Khai, originally passing a few kilometres from Khon Kaen, has been primarily a means for poor rural people to migrate to Bangkok for work.

The recent growth of Khon Kaen is largely a product of central government policies seeking to promote economic development in other major regions outside of Bangkok on the central plain. The government has invested in administrative buildings, a major university, an airport, land and irrigation schemes, and Khon Kaen's transportation infrastructure. It also built a major highway from Bangkok through Khon Kaen to the Laotian border, making the drive to Bangkok a mere four hours. The town has expanded greatly, placing its rail line and the station near the town centre. The Bank of Thailand located its centre for the entire Northeast Region in Khon Kaen.

In part, the recent growth was spurred by the Vietnam War, when the US built air and military bases in the Northeast for its war against North Vietnam. Due to government regional development planning, however, when the Vietnam War ended, Khon Kaen and the rest of the Northeast continued to grow from their own initiative.

Environmental changes are clear and of long standing, but as yet do not appear overly debilitating. The forests of the region have been largely cleared. This process has gone on for centuries, as agriculture in this region is very old, perhaps 4000 years or more. More recently, however, the rate of deforestation has increased. Small villages have also existed in the region for centuries, but only recently have we seen the rise of substantial towns, like Khon Kaen. For the most part these towns appear well supplied with water and energy, and well served with waste disposal, which have provided the population with a relatively healthy environment. Once an isolated region, it has now become closely connected to the rest of the country and the world by railroads, roads, motor vehicles and aeroplanes. There is as yet, however, little of the heavy vehicular congestion and air pollution that plague many areas of rapid urbanization and population growth.

Development has also meant change in migration patterns. For years Khon Kaen was only a way station for rural migrants from the poor Northeast region, travelling to Bangkok to seek work. Today, that migration continues, but has slowed and there is now a new movement back from the central plains to the north-east and to Khon Kaen itself.

The great economic downturn of 1997 hurt Khon Kaen as it did all of Thailand. The baht fell from 25 to 40 to the US dollar. Capital dried up, construction slowed or ceased, and inflated real estate prices and heavy speculation were punctured. This left many people poor, out of work, and bewildered after more than three decades of steady and recently very rapid economic growth. But Thailand has been more resilient and stable than such countries as Indonesia, and now is currently showing good signs of recovery. Khon Kaen continues to grow as a regional centre, and shows relatively little wear and tear from these economic gyrations.

Though it presents real challenges, the future looks good.

POPULATION

The Numbers and the Data

Population data come from the population register, which is believed to be quite complete. As will be immediately apparent, however, the official data produce some strange results. Table 5.1 shows the official counts of population, births, deaths, and migration.

Table 5.1
Demographic History of Khon Kaen City Municipal Area

Year	Pop.	No. Birth	No. Death	In-Migration	Out-Migration	Net-Migration	Birth Rate	Death Rate	Natural Increase	Growth Rate %
1970	31625	625	82	3093	2432	661	19.8	2.6	17.2	–
1971	32393	639	62	27601	2441	25160	19.7	1.9	17.8	2.43
1972	61004	1633	224	5137	3400	1737	26.8	3.7	23.1	88.32
1973	64402	1981	298	5913	4182	1731	30.8	4.6	26.1	5.57
1974	67904	1996	319	6747	4761	1986	29.4	4.7	24.7	5.44
1975	71526	2119	372	6211	4336	1875	29.6	5.2	24.4	5.33
1980	94019	9032	349	8662	13054	–4392	96.1	3.7	92.4	4.55
1985	121784	9305	319	8161	15785	–7624	76.4	2.6	73.8	2.02
1990	143708	11935	1721	8259	11893	–3634	83.1	12.0	71.1	2.18
1995	141911	14794	2078	5116	18237	–13121	104.2	14.6	89.6	–0.87
1997	152601	13409	3307	8136	14386	–6250	87.9	21.7	66.2	5.81

The number and rate of births is especially striking. In 1970 and 1972, there were about 600 births per year, producing rates just below 20 per thousand. These rates were lower than the birth rate for Thailand as a whole, which then registered about 35 per thousand. With the very low death rates for those two years, it appears that the registration process may have been incomplete, and that both births and deaths were underestimated.

Then in 1973 the births increased by about 1000, and the rate jumped to that of the overall national level. The death rate also rose, though it was still less than half the national level. We can assume that the registration process was being strengthened, but we also know that part of the large growth of population from 1972 to 1973 was due to an almost four-fold expansion of Khon Kaen's area, which took in many of the small villages that had become suburban neighbourhoods of the city.

The recorded birth statistics grew gradually through 1977, then took a dramatic turn upward in 1978, when 7800 births produced a crude birth rate of 92.6 per thousand, much higher than found in any average society. This great increase was, however, merely the result of the completion of a new regional hospital, which drew pregnant women from many parts of the province to deliver their babies. This fact represents a major problem in Khon Kaen's data collection and recording, which has been a persistent challenge to our study of the city's population-environment relationship.

Part of the problem lies in the city's recording procedures. Births in the hospital are considered city births, but are also counted as in-migrants if the births are to mothers residing outside of town. When the new babies leave the hospital, they are counted as out-migrants. This method of counting inflates both birth and migration numbers, giving us rates that are, at best, unusual for any normal city. In addition, new college students who enrol in Khon Kaen University each year are counted as in-migrants. When they graduate, usually four years later, they are counted as out-migrants. Both these recording procedures make it difficult to assess the rate of natural increase or migration for the city as a whole. At the same time, these procedures and the results they provide reflect a distinctive character of the city: it is a service-providing centre that serves a population far beyond its own administrative boundaries. This is true for most cities of the world, of course, but for Khon Kaen the situation is especially marked by the nature of official recording.

Strategies: Linear regression or modelling

There are two strategies available for working with the data to examine the distinct urban processes they reflect. The first strategy is to use the data as they are, making trend analyses with linear regression techniques, and essentially assuming that past trends would continue into the future. Alternately, the situation can be *modelled*, using a simulation based on reasonable figures and rates. Each of these strategies will be considered next.

Trend Analysis

Table 5.2
Projected Population, Birth, Death, In-migrants and Out-migrants,
1998–2020 (With linear regression techniques)

Year	Population	Birth	Death	In-migrants	Out-migrants
2000	161,392	16,637	3730	6554	15,936
2005	176,992	19,218	4647	6153	18,149
2010	192,591	21,799	5563	5753	20,363
2015	208,190	24,380	6479	5353	22,577
2020	223,789	26,961	7395	4952	24,790

Table 5.2 shows the results of trend analysis, which used linear regression techniques to project births, deaths, migration and Khon Kaen's total city population. Estimated in this fashion, the population shows a growth rate of about two percent per year, with the total population reaching almost 224,000 by the year 2020. The totals appear reasonable, but both migration and birth rates seem greatly inflated.

Modelling the Population Growth

To model the population of the past, we disregarded Khon Kaen's recorded vital rates and used the United Nations (1996) estimates of crude birth and death rates for Thailand as a whole. The country has gone through the demographic transition from high to low birth and death rates. The crude death rate began to fall rapidly after 1945, declining to 11.4 by 1970 and levelled off below eight by 1980. Fertility decline followed and came very rapidly after it started. The total fertility rate was above six until 1970, fell to 4.99 in 1975, to 2.96 in 1985 and to 1.94, below replacement level, in 1995. In the same period the crude birth rate dropped from 41.8 to 18.1. The period between these two declines was one of very high population growth rates.

It is not unreasonable to apply the overall national vital rates to Khon Kaen City. The birth rate might be an overestimate, since urban rates have usually been below rural rates. By 1980, however, the Thai family planning programme had brought effective contraceptive use to most of the country, with little real difference between urban and rural contraceptive use and fertility. It is also possible that the national figure might underestimate the real rates in Khon Kaen, since the city has attracted in-migrants for many years, and they tend to be younger people of prime reproductive ages. Thus the crude birth rate for the city might have been slightly higher than that for the country as a whole. Given the possibility of both under and overestimation, we can safely use the national figures as they are. Thus we used the national rates from 1970 to 1997 to estimate Khon Kaen's total population, adjusting the migration rates to produce a model total that fits exactly the city's registered population total for that period.

It was more difficult to decide what to do with the migration figures. From the recorded data it appears that there was net in-migration from 1970 to 1977, followed by roughly stable net out-migration, punctuated by wild swings in both rates from year to year. To simplify the process, we decided to leave the in-migration rates as they are listed and to change only the out-migration rates, to provide a total population figure that matched the actual registered population. All of these assumptions are visible and can be examined and changed.

In summary, our model uses UN estimates of Thailand's crude birth and death rates, Khon Kaen's recorded in-migration rates, and adjustments of out-migration rates to model the city's population. Our modelled totals of 1970 to 1997 exactly fit the actual registered population of Khon Kaen for the same period.

To model the future to 2020, we again used UN estimates of birth and death rates, which are separated into high, medium and low variants. We held migration rates constant at six percent in-migration and five percent out-migration for the period. The model results are shown in Figure 5.1 and Table 5.3.

Overall, Khon Kaen's population rose from 31,000 in 1970 to about 150,000 in 1997. For the future, our model's medium variant projects an increase to 233,000. The low variant gave 212,000 and the high variant 240,000. Thus, future growth is expected to be approximately two percent per year, with the increase coming in roughly equal rates of one percent each from natural increase and net migration.

These are similar to the results achieved by simply projecting a two-percent per year increase as in the trend analysis. The model does, however, give us a better picture of the population dynamics as based on vital rates. The migration projections are much less certain. The future of migration will undoubtedly be the result of many factors. Chief among these will be patterns of investment,

Figure 5.1
Modelled Khon Kaen Population, 1970–2020

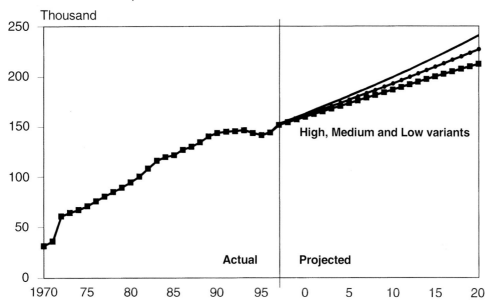

Table 5.3
Modelled Population (Medium Variant) and Components

Year	Total Population	Births	Deaths	In-Migration	Out-Migration
1970	31,625	1110	294	4744	949
1971	36,236	1247	330	25,365	1449
1972	61,068	2058	544	4885	3053
1973	64,415	2126	560	5153	3865
1974	67,269	2173	572	5381	3363
1975	70,888	2240	588	5671	2481
1980	94,490	2372	661	9260	5197
1985	121,558	2808	778	10,697	7293
1990	143,647	2600	876	7470	7901
1995	141,514	2363	934	9198	7783
2000	161,433	2551	1130	9779	8072
2005	177,661	2718	1279	10,845	8883
2010	195,073	2809	1424	11,967	9754
2015	213,471	2925	1580	13,154	10,674
2020	233,131	–	–	–	–

both from public and private sources. These will depend in part on movements of the global economy, over which Thailand will have little control and Khon Kaen even less. Moreover, relatively small swings in the global economy or Thailand's position in it can have large implications for a relatively small-sized city such as Khon Kaen.

Families and Households

The number of families in Khon Kaen grew steadily over the period 1970 to 1997, from about 5500 to 39,000. With Thailand experiencing a rapid modern fertility decline, family size has declined steadily. Khon Kaen followed the rest of Thailand closely; there were almost six persons per family in 1970, declining steadily to 3.9 in 1997.

Unlike families, however, household size in Khon Kaen has not declined. It stood at eight in 1970, declined to six in 1981, then rose again to 8.4 in 1997. Clearly something unexpected happened. We caught a glimpse of the cause while examining vital statistics, and will go into more detail when we discuss the educational system, but the driving force here is essentially the regions' distinctive migration pattern.

Khon Kaen contains a large number of families that retain bases in rural areas. Family relations and ties to the home village give Thais natural staging areas as they move throughout the country (Government of Thailand, 1986; Fuller et al., 1983; Lightfoot et al., 1983). Village people can send their children to relatives in the city for births, health care and education. A Khon Kaen household may often include village cousins who come to stay for varying periods of time. But it is not only family relations that provide the tie. Rural migrants can also visit city dwellers from their village and expect a warm reception. If the city family can accommodate the migrants, they become part of the household, swelling it beyond its own immediate family members. All of this is shown in Table 5.4.

What will the future hold? It is easy to project family size and numbers from what we know of the probable course of fertility. Average family size will likely continue to decline, as it has in the past. It fell from 5.7 in 1970 to 3.9 in 1997. It is easy to foresee a continued decline to 3.0 by 2020. Using the modelled population size for the near future, we calculated the number of families shown in Table 5.4.

It is not easy to project household size, however, and Table 5.4 leaves these

Table 5.4
Family and Household in Khon Kaen

Year	Population	Families	Family Size	Households	Household Size
1970	31,625	5511	5.7	3974	8.0
1975	71,526	13,576	5.3	10,893	6.6
1980	94,019	17,736	5.3	16,416	5.7
1985	121,784	21,946	5.5	17,495	7.0
1990	143,708	29,989	4.8	17,716	8.1
1995	141,911	34,133	4.2	18,076	7.9
1997	152,810	39,182	3.9	18,258	8.4
2000	161,433	42,482	3.8	–	–
2005	177,661	49,350	3.6	–	–
2010	195,073	57,374	3.4	–	–
2015	213,471	66,710	3.2	–	–
2020	233,131	77,710	3.0	–	–

cells blank. At the moment, Khon Kaen has something of a housing shortage. It is likely that many families would prefer to live in single family, nuclear households. If low interest rate mortgages were available and the construction industry had substantial unused capacity, it is likely that there would be a boom in single family housing and a decline in household size. There is also the question of land for housing in the city. Land is now becoming scarce and this restricts the easy expansion of housing. If there is another expansion of the city's boundaries, as in 1972, it is possible that more land could become available for housing and thus have an impact on the average size of the household. But these questions of how open and how large a household would be, and how the housing market might expand, remain open. It seems reasonable to expect that the pattern of temporary visitors to the household will continue. It is not possible, however, to predict how strong these attachments will prove to be, and thus how household size would change in the near future. Thus we left those data cells empty.

Age Structure

Thailand shows a changing age-structure that is characteristic of rapid population growth followed by rapid fertility decline. First the fall of mortality and continued high fertility produce a very young population. Then as fertility rates fall, the population ages: proportions in the young ages decline, while those in older ages increase. There are no surprises in store for Thailand in this respect and no real problems pending in the near future from the increase in the number of older people. While we do not have data for Khon Kaen itself, there are no indications that the pattern has been, or will be, any different from that of Thailand as a whole. Thus we can again use national level data on various age group proportions to estimate age structures for Khon Kaen municipality. When we turn later to educational services and school populations, we shall see that we can use these national level proportions to model the potential school population. This will provide us with a good basis for understanding what the actual school population means.

Figure 5.2 shows one picture of the age structure for the past quarter century, and its probable course for the next. With a successful family planning pro-gramme, Thai fertility rates have fallen very rapidly, and the population under five years of age has declined accordingly from more than 25 percent in 1970, to less than a fifth today, and will decline further to about 15 percent by 2020. The young school-age population, five to 14 years of age, has also declined from just under 20 percent to about eight percent today, and will continue to decline

Figure 5.2
Changing Age-Structure for all Thailand

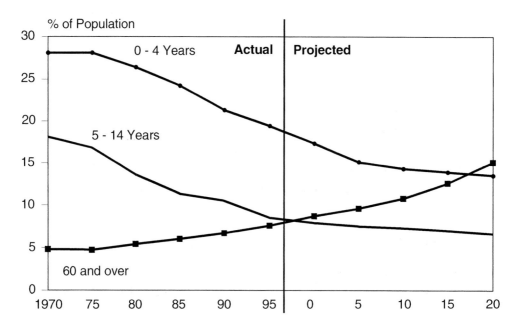

slowly to about six percent by 2020. The population is ageing, and the proportion of people over 60 will continue to grow. For the next generation, however, that growth will remain moderate. The over-60 population was only five percent of the total in 1970. It rose slowly to about seven percent in 1997, and is projected to rise to 15 percent by the year 2020. In effect, Thailand's problems of the ageing population lie considerably in the future. For all of the period of our analysis, the young will considerably outnumber the aged. In 2020, the combined 0–14 population will still amount to 20 percent of the population, while the over-60 group will be just 15 percent. That picture for Thailand will most likely be mirrored in the Northeast Region, but as we shall see in examining the school population, Khon Kaen may have a somewhat different age structure, for understandable institutional reasons.

SOCIAL SERVICES

Health and Health Services

Overall, Thailand's health system has grown steadily over the past half century, providing good quality primary health care throughout urban and rural areas. The result has been a dramatic decline in mortality and a general increase in the quality of life for virtually the entire population. Khon Kaen municipality and province have both participated fully in this progress.

Table 5.5 shows the data available from the Provincial Health Office. Data recording began only in 1981, and it makes no distinction between public and private facilities. Public facilities remain dominant in number, staff and acceptors, but the private sector is growing in the city. In the surrounding rural areas, the public sector provides the great bulk of services.

As Table 5.5 shows, the number of health centres in Khon Kaen steadily increased from about 150 in 1981 to 250 in 1997. The number of staff has also increased in this period, from just under 2000 to just under 3000. Users of these services have increased far more rapidly, however. From just over 1000 in 1981, they grew to almost 30,000 in 1997, with an absolute explosion of numbers after 1993.

Although staff and users have grown, they have not grown more rapidly than the population. The staff per 1000 population remains around 20. The fluctuations of 1987, 1991 and 1992 are not explained, and probably represent some error in the recording. Figure 5.3 shows the statistical movements over time.

Table 5.5
Health Services and Acceptors

Year	Number of Health Clinics	Number of Staff	Number of Service Acceptors
1981	159	1926	1194
1982	162	2002	1687
1983	167	2014	2082
1984	203	2132	2449
1985	190	2365	3230
1986	190	2477	3718
1987	193	3119	3782
1988	196	2873	3998
1989	198	3523	4334
1990	198	2850	5868
1991	206	2449	4521
1992	203	3671	3951
1993	210	2597	4497
1994	213	2491	6343
1995	229	2590	12,044
1996	232	2605	18,094
1997	250	2994	28,217

For the future, Khon Kaen will have to increase the staff from between 4500 to 5000 if it is to retain its same staff per population ratio. It is difficult to project the number of users, since they have risen so rapidly in the past few years. If they keep rising at this rate, the numbers would be astronomical and unbelievable. Trend analysis can be used to make a more reasonable statistical projection, which would see users rising to over 50,000 by the year 2020. This would imply a ratio of about 200 users per 1000 population, just slightly more than the figure for 1997. This is merely a statistical projection, however, uninformed by the needs of the users or the character of the services provided. To make a more informed projection, it will be necessary to know more about who the users are and what services they are using. At this time, we can make only a modest start on this set of questions.

Figure 5.3
Health Services: Staff and Users

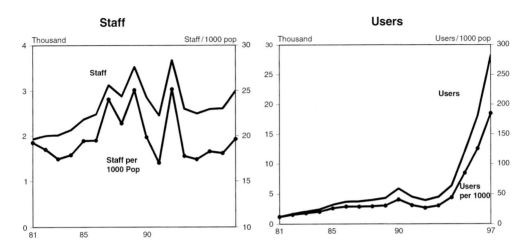

First, we know that in all of Thailand, mortality rates have been falling steadily since 1950. The Infant Mortality Rate was cut in half from 135 in 1950 to 65 in 1970, and halved again to 32 in 1990. Life expectancy has increased for both males and females, but slightly more rapidly for women. Since life expectancy for women is influenced by the maternal mortality rate, we can assume that the maternal mortality rate has been falling as well. It is reasonable to assume that all parts of the country have participated in this general increase in the physical quality of life.

For Khon Kaen, specifically, we can begin with two sensitive mortality rates, infant and maternal mortality rates, shown below. Both conditions, childbirth and infancy, are vulnerable conditions, and both are strongly affected by the quality of primary health care services. These services provide the pre- and antenatal care that reduce the risk of death from child-bearing and the vaccinations that protect against early childhood diseases. Other public health investments, such as for water and sewage, also have a major impact on child and maternal mortality, but they lie outside of the specific health services we are examining here and were not considered. Still, the general progress of economic development and expanding physical infrastructure that the city and province have experienced over the past few decades have surely contributed to the reduction of mortality, along with the provision of good primary health care.

Table 5.6 shows the movement of Khon Kaen's infant and maternal mortality rates since 1981, when locally-collected data become available. The infant mortality rate stood at 9.33 in 1981, and fluctuated around that level for the next 18 years. Maternal mortality was 60 in 1981 and fluctuated wildly from a high of 176 to a low of ten for the next 18 years. The high figures for 1986 and 1993 to 1994 are explained by an error in recording, which counted all female deaths in this period as maternal deaths. Thus, those figures can be ignored. In any event, there is no clear trend in either rate. The average for these 17 years is nine for infant mortality, and 57 for maternal mortality.

Both rates are low by the standards of developing countries. For example, Thailand is in the group of developing countries with high human development indices[1]. For these countries, the average of infant mortality is 29 and 148 for maternal mortality. Note that many of these countries are substantially wealthier than Thailand. For countries with moderate or low human development indices,

Table 5.6
Mortality Rates for Mothers and Infants, 1981–97

Year	Maternity/100,000	Infant/1000
1981	60	9.33
1982	61	11.34
1983	29	15.34
1984	43	9.84
1985	41	9.93
1986	176	7.38
1987	75	5.99
1988	35	9.00
1989	10	8.10
1990	55	8.80
1991	20	13.20
1992	10	5.50
1993	80	8.60
1994	87	8.76
1995	55	2.45
1996	60	8.83
1997	80	10.60

but near the same level of wealth as Thailand, average infant mortality rates are 40 and 90; maternal mortality rates are 210 and 766 (UN, 1998). Thus the Thai measures are quite favourable overall. This, too, is evidence of the progress Thailand has made in primary health care over the past few decades.

Next, we examined rates for two infectious diseases common in poor countries, respiratory and gastrointestinal diseases, which are strongly influenced by primary health care and public health investments. Table 5.7 shows the number of patients treated for these disease symptoms from 1981 to 1997.

The numbers are actual treatments, thus an individual receiving four or five treatments will be counted four or five times. In the case of both diseases there has been steady and substantial growth in the number of treatments. It is difficult to know what to make of this trend. Death rates have been going down, but the treatment of these two common infectious diseases is rising rapidly. It is difficult to think that the incidence of these diseases is actually rising, especially

Table 5.7
Number of Treatments for
Respiratory and Gastrointestinal Diseases, 1981–97

Year	Respiratory	Gastrointestinal
1981	1803	4284
1982	2642	5341
1983	3549	6687
1984	6793	9046
1985	6998	10,809
1986	8584	10,013
1987	9643	12,638
1988	9535	11,342
1989	9450	12,590
1990	10,453	13,216
1991	11,295	12,274
1992	12,117	15,862
1993	12,412	18,584
1994	15,208	20,992
1995	21,734	30,970
1996	22,926	34,169
1997	26,873	38,874

at the rates shown here. A better explanation probably lies in better treatment. With the advent of good primary health care centres that provide free or very low-cost service, people are now receiving treatment for ailments that before went untreated. This is mere conjecture, however. Clearly the issue needs further study. It would be inappropriate to project these numbers into the future until more is known about what they actually mean. Here is a good case for some detailed epidemiological work in and around Khon Kaen. Figure 5.4 shows these past movements more clearly.

Figure 5.4
Numbers of Treatments for Respiratory and Gastrointestinal Symptoms

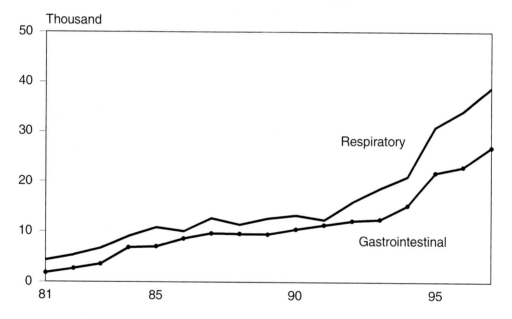

Education

Overall, Thailand has made much progress in the past half century in extending education to its population. By the beginning of our period of analysis, 1970, Thailand had achieved nearly universal primary education. It continues to expand educational services at all levels, and just recently mandated free education through secondary school, to age 18. Khon Kaen has participated in this overall expansion of education, and in addition has benefited by being designated the major university centre for the Northeast Region. Educational data for Khon Kaen are shown in Table 5.8.

Table 5.8
Numbers of Students Enrolled in Educational Institutions

Year	Primary	Secondary	Tertiary	Primary & Secondary
1970	Not available	Not available	1165	Not available
1971	Not available	Not available	1434	Not available
1972	Not available	Not available	1667	Not available
1973	Not available	Not available	1786	Not available
1974	Not available	Not available	2062	Not available
1975	Not available	Not available	2201	Not available
1976	Not available	Not available	2650	Not available
1977	Not available	Not available	3035	Not available
1978	Not available	Not available	3356	Not available
1979	Not available	Not available	3715	Not available
1980	Not available	Not available	4073	Not available
1981	Not available	Not available	4169	Not available
1982	39,355	26,782	4095	66,137
1983	41,433	25,521	4652	66,954
1984	37,784	19,323	5051	57,107
1985	19,750	18,863	5435	38,613
1986	38,059	28,766	5757	66,825
1987	37,323	24,534	5747	61,857
1988	19,806	17,948	6026	37,754
1989	34,438	34,263	6508	68,701
1990	34,438	34,263	7815	68,701
1991	34,887	32,401	7725	67,288
1992	34,390	39,960	8334	74,350
1993	34,596	41,999	9138	76,595
1994	34,078	43,361	9788	77,439
1995	36,420	47,145	10,752	83,565
1996	38,762	47,416	12,082	86,178
1997	34,893	49,466	13,305	84,359

The data provided for education in Khon Kaen present a number of problems. Data for both primary and secondary students became available in 1982. That year there were 39,355 primary and 26,782 secondary students. In the next four years primary students went to 41,000, 37,000, 19,000, and 38,000; secondary students to 25,000, 19,000, 18,000, and 28,000. Thus, 1984 and 1985 showed strange deficits of secondary and primary students. The year 1988 also showed a sharp drop for both from the year before. In addition, the numbers appear too high for the size of the population. While the trends for primary enrolment per family show a steady decline, the numbers are greater than the estimates of family size. Trends for secondary enrolment remain steady, despite the real decline in family size. Finally, the ratio of primary and secondary school students to families shows a considerable excess over the actual and projected family size.

Although the sharp declines in the years 1985 and 1988 remain anomalies and are probably errors in reporting, we have determined what is happening in the numbers and trends. As noted above, Khon Kaen families often host children of relatives and fellow villagers so that they can receive the advantages of urban educational services. This influx of rural children inflates Khon Kaen's school population.

How large in this influx? To answer this question, we modelled the school population to develop a number that would be expected for a city this size. The expected population can then be compared to the actual to estimate the size of the influx. For this, we required a number of estimates:

- The number of children in age groups 0–5, 6–11 and 12–17
- The survival rates from each age group to the next
- The proportion of the total population that is 0–5 years of age
- The proportion of primary school students who advance to secondary
- All estimates from 1965 to 2020

A technical note at the end of this chapter indicates how these estimates were made, using the UN 1996 estimates of age-sex distributions for Thailand. With these estimates, we have modelled the entire period 1970 to 2020 for both primary and secondary school enrolments. The results of our model and the actual recorded data are shown in Figure 5.5.

Uses of Modelling

The model shows what the school population might be for a city with Khon Kaen's vital rates, survival rates and school advancement (or drop out) rates

Figure 5.5
Khon Kaen Primary and Secondary School Populations:
Actual, Recorded and Modelled

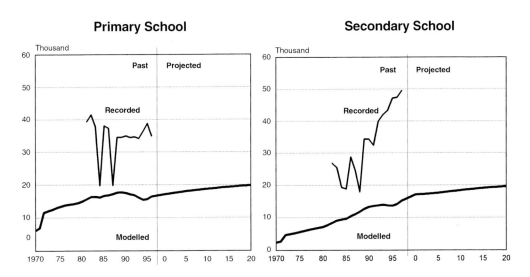

under what we consider normal conditions. We can match the output against official school enrolment records at any time to assess actual excesses or deficits from the proposed. The two charts in Figure 5.3 show these estimates for the entire period. For the most part, the official record is considerably in excess of the modelled or expected condition. Often the official count is three to five times the size of the modelled, but it is reasonable to view this excess as the result of a rural population sending children to the city to stay, allowing them to take advantage of the better schooling available there. This is a normal and expected condition in all Thai cities, including Bangkok.

There are at least two ways to look at this situation, each of which implies the need for more resources for education in Khon Kaen. On one hand, we can see a school population that is much more than double what it should be for the size of the city. Extra students require additional resources.

On the other hand, we could ask what size city would produce this recorded school population. Simulations can be run with different initial city sizes to obtain a population that produces the recorded school population. In effect, the school populations observed in Khon Kaen would be expected of a much larger city, with a population in 1970 in excess of 250,000, or about eight times the actual size of the city at that time.

Either way, the data make a good case for more national resources to be directed to Khon Kaen's schools, which obviously serve a larger area than the city itself.

Data for university students are not problematic. They are available from 1970, when there were 1165 students enrolled in Khon Kaen University. That number grew steadily to 13,305 students in 1997, and is projected to continue its steady growth through the year 2020, when it may reach 26,235.

WATER

The multiple links between population and the environment are especially clear in the case of water. People use water and also produce wastes that pollute water, causing disease and death. In the last section we saw the high rates of treatment for gastrointestinal diseases. These rates could indicate either an increase in water-borne disease, or an increase in effective treatment, or a combination of the two. To understand what is happening more fully, we need to know something about the quantity and quality of water and how it has changed over time.

Data on water quantity are available for the period 1970 to 1978 and they illustrate the point made in the introduction: Khon Kaen is a well-watered city. Its three rivers provide sufficient water, and infrastructure development for water has kept considerably ahead of the city's population growth. The data are shown in Table 5.9.

Table 5.9
Water Available and Consumed, 1970–78 (cubic metres)

Year	Water Withdrawals from Rivers	Tap Water Consumed	Per Capita Consumption
1980	10,927,945	7,340,443	78
1981	17,919,785	8,489,058	85
1982	–	–	–
1983	23,404,820	10,899,577	94
1984	21,069,490	11,837,507	99
1985	25,243,280	12,988,735	107
1986	28,376,120	14,837,667	117
1987	30,394,184	15,762,082	121
1988	28,857,385	15,355,843	114

Clearly production has kept far ahead of demand. The quantity of water should pose no problem for Khon Kaen for the near future. Using 120 cubic metres per capita as the norm for consumption, we can calculate total needs over the 50-year period using the modelled population. This shows that water production in 1988 was sufficient even for the high variant population projection through the year 2020. Figure 5.6 shows these figures.

Figure 5.6
Water Production and Modelled Requirements, 1970–2020

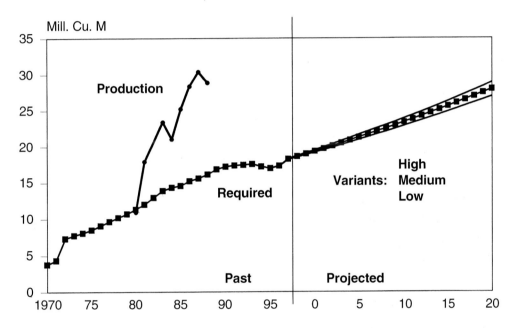

Table 5.10 shows the data the city can provide on measurements of water quality. The data provide a general picture of progress in water quality, but also raise serious questions about accuracy. Dissolved oxygen increased slightly since 1983, and the other three measures have declined. At the same time, some of the measures look suspect: all four measures are exactly the same for eight of the years: 1985 to 1987, 1989, and 1991 to 1994. Moreover, the dramatic drop in fecal coliform in 1994 to 1995, from 17,182 to 185, suggests that different measures were being used.

The data do suggest that water quality is improving, which would support the interpretation presented above, that the rise in number of treatments for gastrointestinal diseases is the result of better and more widely-available treatment rather than

Table 5.10
Water Quality Measurements, 1983–97

Year	DO	BOD	COD	Total Coliform
1983	3.060	30.92	77.21	60137.5
1984	3.170	38.24	99.66	38405.00
1985	4.740	12.94	51.50	17182.40
1986	4.740	12.94	51.50	17182.40
1987	4.740	12.94	51.50	17182.40
1988	4.100	8.60	51.50	9700.00
1989	4.740	12.94	51.50	17182.40
1990	4.740	2.20	51.50	11000.00
1991	4.740	12.94	51.50	17182.40
1992	4.740	12.94	51.50	17182.40
1993	4.740	12.94	51.50	17182.40
1994	4.740	12.94	51.50	17182.40
1995	8.150	5.69	33.81	185.00
1996	4.130	2.03	19.70	340.86
1997	5.830	2.92	26.61	418.45

a real increase in the incidence of the disease. But the data still raise serious questions about accuracy.

In any event, the city does recognize the importance of clean water and is now building stabilization ponds with a capacity of 25,500 cubic metres per day to treat household and commercial wastewater. It is most likely that this will further increase water quality. We can hope that with time the measurement technology and control will also improve.

AIR QUALITY

As in all large cities, air quality is becoming a serious concern for Khon Kaen's managers. Systematic monitoring of air quality, however, was initiated only in August 1996, and even then only on a sample basis. Eight samples of air monitoring for specific pollutants were undertaken in January 1998. The results are shown in Table 5.11.

Table 5.11
Results from Selected Air Quality Monitoring, 4–27 January 1996

Date	Small Particle	Lead	Iron	Manganese	Copper	Zinc	Chromium	Cadmium
Jan 4	301	0.101	1.89	0.09	0.04	0.19	–	0.003
Jan 5	393	0.090	2.19	0.12	0.06	0.41	0.016	0.003
Jan 6	167	0.039	1.83	0.06	0.04	0.02	0.008	0.001
Jan 7	188	0.030	1.91	0.07	0.03	0.25	0.009	0.002
Jan 16	211	0.033	2.01	0.08	0.03	0.29	0.015	0.002
Jan 19	202	0.030	1.91	0.07	0.03	0.24	0.007	0.002
Jan 22	269	0.210	1.82	0.08	0.02	0.13	0.005	0.003
Jan 27	106	0.040	1.21	0.04	0.02	0.29	0.004	0.001

Table 5.12
Results from Selected Air Quality Monitoring, August 1996–September 1997

Date	Sulphur Dioxide		Nitrogen Oxides		Carbon Monoxide		Ozone		Small Particle	
	Max	Ave	Max	Ave	Max	Ave	Max	Ave	Max	Ave
Aug 96	22	4.7	40.0	12.4	3.4	0.8	41.0	11.5	141.2	69.3
Sep 96	68	7.2	42.0	15.3	3.9	1.2	34.0	9.6	115.7	76.0
Oct 96	36	4.9	46.0	18.6	2.9	1.1	34.0	12.8	119.3	95.1
Sep 96	19	7.6	50.0	20.4	6.3	1.4	32.0	10.7	172.9	106.3
Dec 96	21	6.3	69.0	29.3	8.9	1.6	41.0	15.4	194.6	131.2
Jan 97	29	6.2	94.0	31.2	8.7	1.8	79.0	15.9	262.2	150.6
Feb 97	20	5.6	86.0	29.1	5.9	1.6	70.0	17.3	77.6	137.0
Mar 97	3	6.8	86.0	30.3	9.8	1.4	80.0	24.2	249.0	137.0
Apr 97	14	5.8	64.0	23.8	2.9	0.9	64.0	27.0	158.9	98.6
May 97	18	4.6	57.0	18.1	4.9	0.7	61.0	23.9	141.8	84.5
Jun 97	12	4.2	72.0	16.2	4.3	0.8	57.0	20.4	168.1	86.6
Jul 97	11	3.6	39.0	11.8	2.8	0.7	37.0	14.7	96.0	49.1
Aug 97	13	3.8	43.0	12.6	3.2	0.7	39.0	13.2	55.9	42.5
Sep 97	12	3.7	62.0	16.2	5.0	1.0	38.0	11.1	130.5	73.0
Standard	300		170		30		100		120	

Figure 5.7
Khon Kaen's Five Major Air Pollutants, August 1996–September 1997

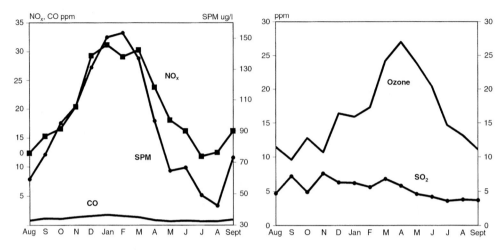

All levels, except that of suspended particulate matter, were found to be below WHO standards. This indicates relatively good air quality in Khon Kaen, despite the rapid increase in vehicular traffic. It should also be noted that these measures were taken during the dry season, when the air is not washed daily by the rains that come in the rainy season.

In addition, since August 1996, monthly monitoring samples have been taken of five pollutants: sulphur dioxide, nitrogen oxides, carbon monoxide, ozone and suspended particulate matter. The maximum and average values for these are shown in Table 5.12 and Figure 5.7.

Figure 5.7 shows the movement of these five main pollutants over the year. The three on the left come primarily from vehicular traffic: suspended particulate matter, carbon monoxide and nitrogen oxides. Those on the right are from industry as well as vehicles. When displayed in this manner these data show a distinctive seasonal trend. They show the heavy influence of the south-west monsoon winds, which bring the rains that last from May through October. Washing the air daily, the rains substantially reduce all pollutants, but especially suspended particulate matter, nitrogen oxides and ozone. During the dry season of the north-east monsoon winds – November through April – all pollutants rise.

There does not appear to be a long-term secular trend, which we might expect given the rise of motor vehicles in Khon Kaen. At the same time, it would take more than one year of monitoring to determine if there is a trend.

TRANSPORTATION

Like virtually all cities, Khon Kaen has experienced a rapid growth of vehicles. Data on car and motorcycle registration are available since 1970, but the figures provided are those for the province as a whole. The year 1994 stands out for the extremely large number of cars. They increased from 44,000 in 1993 to 182,973 in 1994, and back to 61,202 for 1995. There is obviously an error in recording. Until we can determine the source of the error and a more reasonable figure, we shall assume the figure of 53,973. It is estimated that about 50 percent of all cars and 20 percent of all motorcycles registered in the province are from Khon Kaen City. The growth of vehicles in Khon Kaen City is quite remarkable. From a mere handful of vehicles of less than 5000 in 1970, the number has grown to about 100,000. This growth can be seen in Table 5.13 and Figure 5.8.

The implications for urban life quality include the impact on ease of movement, vehicle congestion, air quality and vehicle accidents. There is as yet no way to assess the ease of travel that the vehicles have brought, but it must be considerable. Surrounding villages that were once largely cut off from the city are now in direct daily contact. Thus, villagers can easily sell their products, purchase what they need, find health and educational services and take part in the rich entertainment life of the city. This no doubt enhances the quality of urban (and rural) life, which is not directly measurable at this time.

Vehicle congestion, however, can be measured directly by the ratio of vehicles to road area. Data indicate that road area has increased only slightly over the past 25 years, from six to seven square kilometres. This means that total vehicles per square kilometre has increased considerably, from about 600 to about 13,000. Does 13,000 vehicles per square kilometre of road imply congestion[2]? Though it might seem so, we cannot say, as there are at this time no comparable statistics. Visual impressions, however, indicate there is no substantial road congestion in Khon Kaen. There are none of the severe traffic jams with long waits that one finds in Bangkok or Chieng Mai. To be sure, much of Khon Kaen's traffic – about half – is made up of motorcycles, which take little space and contribute little to the creation of traffic jams. Thus, until we have more valid standards for assessing traffic congestion, we can only say that while the numbers appear high, the visual impression is that of no substantial congestion. Figure 5.9 shows the movement of roads and road density.

Finally, as to air quality, we saw above that there is no apparent secular rise in vehicular air pollution. This must be a highly tentative conclusion, of course,

Table 5.13
Numbers of Registered Vehicles, 1970–97

Year	Passenger Cars	Motorcycles	Public Vehicles
1970	4191	4156	Not available
1971	4470	4743	Not available
1972	5198	4725	Not available
1973	6519	4835	Not available
1974	7521	5208	Not available
1975	8006	5153	Not available
1976	9422	6730	Not available
1977	13,240	11,203	Not available
1978	14,211	7443	Not available
1979	14,657	8242	Not available
1980	14,300	11,751	Not available
1981	10,675	12,231	Not available
1982	12,884	19,918	Not available
1983	14,813	26,393	Not available
1984	15,565	60,071	Not available
1985	27,412	60,071	Not available
1986	27,412	60,071	Not available
1987	27,412	60,071	Not available
1988	30,644	78,781	665
1989	23,913	77,714	463
1990	28,829	94,646	499
1991	30,692	97,556	534
1992	35,487	109,225	1867
1993	44,930	152,337	3565
1994	182,973	190,746	2907
1995	61,202	203,912	2492
1996	73,537	243,992	2622
1997	78,318	260,007	2988

Figure 5.8
Estimate of Cars and Motorcycles, 1970–97

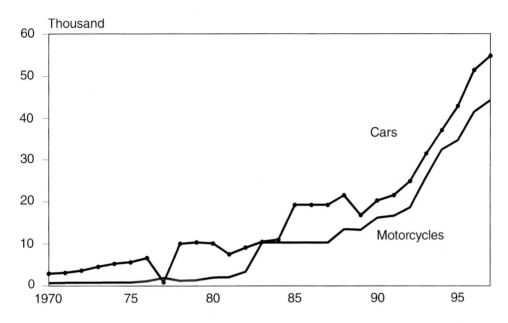

Figure 5.9
Road Area and Vehicles per Area, 197–95

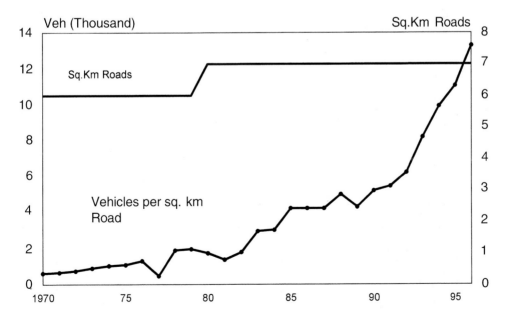

since we have only one year of data on which to base this conclusion. Data on accidents and injuries are not readily available.

What does the future hold? We have modelled the Khon Kaen situation using procedures worked out for other cities in this study. That is, we have estimated the rates at which vehicles are purchased and disposed of. These were estimated for the period 1970 to 1997, for which recorded data are available. Our estimates of purchase and disposal rates produced a modelled number of vehicles for 1970 to 1997 that exactly matched the recorded numbers, essentially validating our model.

For the future, we must also assume specific purchase and disposal rates, but this is extremely difficult because of the steep economic decline of the Thai economy from late 1997. As we shall see in the section on the economy, the value of the baht declined substantially from 25 to 40 to the US dollar. The country's total output declined by about eight percent in 1998. In 1999, the economy is expected to register a 0.5 percent decline, but the projection for 2000 is 2.2 percent overall growth. The overall shape of the economy will certainly have a major impact on the rate of vehicle purchase and disposal.

The economy has had a major impact on vehicle numbers in the past. As the Thai economy grew rapidly, at rates near ten percent per year, foreign banks competed with one another to obtain a share of the country's loan market. Interest rates were low and loans were made on highly speculative real estate ventures. This was one of the reasons for the collapse of the baht in late 1997, and all manner of credit was overextended, often for loans with no capacity for repayment. The automobile and motorcycle market was highly stimulated by this easy credit. Cars and motorcycles could, after all, provide something like collateral, since they could be repossessed for default on payment. Thus, times of easy credit would see a sharp rise in the number of vehicles, and times of economic downturn could see almost equally sharp declines. This is one of the reasons for both rapid growth and radical change in the number of vehicles registered.

Whatever the economy does, however, it seems unlikely that the number of vehicles will decline in the future. Vehicle purchase will certainly reflect the economy, but perhaps not with the sharp swings of the past, as lessons of overextended credit have been learnt. Still, if the economy grows in the future, which it is expected to do, vehicle purchase will grow; if the economy remains moribund, purchases will slow, though they are not expected to reach zero. As to vehicle disposal, however, the opposite can be expected at least in part. Two different forces will be at work. If the economy remains moribund, there may be an increase in the repossession of vehicles purchased on credit, causing their numbers to decline. Countering this trend, people can be expected to work hard to keep their old cars and motorcycles going, causing disposal rates to decline, perhaps even approaching zero. If the economy grows, the disposal rate will undoubtedly rise, in part because there is a good used-car market nearby in Laos. Disposal is not expected to rise as rapidly as the economy, however, especially since the recent collapse has made people wary of extending themselves too far. Thus, even if the economy rises, we expect the disposal rate to remain moderate, and substantially below the purchase rate.

With these considerations, we have modelled the period to 2020 assuming a modest economic growth of two to four percent per year. This will translate into a modest increase in the purchase of new vehicles. But we believe the effects of the 1997 downturn will lead to a substantial reduction of the disposal rate, which will imply a continued growth in car numbers, and a probable saturation of motorcycles. Our projections for Khon Kaen are shown in Figure 5.10.

Figure 5.10
Cars and Motorcycles: Past and Projected

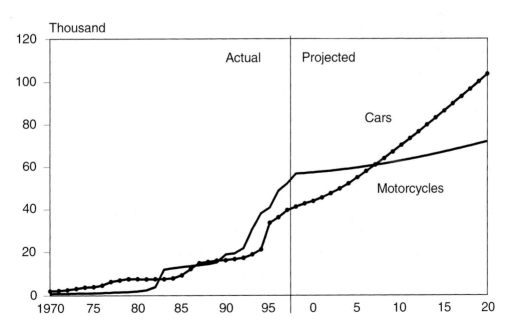

LAND USE

Khon Kaen experienced a major expansion of its administrative area in 1972, adding some 33 square kilometres of land and growing from 13.5 to 46 square kilometres. This expansion added some agricultural land and expanded the area for institutions, such as the Khon Kaen University, by about two square kilometres. Open lands in the city, especially those fit for recreation, include a large reservoir and new parks, together provide some five square kilometres of area. Road area and residential housing have increased slightly, each adding about one square kilometre of area. At present, the city does not appear densely packed or overcrowded.

Table 5.14
Land Use Pattern in Khon Kaen City Municipal Area, 1971–86

Types	1971		1983		1986	
	Area Km^2	Percent	Area Km^2	Percent	Area Km^2	Percent
Agriculture	1.5	33	13	28	11	24
Housing	5	11	6	13	7	15
Commercial	1	2	1	2	1	2
Industry	1	2	1	2	1	2
Institution	12	26	14	30	14	30
Road	6	13	7	15	7	15
Recreation	0	0	0	0	1	2
Reservoir	6	13	4	9	4	9
Total	46	100	46	100	46	100

Housing area has grown and there has been a great deal of construction in the city over the past three decades. We do not, however, have separate figures for the number of residential buildings constructed. All construction requires city permission, but records of permits do not indicate building use, so there is no way of knowing the housing situation with any precision. There are two impressions, however, which can be reported here. One is that though there is low income housing, there are no extensive slum areas that lack city services and well-built houses. There does, however, seem to be a housing shortage.

Figure 5.11
Families and Households: An Estimate of Housing Shortage

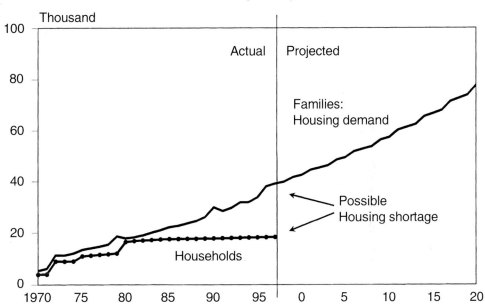

We can use the analysis of numbers of families and households to provide a rough estimate of the magnitude of the housing shortage. Figure 5.11 shows the results of this estimate.

There are now some 40,000 families in Khon Kaen, with less than 20,000 households. While the number of families has continued to grow, the number of households has remained roughly constant for the past decade and more. This is admittedly a very crude estimate, which is confounded even more by what we saw previously in the analysis of the school population. It is possible that many households contain young school-aged people from the rural areas who are only temporarily residing in the city. In any event, both this analysis and general impressions in the city do indicate a housing shortage. Whether this problem will be alleviated in the near future is impossible to say, since it will rest on both the kinds of housing policy the central and provincial governments support, and on the level of foreign investment that flows into the country.

THE ECONOMY

Khon Kaen's economy, like that of Thailand as a whole, has grown steadily over the past three decades and more. For the past decade, the city's economy has registered seven percent per year growth. This is more rapid than for the North-east Region as a whole, where the annual growth rate registered only six percent for the past decade. With an annual population growth rate of around one per year, this translates into a six percent per year growth in Khon Kaen's per capita income, or a doubling of the standard of living every 11 years. That statistical estimate is validated by general observations. Anyone familiar with the region has seen very rapid growth in less than a generation. The improvements in the physical infrastructure are dramatic and visible: from roads and government offices to shops and private homes. Material goods, food and personal services have all also increased.

The city records three specific measures that reflect the wealth of its citizens. There is an estimate of per capita income, data on taxes collected, and information on bank deposits. Table 5.15 provides the data, while Figure 5.12 gives a graphic representation of both income and tax collections.

Table 5.15
Economic Data (baht)

Year	Per Capita Income	Collected Tax	Bank Deposit (million)
1982	3467	54,523	3476
1983	3875	26,499,241	4516
1984	3930	34,125,258	5200
1985	4196	41,751,275	5812
1986	10,302	49,377,292	6130
1987	11,513	57,003,309	6862
1988	13,507	64,629,326	7899
1989	14,921	72,255,342	9590
1990	17,230	79,881,359	12,019
1991	20,101	87,507,376	14,267
1992	24,044	75,978,248	17,517
1993	25,714	87,259,496	20,174
1994	29,644	103,000,000	22,786
1995	34,271	121,000,000	27,014
1996	39,139	142,000,000	30,696
1997	32,979	154,000,000	33,291

Figure 5.12
Khon Kaen Per Capita Income and City Tax Collections, 1982–97

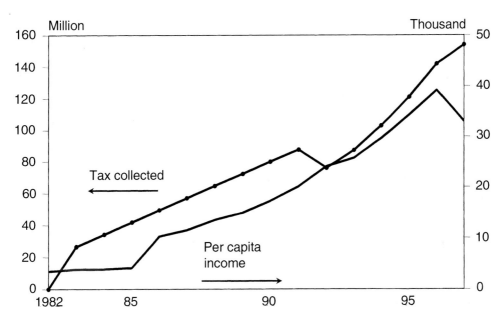

Thus, in a decade and a half, per capita income and bank deposits have both grown by a factor of ten. City tax revenues have grown by a factor of six, if we omit the very low figure for 1982, or by almost 3000 if we include that figure. In effect, for this period, the per capita income of the city has grown at about ten percent per year, while the tax collections have grown at about 12 percent. City services have grown accordingly, and the citizens have a right to expect increased services for the increase in taxes they pay.

The 1997 downturn is reflected in the 15-percent decline in per capita income, which will most likely be reflected in the 1999 tax collection and bank deposits. It is difficult to see what lies ahead in any real detail. Thailand is making major adjustments in its financial and governmental institutions, and there is considerable optimism about how things will turn out. In Khon Kaen, we expect steady progress in the general character of the economy. There is an abundant and increasingly well-educated labour force, but its growth has slowed considerably due to reductions in fertility. Thus, we do not expect a great increase in unemployment, or a great increase in demand for jobs.

THE QUALITY OF LIFE

We began this analysis with questions about data. Data problems have, indeed, plagued the analysis throughout. We know the city's population has grown, and both mortality and fertility have declined dramatically. We know this is true for Thailand, the Northeast Region, Khon Kaen Province and Khon Kaen City. Unfortunately, when we look at the data for Khon Kaen City itself, we cannot determine how rapidly fertility has fallen, because the city is a major health service centre for the entire province. Births have grown rapidly, and the recorded birth rate is far beyond what any society has ever shown. Nor do we know the real picture on migration, since the city counts entering university students and new births to mothers from outside the city as in-migrants. Similarly, newborn babies who return to their rural homes and graduating university students are counted as out-migrants. Thus, to try to get a good sense of the vital rates and migration in the city itself, we had to develop a dynamic model, which we feel may provide better measures than the recorded data of the city itself.

We also know that, for the immediate as well as for the longer past, Khon Kaen has been a migrant way station. Rural people from the relatively poor Northeast Region have come to Khon Kaen on their way to Bangkok, looking for jobs, income, and better educational and health services. How many have come and then gone on is something we do not know. Personal impressions tell us that the almost exclusive out-migration of the past may have changed. Many people are staying in Khon Kaen, and some are returning from the Bangkok/Central Plains area to the city. Until we have better data collection processes, however, we are left with little more than observations and guesses about the magnitude of the migrant streams.

We know that death rates have gone down, especially for the most crucial periods of life: infancy and childbirth. Infant mortality and maternal mortality rates are at low levels and have declined. Even in this relatively poor region of the country, these rates are lower than those of many countries with much higher levels of per capita income. We know from experience why this has happened: the Thai government has built an extensive primary health care system that has reached all rural areas, reducing infant and maternal mortality throughout the country.

That health delivery system has also carried both the message and the supplies for fertility control. Thailand has had one of the world's most successful national family planning programmes, which has helped to produce one of the world's most rapid declines in fertility. The fertility decline was accomplished without coercion and without high rates of abortion or maternal mortality. This indicates that the family planning programme has been an outstanding success, not only in lowering fertility and population growth, but also in increasing the quality of life for poor rural women and children, who are usually excluded from modern development programmes. We know this excellent family planning programme and its benefits have been extended to Khon Kaen, even though the inflated data collection process does not show this. To get closer to a reasonable picture of birth and death rates, we used dynamic modelling. But the increase in the physical quality of life over the past two decades and more is unmistakable.

Education provides the same picture of increased quality of life with data that once again do not show a clear picture for Khon Kaen itself. Primary school education is essentially available for all children. Secondary school education is expanding rapidly, and will shortly also be available at no cost to all children. University education is expanding, especially since the major regional university was built in Khon Kaen in the early 1960s. But the data on education in Khon Kaen City are highly inflated. Again, dynamic modelling provided insights that are not available from the actual recorded data.

Air and water quality again present problems. Death rates would suggest that the quality is good for both. But again there are problems with the data. Air quality data are available only for one year, and they show the major influence of the seasonal rains. Air quality is high when the rains wash the air daily; it declines in the dry season. Without a longer time-series of air quality monitoring, however, future projections are hazardous. Water quality is more problematic. Data have been collected for a longer period of time, but the measures themselves raise serious questions of accuracy. There does seem to be a trend toward improved water quality, but data problems make this assessment quite uncertain. Nor is there here any effective way to model the condition. The data are very weak, though there is some indication that they are getting much better.

Transportation presents another paradox. Data on vehicle registration are for the province as a whole and not for the city, and they show what we know has been the case: a great increase in pick-up trucks, cars and motorcycles. Here, the data are sufficient for us to employ a modelling exercise to suggest both how rapidly the numbers have grown in the past and how rapidly they might grow in the future. Despite the rapid growth of motor vehicles, however, visual impressions show little or no congestion, and there is no sense that air quality is being negatively affected.

Land use showed two improvements. Open spaces and recreational land have increased. Housing has also increased, though there are indications of a possible housing shortage. Again visual impressions are partly supported by the data, which are admittedly deficient. Families have grown far more rapidly than households, and this suggests a housing shortage. Exactly how large that shortage is we cannot say. Nor do we know why the number of households and the size of households – seven to eight – have remained the same over most of the past two decades. There is the sense, however, both from the data and from personal observation, that with proper financial assistance in the form of mortgage guarantees, there could be a major building boom that would satisfy what seems to be a substantial demand for housing.

All of this adds up to an interesting exercise. We use visual impressions, recorded data and dynamic modelling to try to tell what has happened over the past two decades, and what might lie in store for the city in the next quarter century. Overall, it is clear that the quality of life has improved, and we can look forward to further improvement. There are also many questions both about the existing data, and about conditions for which we have no data. Khon Kaen stands at an interesting juncture. We believe the city will continue to grow and the quality of life of its citizens will continue to improve. But the data problems are such that it is unclear whether the city itself will have the information it needs to plan its future for itself.

The future looks good, but it also presents many challenges.

TECHNICAL NOTE: ESTIMATING KHON KAEN SCHOOL POPULATIONS

The data for education in Khon Kaen, shown in Table 5.8, are erratic and inflated. Data are available from 1982, and show large and unexplained drops in the years 1984, 1985 and 1988. Moreover, the numbers of primary and secondary school children are apparently inflated, since they are larger than the average family size for the city. Given these problems, it appeared useful to attempt to model the number of school children we could reasonably expect from a city the size of Khon Kaen. Modelling requires first an estimation of the number of children in relevant school ages. The following estimates were required:

- The numbers in age groups 0–5, 6–11 and 12–17
- The survival rates from each age group to the next
- The proportion of the total population that is 0–5 years of age
- The proportion of the primary school students who advance to secondary education
- All estimates from 1965 to 2020

Numbers

To estimate the size of the two six-year age groups, we adjusted the four five-year age groups provided in the UN age-sex distributions to three six-year age groups. That is, the 0–4, 5–9, 10–14 and 15–19 age groups in the UN data were changed to 0–5, 6–11 and 12–17 respectively. We used a simple straight-line disaggregation of each five-year group to reassign one or two year groups to other categories. First, one-fifth of the 5–9 group were reassigned to the 0–4 group to raise the total to ages 0–5, or the pre-school group. Second two-fifths of the 10–14 group were reassigned to the 5–9 group to give us a group that includes the years 6–11. Third, three-fifths of the 15–19 year group were assigned to the remainder of the 10–14 group to give us the estimates for the 12–17 age group. All calculations may slightly underestimate the numbers to be assigned, but the errors will be small.

Survival

Next, we used the new six-year age groups to calculate the survival rate from one group to the next. These survival rates were used in the STELLA model to reduce the 0–5 population surviving to the primary school age, and the primary school population surviving to secondary school age.

Proportion

Finally, we calculated the percentage the 0–5 age group was of the total population. Its dramatic decline from 21 to 8.8 percent reflects Thailand's rapid fertility decline after 1965. This series of percentages were used to estimate the size of Khon Kaen's 0–5 age group from its modelled total population.

Advancement

One further calculation is needed: the rate at which students advance from primary to secondary school. For this we began with the published school enrolment data for 1980 to 1981. These figures were used to estimate the potential secondary enrolment for 1981. The actual new secondary enrolment was divided by the potential to give us an estimated rate of advancement. The following calculations were used:

Year	Primary	Secondary
1982	39,355	26,782
1983	25,521	

Potential primary students advancing to secondary school:

39,355 / 6 yrs = 6559 × 0.979 survival rate = **6421**

Actual secondary students in 1982:

1982 school-leavers (26,782 / 6)	4464
1983 minus leavers (26,782 − 4464)	22,318
1983 actual enrolment	25,521
New advancers	**3203**

Advancement Rate (3203/6421) in 1982–3   49.9%
$\approx$ **50%**

For the STELLA modelling, we assumed that the advancement rate would have been lower (35 percent) in 1965, when we begin the analysis, and that it will move to 100 percent by the year 2000, in accord with the new law mandating free education through secondary school.

Notes

1. The Human Development Index is a relatively recent development of the United Nations Development Program. It combines measures of wealth, health and education, GNP per capita, life expectancy and school enrolment, to provide a measure of the quality of life beyond mere wealth. On this measure Thailand does very well. Its ranking on the human development index is considerably higher than on GNP per capita.
2. At roughly two square metres per vehicle, admittedly a high estimate, Khon Kaen would appear to have about 26 square metres of vehicles per 1000 square metres of road surface. By this calculation, vehicles would fill only about 2.6 percent of the city's road surface.

Chapter 6

Cebu City:
Heart of the Central Philippines

Prof Wilhelm Flieger

THE URBAN SETTING[1]

Approaching from the east, as Magellan did almost five centuries ago, the course runs between Leyte and Mindanao islands, north of Bohol, to reach the centre of the long, north-south splinter of Cebu Island. Ahead is the low-lying protective shield of Mactan Island, taking the fury of the eastern storm track. Swinging south around Mactan and avoiding its coral shoals, the course leads north into the deep protected bay off Cebu City. On a small alluvial plain, nestled against steep slopes that run to cloud-capped mountain peaks 1000 metres above sea level, the city offers a well protected port, a bustling economic and cultural centre of the Visayan Islands. Lying some 300 miles by air south-east of Manila, the Visayas are a tightly clustered island group that divides the larger island of Luzon in the north from Mindanao in the south. The Visayas also divide the overwhelmingly Christian north and centre from the south where the country's almost three million Muslims are concentrated.

Geography

The narrow island of Cebu covers an area of 4400 km^2, with a length of 220 km and an average width of only 25 km. A steep mountain range runs along the island's roughly north-south axis. Close to one half of the island's surface is 200 or more metres above sea level, and about one-eighth is at altitudes of more than 500 metres. More than half of the island is covered by slopes steeper than 18 percent (ca. 10 degrees), and one-sixth of the island's area has slopes in excess of 44 percent (24 degrees). Rivers, running East and West from the main water divide in the island's centre, are relatively short. During the dry season, they carry little or no water.

Geologically, Cebu island consists of a number of overlaid rock formations of both volcanic and limestone origin. The porous coral limestone does not hold water well and thus is of relatively little agricultural value. Only the highly elevated central portions of the mountain range contain spots of fertile soil. It is these relatively limited areas that today supply vegetables, fruits and flowers to the city. Some sections of the island's coast are lined with narrow strips of flat alluvial deposits. On the largest of these is the crowded downtown portion of Cebu City.

In their foothills and lower elevations, the mountains of Cebu are dotted with coconut palms and banana plants. At altitudes above 400 metres, higher rainfall and lower temperatures make for lush vegetation. The tropical virgin forests that used to cover large parts of the island's mountains have been reduced to a mere 90 hectares according to 1997 estimates[2]. A century of deforestation has left the island empty of trees and subject to severe erosion.

Cebu's climate differs by altitude, not latitude. The lowlands suffer from a severe dry season extending from March through May. Rainfall is concentrated in the middle and at the end of the calendar year. With increasing altitude, however, the dry season decreases in length and severity. At altitudes above 600 metres, there is no dry season.

Because of its mountainous nature and the dearth of arable lands, and exacerbated by a century of radical deforestation and soil erosion, Cebu Island has never been a major agricultural centre. Slightly less than 30 percent of the island was suited to agriculture in the middle of the 20th century (Wernstedt & Spencer, 1968, p. 471). The main advantage of Cebu is its geographical location in the centre of the Philippine archipelago, and its deep and well-protected harbour.

Cebu Province comprises 53 administrative units. There are 44 such units on Cebu Island: Cebu, a chartered city, four other cities, and 39 municipalities. In addition, one other city and eight municipalities are located on offshore islands. Originally, all of Cebu City was located on the narrow alluvial plain on the island's East Coast. After Cebu became a chartered (province-free) city in 1936, extensive portions of the mountainous hinterlands were included in the city limits. The official city area as currently defined covers some 280 km^2.

Administratively, the city is divided into 80 *barangays*. Originally, these were scattered settlements that grew together over time, at least in the lowland section of the city. Some 30 mountain *barangays* of the city are still separated by large stretches of open land from the built-up core of the city. Substantial portions of Cebu City's mountain territory, aside from not being well suited for urban 'development', are officially classified as *protected areas*. Either partially or totally included in these protected areas are three watersheds vital for the water supply of Cebu City and environs, reforestation areas and one national park. Despite their rural character, all mountain *barangays* of the city are officially classified as urban because of the definition of 'urban' currently applied in the Philippines. According to this definition, any *barangay*, regardless of its demographic, social and economic characteristics, located in a city or municipality with an average population density of 1000 per km^2 is automatically designated as an urban place (Philippines National Statistics Office, NSO, 1992). This 'overboundedness' is not unique to Cebu City; it is common to Philippines cities and is rooted in the politics of urban definitions. Philippines cities are ranked by the size of their tax base, which determines the salaries of city officials. All cities, therefore, have a strong incentive to include large rural areas in order to raise their potential tax base, and thus place them in a higher ranking.

Figure 6.1 illustrates the topography of Cebu City. Overlaid over the topographical map are the boundaries of the 80 city *barangays*. The dark grey portion at the bottom of the map indicates the lowland portion of the city. Here is the old city, the 16th century fort, a busy waterfront with small ships from the outlying islands and larger ones from Manila and the rest of the world. Narrow streets are crammed with cars, trucks and the Jeepney, the Philippines' most distinctive form of transportation. Originally converted from World War II jeeps, elongated and brightly decorated, Jeepney provide a colourful and efficient, if somewhat chaotic, privately-owned public transportation system for the city, as throughout the country. They also add greatly to the heavy traffic congestion of the downtown area. Older houses, shops and official buildings compete with newer buildings for space. Few parks relieve the hot, dusty character of the city, made dustier by the predominance of dirt and gravel roads. It is a bustling city that seems never to sleep.

History[3]

After Magellan it was almost half a century before Spain returned to make good his claim. The Spanish explorer, Miguel Lopez de Legaspi, arrived in Cebu in 1565 and established Spanish rule in the Philippines. He found a modestly sized,

152 *Five Cities*

Figure 6.1
Cebu City: Showing Topography and *Barangay* Boundaries

prosperous entrepôt with well-established trade links with China, parts of Southeast Asia, and other areas in the Philippine archipelago. It was a city Legaspi intended to make the capital of a far-reaching territorial empire. Antonio Pigafetta, who accompanied Magellan on his 1521 to 1522 voyage to the Philippines, estimated that the port contained at least 2000 people. On 8 May 1565, Legaspi laid out a Spanish town and ground was broken for a triangular fort. For the next four years, the town served as the Spanish base of operations in the Philippines.

In 1571, the Spanish colonial capital was moved to Manila, which became the transshipment centre for the Spanish Galleon trade where silver from New Spain (Mexico) was exchanged for luxury goods from Asia. Colonial wealth came from the Galleon trade, and turned attention away from the development of local agriculture or other products. As a result, Cebu's role as a regional trading centre was drastically undermined, and the city remained an economically depressed backwater.

It was not before the middle of the 19th century that Cebu began to re-emerge as a major Visayan port. The initial impetus for this development came from attempts by the Spanish crown to increase trade between Spain and the Philippines and to spur agricultural development of export crops, especially sugar and tobacco, to make the colony less dependent on subsidies from the Spanish homeland. While these attempts were not successful and were eventually abandoned, they did lead to increased trade for Cebu, first in the domestic market and to the larger world after the Cebu port was opened to international trade in 1860. Around 1850, the population of Cebu City and the nearby settlements of Pari-an (Chinese) and Lutaos (non-Muslim refugees from Mindanao) is given as 10,921. By the end of the Spanish period, Cebu City had become more closely linked, economically, to its hinterland and surrounding islands than at any other time in its history. Through the port of Cebu, the provincial towns were now tied to the international market for sugar and were consequently vulnerable to changes in world prices.

Since then, the fortunes of Cebu City have changed with prevailing economic climates and wars. During World War II, Cebu City was largely destroyed. Unfortunately, from a city planner's point of view, the city was rebuilt in its old moulds, with few thoroughfares and many narrow streets and alleys utterly unsuited for modern-city traffic. Despite these deficiencies, Cebu City has continued to function as the demographic and economic centre of the central Philippines.

Data Problem

The Philippines has no lack of data, but there are many problems, especially in locating data for local urban planning. Characteristic of the country's high degree of administrative centralization, most data are collected locally and forwarded to Manila for collation and publication. They become available usually long after the fact, if at all, and are presented in highly aggregated form, for the nation as a whole, or for a region of many provinces. Local level data collected by specific organizations are usually not available publicly. Moreover, there are many data collection agencies, both governmental and private, and there is little or no attempt to draw these different sources into a coherent system.

Data collection is often problem-driven and thus must wait until problems are recognized or become acute. Cebu has suffered from a severe water problem for decades because of population growth and radical deforestation. Data relating to that problem exist, but they are held by private research organizations. Some have become available through the Water Resources Center of the University of San Carlos. Air pollution has been bewailed as a health threat for some time, but no systematic public monitoring or documentation has been introduced, though the University of San Carlos department of Chemistry does collect some air pollution data. Electricity is provided not by communities such as Cebu City but by a central semi-government corporation and by private cooperatives. These sources started pooling their resources ten years ago when the power plants in the country started to fall apart due to lack of maintenance. Nonetheless, information on demand and supply has not yet been pooled. Roads in the city are classified by the agencies responsible for maintaining them: there are national roads, city roads and *barangay* roads. It is difficult to sort out just who is supposed to keep track of what and who collects data for which roads. Another data-related problem specific to Cebu City is that the city is tied into a larger geographic system: Metro Cebu. The latter usually serves as development unit, thus much information is assembled for the larger unit but not the city.

CEBU'S POPULATION: PAST AND FUTURE

Growth Rates

The first census of the Philippines, under American auspices in 1903, counted 45,994 inhabitants of Cebu City. The City more than doubled its population in the next two decades, grew very slowly during the war and Japanese occupation, and after 1945 returned to rapid growth again for more than three decades.

In 1995, the city had a population just over 650,000 people but its growth rate has slowed dramatically. At a mere 1.5 percent per year since 1990, the city is now growing more slowly than the province or the Philippines as a whole. Populations and comparative growth rates are shown in Table 6.1 and Figure 6.2.

Table 6.1
Population and Comparative Growth Rates

Date	Cebu City		Cebu Province	Philippines
	Population	% growth	% growth	% growth
1903	45,994	–	–	–
1918	65,502	2.30	1.75	1.90
1939	146,817	4.04	1.11	2.20
1948	167,503	1.35	0.52	1.89
1960	251,146	3.56	1.51	3.01
1970	347,116	3.16	2.05	2.96
1980	488,255	3.42	2.47	2.71
1990	604,407	2.13	2.35	2.30
1995	654,839	1.50	1.82	2.29

The slowing of Cebu's growth rate is not due to reduced economic activity, but to severe crowding in the central city. The city's low-lying delta now contains over 88 percent of the city's population, with an average density of 9500 persons per square kilometre. The other 12 percent of the population live on the steep slopes of the upland *barangays*, which have a density of only 353 persons per square kilometre. Crowding is producing out-migration into the steep slopes, causing problems of erosion and flooding in the lowlands.

There is also a set of rapidly growing alternate urban centres nearby that have taken growth from Cebu City. Mandate, just to the north along the coast, and Lapu Lapu on Mactan Island have grown rapidly as adjacent urban areas. From 1970 to 1990, Mandate grew at rates above five percent per year, reaching a density of over 6000 per square kilometre by 1990. As in Cebu, crowding brought rapid growth to a halt, and the city is now growing at just over one percent per year. Lapu Lapu City continues to grow in excess of three percent per year.

Figure 6.2
Population Growth and Growth Rates

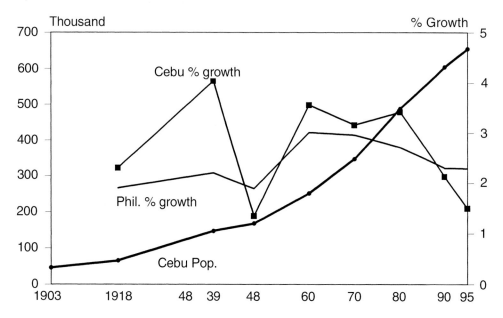

Mandate and Lapu Lapu, together with seven other adjacent municipalities, now make up the greater Cebu metropolitan area of 1.5 million people on 722 square kilometres of land. Although the larger metropolitan area is not an officially recognized administrative entity or planning unit, it has acquired a life of its own and developed its unique ecological and economic dynamics.

The source of past growth has included both natural increase and net in-migration. Unfortunately, migration data are almost non-existent. The census contains questions about former residence, from which an estimate of in-migration can be made, but there are no data on out-migration. It is known that Philippines fertility has declined over the past few decades, and the current total fertility rate for Cebu City is estimated at 3.2, indicating a substantial decline from the Philippines 1950 level of about 7.3. The current rate is also somewhat below that for the Philippines as a whole, which is estimated at 3.62 for the period 1995 to 2000 (UN, 1996). The crude birth rate for the city is estimated at 30.1 per 1000 population. With an estimated crude death rate of seven, this implies a rate of natural increase of 2.3 percent. This is higher that the city's growth rate of 1.5 percent for 1990 to 1995, suggesting net out-migration. But the data are contradictory.

Migration estimates are highly problematic. It is certain that in-migration contributed to Cebu City's growth in the past. Age-sex data show a considerable bulge of the young productive age population, which matches the lower levels, or 'hallows', in these ages in the Province as a whole, and in surrounding municipalities. After 1990, the slower overall growth suggests net out-migration, but intercensal data by *barangay* show a different picture. They show that 20 lowland *barangays* at or near the old city centre lost some 20,000 people, while the 60 remaining *barangays*, more than half of them located in the uplands, gained some 70,000 people. Even under the assumption that all 20,000 out-migrants from the old city centre moved into the city's mountains, there still would be a net in-migration of 30,000, giving the city an almost one percent growth rate without any natural increase. With the latter added in, substantial net out-migration is again suggested.

The age-sex data show a considerable difference between the lowland and upland *barangays*. The lower fertility of the lowland and the bulge of the young productive age population are not seen in the upland populations. There continues to be a large number of very young children and no surplus in the productive ages. Projections for the near future expect to see a continuation of the movement from the crowded city centre to the upland areas, as Table 6.2 shows.

Table 6.2
Lowland-Upland Projections for Cebu City

Area	Year	Population (000)	% Growth	% of Population
All Areas	1970	348	–	–
	1995	655	2.5	–
	2020	907	1.3	–
Lowland	1970	289	–	83
	1995	490	2.1	75
	2020	612	0.9	67
Upland	1970	59	–	17
	1995	165	4.1	25
	2020	295	2.3	33

These projections do not take account of environmental problems caused by the move to the steep slopes of the upland *barangays*. There are already problems with erosion, flooding and excessive water withdrawals, which will most likely worsen as the development of the slopes proceeds. There seems little political will or administrative capacity to deal with this type of urban sprawl, making the future quite precarious for the city's environment.

Age Structure

Cebu City and the Philippines continue to show the relatively young population of a society that has not yet completed its demographic transition. Nor is this expected to change very much in the next quarter century. The problems of an ageing population still lie considerably far in Cebu's future. Table 6.3 shows our estimates based on the life table discussed in the next section.

Table 6.3
Age Structure of Cebu City, 1995 and 2020

Year	% under 15	% 15–64	% 65+	Mean age
1995	33.4	63.5	3.1	24.6
2020	28.0	68.8	3.2	26.1

Projections

In the absence of accurate fertility and any migration data, population projections for Cebu City are difficult to produce. The projections shown below are based on extrapolated population growth trends implied in the census counts of 1970 through 1995, and a number of somewhat arbitrary assumptions. They essentially project the persons in each five-year age-sex group separately, using as starting point average age-specific growth rates that had been in force between 1994 and 1995. The medium (M) variant assumes that the annual age-specific growth rates decline at an even pace during the 1995 to 2020 period, so that the projected population for the year 2020 comes close to the extrapolated population for the year 2020 shown in Table 2. The high (H) projection assumes that the age-specific growth rates remain at the level of 1995 during the entire 25-year projection period, and the low (L) projection assumes that the population growth rate approximates zero by the year 2020. The high projection shows

Figure 6.3
Cebu City Population, 1913–2020
(With High, Medium and Low Variants)

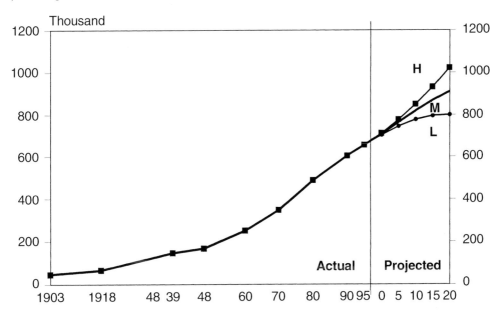

a population of just over one million by the year 2020, i.e. 100,000 persons more than the medium variant, and the low projection indicates a population which is by 100,000 lower than the medium. None of the three projections predicts the future population course, but it is reasonable to expect that the actual growth will be within the 'growth area' delimited by the two extreme projections[4].

SOCIAL SERVICES

Health

Lacking detailed published data for Cebu City, we examined death records issued by the city for 1994 to 1995 and constructed a life table for the city itself[5]. This table provides us with the basic data on the health of Cebu's citizens: death rate, infant mortality rate and life expectancy. The overall death rate is very low, 6.4 per 1000, due both to the young age of the population and to the expansion of public health and medical services that have brought down deaths from infectious diseases. The infant mortality rate is 28.6 for boys and 24.0 for girls, or 26.3 for both sexes. This is slightly lower than the infant mortality rate for the country as a whole, which stood at 35 for the period 1995 to 2000 (UN, 1996). Life expectancy at birth was 63 years for males and 69 years for females. Compared to the rest of Southeast Asia, these rates indicate a level of health near the same as Indonesia, Thailand and Vietnam, somewhat better than Myanmar, Cambodia or Laos, but substantially below Malaysia or Singapore. Overall, they reflect a rather healthy population.

From the same death rate data used above, we examined causes of death. Of the ten most common causes, pneumonia (19 percent) tuberculosis (8 percent) and bronchitis (5 percent) were the most prevalent infectious diseases which still accounted for one-third of the deaths in 1994 and 1995. Gone, however, were the gastrointestinal diseases marking a poorer society with a less developed health system. Degenerative diseases have begun to take their toll, with stroke (14 percent), heart diseases (10 percent) and hypertension (5 percent) leading. Cancer and cirrhosis follow, making up nearly ten percent of death causes.

The most frequent causes of infant deaths, aside from pneumonia and bronchitis, are related to prematurity, birth defects and pregnancy complications. The only deaths attributed to malnutrition during the two-year period (17 cases) occurred to children aged one to four. It was this same age group (30 cases out of 75) that was most affected by deadly dengue fever outbreak in 1994 and 1995. In effect, the major part of the epidemiological transition has been completed, taking away gastrointestinal diseases, though the city is left with a serious problem in respiratory diseases. A return of infectious diseases remains a concern, as reflected in an outbreak of dengue fever in 1994 and 1995, which claimed 57 lives and has alarmed city health officials.

The progress of the epidemiological transition depends on the effectiveness with which communicable diseases can be controlled, and the access the population has to medical services. While the latter is primarily a function of economics and government policies and programmes, the direct control of communicable diseases also requires behavioural change on the part of the population with respect to sanitation, hygiene and environmental cleanliness.

Access to medical services is provided by the government and the private sector. Since 1994, government-provided health services are financed through and supervised by local governments under the overall direction of the country's Department of Health. In the countryside, government health services concentrate on public health and primary health care through a network of municipality-based Rural Health Centers, from which Barangay Health Stations, spread over the municipalities, are serviced. Through the primary and secondary schools, the government reaches out to children for immunizations. The services and supplies dispensed by the primary health care system are free of charge, but patients are often asked for donations. In cities like Cebu, this system is augmented by government hospitals. Hospitalization in government-operated health centres is not free of charge. To help pay for hospitalization and hospital services, salaried employees and their employers contribute to mandatory 'insurance' systems, which cover the employed person and dependants. The benefits contributed by these mandatory insurance systems to hospitalization costs are relatively small and rarely, if ever, pay for everything. The greatest drawback of the existing system is that it covers only salaried employees; the agricultural populations as well as fishermen are excluded. Private health insurance, which is slowly becoming more widespread, is affordable only for members of the middle- and upper-income groups.

Under the governmental primary health care system, Cebu City is divided into five *health areas*: north, west, south, east and central. At the beginning of the current year (1998), some 75 Barangay Health Centers were distributed over these five areas, each one serving, on average, a population of 9000. The field personnel manning the health stations consisted of the following members:

Medical officers (physicians)	45
Dental officers	28
Public health nurses	57
Public health midwives	96
Ancillary personnel	91
Total	317

The largest hospital maintained by the city government is the Cebu City Medical Center, with 200 beds. Connected with the medical centre are two small hospitals with very few beds; one of them is located in a very crowded city *barangay* and the other in the mountains of the city. There is also a Cebu City TB Sanatorium with 50 beds, and the main Provincial Hospital, financed by the Province of Cebu, with 450 beds.

Private groups maintain ten hospitals in Cebu City with bed capacities ranging from 20 to 300 for a total capacity of 1560 beds. With the 700 beds in government hospitals, the total bed capacity of all hospitals in the city amounts to 2260. If these hospitals were serving only Cebu City, the average number of persons per hospital bed would be just below 300, a relatively good number by world standards. However, Cebu City is not only the educational centre of the southern Philippines but also its medical hub. As such, its hospitals serve a population much larger than that residing in the city; it is difficult to estimate this number. In the Cebu City Medical Center and some private hospitals of the city, people bring their own beds and put them up in the hospital corridors. According to the World Bank's 1997 World Development Report (1997, p. 75), the increase in the number of hospital beds in the country is not proportional to the increase of the population: between 1980 and 1993, the number of people per hospital bed increased from 589 to 780.

It is close to impossible to determine the number of physicians operating in Cebu City. The Cebu Medical Society has a list of 1003 currently active members, though the location of their practices is not known. What is known is that the number of persons per physician in the Philippines is also increasing: from 7800 in 1980, it grew to 8300 in 1993.

Family planning services are freely available in Cebu City as well as elsewhere in the country. In the late 1980s, the Philippine Department of Health (DOH) was given the overall responsibility for family planning services, a responsibility previously exercised by the Commission on Population. Ever since the early 1990s, when the central authority of DOH was devolved to local government units, local health departments in cooperation have provided family planning services, along with a number of Philippine and foreign-funded non-governmental organizations (NGO).

Contraceptive prevalence rates in Cebu City are substantially higher than comparative rates for the country as a whole. In 1996, the prevalence rate for modern methods among currently married women in Cebu City was 39.9 percent; that for traditional methods, 21.3 percent. Corresponding national figures estimated by the 1993 National Demographic Survey (Philippines NSO, 1994) were 24.9 for modern and 15.1 for traditional methods.

Over the following decades, epidemiological transition and population ageing will proceed slowly but consistently in Cebu City. With the expected recovery from the 1997 economic downturn, these two processes will accelerate. For the City's health system, the expected developments imply a continuous decline of communicable diseases, a slowly growing proportion of elderly people in the city and an increasing need for modern medical services and facilities, for people suffering from degenerative and/or lifestyle-related diseases. If Cebu City is to continue to serve the *current* health needs of its population and that of the region, more staff and facilities will have to be made operational by the city government.

Education

Table 6.4 provides the basic data on schools and students in Cebu City during the past four years.

Table 6.4
Educational Services

Year	Public		Private		Total	Percent	
	Schools	Students	Schools	Students	Students	Male	Female
Elementary Schools							
1995/96	65	84,981	62	22,452	107,433	51.5	48.5
1996/97	66	87,301	64	22,444	109,745	51.4	48.6
1997/98	66	91,294	69	22,686	113,980	51.5	48.5
1998/99	67	92,965	60	22,542	115,507	51.3	48.7
High Schools							
1996/97	33	32,482	33	29,536	62,018	48.9	51.1
1997/98	34	34,467	29	29,780	62,247	49.6	50.4
1998/99	36	36,470	37	28,955	65,425	49.1	50.9
Colleges and Universities							
1996/97	4	10,783	31	105,369	116,152	–	–
1998/99	4	5,397	31	90,271	95,668	–	–

Source: Tabulation of unpublished data, Dept of Education, Culture and Sports, Region VII, Cebu City, 1998

During the present school year (1998/99), some 67 public and 60 private elementary schools serve about 115,000 students in Cebu City. With roughly equal numbers of schools, the public sector serves about four times the number of students served by the private schools. Public elementary schools encompass six grades; some private schools have added a seventh. Before World War II, elementary schools in the country covered eight grades, but the last two were eliminated after the war because of lack of funds. Today, serious consideration is given to restoring at least the seventh grade.

Private schools have two types of clients: children from economically better-off families who can afford the often stiff tuition fees, and children of less well-off families whose schooling is subsidized by church-related or philanthropic associations. In public elementary schools, no tuition is charged, but parents have to pay for school uniforms where required and are often asked for 'donations'. Generally, big city schools are better equipped than small schools in outlying *barangays*.

The number of high schools and high school students are roughly evenly divided between the public and private sectors. Most high schools cover four years and offer day classes; a few offer night classes and fewer still both types of classes. Of special importance are national or city-operated science high schools catering to gifted students: Cebu City has one of these.

School enrolment in Cebu City has increased by slightly less than two percent annually over the last four school years. At the same time, the population of elementary and high-school age, here taken as six to 16 years, was increasing by a little more than one percent annually, and this growth rate can be expected to slowly decline further.

The clientele of the city's elementary and secondary schools consists predominantly of city residents. In 1995, the census of population counted 82,232 children aged six through 12, and 56,944 children aged 13 through 16. These two age groups corresponded approximately to the ones eligible for elementary and high school in 1995. The number of students actually enrolled in elementary school in Cebu City in 1995 exceeded the number of eligible city residents aged six to 12 by some 25,000, and the number of enrolled high school students is larger than that in the 13–16 grouping by 5000. The 'excess numbers' of elementary school students is explained by the number of children older than 12 who have not completed their elementary schooling. For high school students, a similar explanation holds, but out-of-town students also increase the number of enrollees. The enrolment figures for the past three or four school years reveal no gender bias: in elementary schools, the sex ratio of the students corresponds to the population sex ratio for the included age group; in high schools, girls slightly outnumber boys.

Cebu City is the second-largest educational centre of the country after Metro Manila. The 35 colleges and universities located in Cebu City (including seven full-fledged universities and four medical schools) draw their clientele primarily from the three Visayas regions and from northern Mindanao. Unfortunately, enrolment figures by gender are not available.

School population growth is dependent not only on general population growth but also on the growing desire of the population to obtain more education. The implication is that the pressure to provide additional facilities for elementary schooling in Cebu City will most likely decline slowly. The need for additional high school and college facilities may not decline, however, because such facilities serve both Cebu City and out-of-town students in search of higher education.

The realization of the desire to continue on to higher levels of education is very much a function of economics. Table 6.4 points this out with respect to college and university enrolment in Cebu City over the past two school years. Enrolment for school year 1998/9 declined by almost 20 percent, largely due to the economic crisis that hit Southeast Asia in mid-1997.

Because of Cebu City's function as educational and commercial centre of the southern Philippines, the educational level of its population exceeds the average education of the country's population by a good amount. What is noteworthy is that the proportion of college-degree holders in Cebu as well as the country is larger for women than for men. This condition can be seen in Table 6.5.

Table 6.5
Educational Achievement in Cebu City and the Philippines
(% Population Age 6–29 by Years of School Completed)

Highest Grade Achieved	Cebu City		Philippines	
	Male	Female	Male	Female
No schooling	3.3	2.8	7.3	6.7
Pre-school	3.4	2.7	4.4	4.2
Elementary	38.2	35.4	50.3	45.0
High School	29.8	33.4	25.1	28.4
Some College	14.4	14.2	6.3	7.2
Aca. Degree	8.4	9.5	3.5	5.5
Others	2.5	2.0	3.1	3.0

Source: Philippines NSO, 1995

WATER[6]

Cebu's water situation is precarious and its future seems even more so. The main source of water is a coastal limestone aquifer under a land surface of 180 square kilometres. It stretches along the coast from the municipality of Compostela north of the town of Talisay in the south, a distance of about 30 kilometres. The average rainfall in Cebu is 160 cm, of which approximately 30 percent infiltrates to charge the aquifer. Thus the estimated available water in this aquifer is about 86 million cubic metres per year. To maintain the health of the aquifer, no more than two-thirds of its volume should be drawn down, implying an availability of about 58 million cubic metres per year. In 1996, it was estimated that some 85 million cubic metres were extracted, exceeding the limit by 45 percent.

Deforestation and urban development worsen the situation. Deforestation has reduced the soil's capacity to absorb water and thus recharge the aquifer. Urban development has increased impermeable surfaces, blocking water infiltration. The result has been flooding and erosion and a weakening of the natural forces that recharge the aquifer.

Since this is a coastal aquifer, the immediate impact of heavy extraction is the incursion of seawater and the increasing salinity of the water. The normal salinity of ground and fresh surface water is 40 milligrams per litre (mg/l). WHO recommends 250 mg/l as a maximum for safe drinking water, but it is typical to measure seawater incursion into aquifers by the lower level of 40 mg/l. The isochloride line, which divides fresh water in the aquifer from seawater incursion, was 2.5 kilometres inland in 1983. In 1995, it had moved 0.75 kilometre farther inland. Continued population growth and economic development will both increase water extraction and further impede infiltration and aquifer recharging. It is expected that by the year 2000, the 40mg/l isochloride line will have advanced another kilometre inland.

In addition to the problem of water quantity, there are problems with quality. The Metro Cebu Water District (MCWD), which manages the city's water, estimates that less than a third of households are connected to its services. Possibly an equal number are connected to other private services, including an estimated 18 to 19 percent who use their own deep wells. Others rely on shallow wells, rivers, springs, rainwater and peddlers, which are considered unsafe. Perhaps as many as 14 percent of the inhabitants use unsafe water.

Cebu City and its environs have problems with surface water as well as with ground water. Water samples taken from some of the major rivers revealed that they contained heavy metals such as lead, nickel, zinc and mercury and the toxic substance, arsenic, in concentrations that far exceed acceptable limits (Israel, 1996, p. 382). The marine waters of metro Cebu are as polluted as its ground and surface waters. Water samples taken at the beaches in Talisay, a municipality immediately adjacent to Cebu City, are heavily contaminated by fecal coliform (Israel, 1996, p. 383).

Projections of water demand only show a more serious situation. For Cebu and Mandate Cities, the total water demand in 1995 was 126 million cubic metres per year. It is expected to rise to 207 million by 2010.

The main source of Metro Cebu's future water supply will be the rivers in the mountains of Cebu. Three watersheds in central Cebu Island drained by the Mananga, Kotkot and Lusaran rivers are especially important for the city. Twenty-two of Cebu City's 80 *barangays* are either entirely or partially located in these combined watershed areas of some 200 km^2. By law, watersheds are protected areas and not open to private ownership and agricultural or other exploitation. In reality, however, they are areas in which conflicting interests compete: those of farmers living and cultivating fields in them, of developers looking for lucrative project sites, and of local politicians promoting or protecting specific interest groups.

In summary, the combined pressures of population growth and economic development place severe pressures on both current and future water supplies. Facilities must be developed to connect all the city's population with safe water. They must also be expanded to provide for what appears to be certain continued growth. Moreover, sewage facilities must be developed to keep rivers and beaches free of human pollution and toxic industrial wastes. The national government's Department of Environment and Natural Resources is requiring manufacturing establishments to make provisions for specific pollution control measures before they are given a permit to operate. Environmental protection laws are probably adequate to the task of securing safe water, but their implementation is extremely weak. The MCWD supposedly has the capacity to plan for adequate clean water for the future, but again, implementation is weak. Ideas have been proposed for importing water in sea-bottom pipes from nearby islands, but there are objections from potential donor sites, and no real planning seems to be going on for such piping.

One of the more promising developments at this time is the emergence of a citizens' advocacy group. The Cebu United for Sustainable Water is a non-governmental organization formed to exert pressure on local governments to formulate integrated water management and land use plans for watersheds. It is trying to protect watersheds and guarantee sufficient water for the larger Cebu area in the future. The group has much to do.

AIR QUALITY, TRANSPORTATION AND PARKS

In 1987, the national government began an inventory of the sources of air pollution in Metro Manila (Fuentes, 1993). Following this, in 1993, the government established a series of five air pollution standards: for suspended particulate matter (SPM), sulphur dioxide (SO_2), nitrogen oxides, ozone and carbon monoxide. The standards are to be applied to the entire country. There is no systematic monitoring of air quality in Cebu City, but there have been sporadic measurements of SPM in six locations throughout the city. From July 1996 through December 1997, there were 24 measurements taken in one area, 11 in a second, nine in a third and one each in the other three areas monitored. Of the 47 location-days of measurements, 14 were found to be above the level at which an 'alert' is issued; eight were at a level considered hazardous. Daily measurements are highly erratic, moving from 'good' to 'hazardous' levels within a few days.

Sulphur dioxide levels were measured once in 1996, using three one-hour sample periods. They showed, respectively, 217, 25, and three micrograms per cubic metre. Levels of 181 to 650 are considered 'poor', and only become 'hazardous' above 2360.

One can make little of these measures. Without systematic monitoring over time in standard locations, it is impossible to know whether the situation is improving, deteriorating or remaining stable. Popular impressions, however, are that air pollution in the city is a serious problem, is worsening, and is the cause of much complaining.

Cebu City has little heavy industry, thus air pollution from industry is not a real problem. The most important stationary source of air pollution in the city is smoke emissions from households and restaurants that use wood and charcoal for cooking. The estimated 94,000 metric tons of wood and charcoal used for cooking raise SPM levels perceptibly. In the rainy season, the air is cleaned daily by the heavy rains, but in the long dry season the smoke can lay heavily on the city for days.

Most probably a greater source of air pollution comes from the combination of vehicular traffic and roads. An estimate made in the City's Geographic Information System Office in 1993 showed that only 52 of the city's 627 kilometres of roads were paved with concrete or asphalt. The great majority of roads in and around the city are dirt or gravel, which spew clouds of dust from moving vehicles. Further exacerbating the problem is the lack of a perimeter road that could divert the island's north-south traffic from the city centre[7]. All of this traffic passes directly through the centre of the city, adding both to congestion and air pollution.

Data on the number of vehicles in the city are not readily available, but a count of the register in 1996 showed a total of 92,000 vehicles registered in the City. Of these, there were 81,000 private vehicles, including 20,000 cars, 44,000 trucks and 17,000 motorcycles. There were almost 12,000 public vehicles, including 3600 taxis and 4500 Jeepneys. In addition, there are some 48,000 vehicles registered in adjacent Mandate and Lapu Lapu cities. There is no real mass transit system in the city. Public transportation is provided for primarily by the Jeepney, that most distinctive Philippines form of public transport. Though the city shows a registration of some 92,000 vehicles, it is estimated that as many as 130,000 cars and trucks use the city's limited road area. Of Jeepneys, the estimate is 10,000 that use the city daily.

The heavy traffic congestion together with poor roads leads to a relatively high incidence of accidents. On average, about 1100 accidents are reported monthly. The best that can be said here is that few involve personal injuries or deaths. The greatest damage is to property, usually other vehicles.

Finally, contributing to the poor air quality is the lack of open green space in the city. In 1997, the city showed just 4.5 hectares of parks, no more than tiny patches of green, often parched, hemmed in by a bustling city. The hills behind the city offer only little respite. They are treeless slopes covered by scrub bush, with little access, even to the one National Park, a steeply sloped area designated by the government as a protected area.

ENERGY

Energy use in Cebu City provides a picture of contrasts. Electricity is apparently in abundant supply and the great majority of households (88 percent) are connected to the supply grid. Most use electricity for lighting. At the same time, the great majority of households (66 percent) in the city use wood and charcoal for cooking. Only four percent use electricity for cooking. Liquefied petroleum gas and kerosene make up the other 30 percent. By the count of electric connections, Cebu City appears a well-off city in a rapidly developing nation. By the count of cooking fuels, it appears more like a poor city in an underdeveloped country.

The figures are not easy to reconcile either. A private company, the Visayan Electric Company (VECO), provides electricity, but it is merely concerned with distribution. Power is purchased from a semi-governmental entity, the National Power Corporation (NAPOCOR), which operates a coal/diesel generator south of Cebu City in Naga. Residential and commercial/industrial connections and power consumption are shown in Table 6.6, which shows data from the past few years, compiled from the unpublished records of the company.

Table 6.6
VECO Electric Connections and Consumption, 1993–97

Type	1993	1994	1995	1996	1997
Service Connections (000)					
Residential	157	164	176	181	191
Comm./Ind.	11	12	13	14	16
Other	1	1	1	1	1
Consumption (Bill.WHrs)					
Residential	205	218	245	269	308
Comm./Ind.	455	496	554	596	632
Other	14	17	18	19	20
Consumption (KWH) per Connection					
Residential	1,301	1,329	1,394	1,492	1,614
Comm./Ind.	42,583	42,463	42,480	43,140	40,115
Other	12,853	16,380	15,945	16,766	17,205

The level of consumption is shown more graphically in Figure 6.4, which also carries the company's projections to the year 2002.

In 1992, an FAO study (FAO, 1993) showed that the type of fuel used for cooking is a matter of economic status. Upper and upper-middle class households use LPG and, to a lesser extent, kerosene. Poorer households use charcoal or wood. That study also found that some 68,635 tons of wood were used annually, with households counting for two-thirds of the total and commercial establishments the other one-third. Another 13,000 tons of charcoal were used, with households and commercial establishments having equal shares. This level of household consumption of fuel wood signifies a substantial demand on the environment and explains the treeless nature of the hills of Cebu. The extensive

Figure 6.4
VECO Electricity Consumption, 1993–2002
(Residential and Commercial/Industrial)

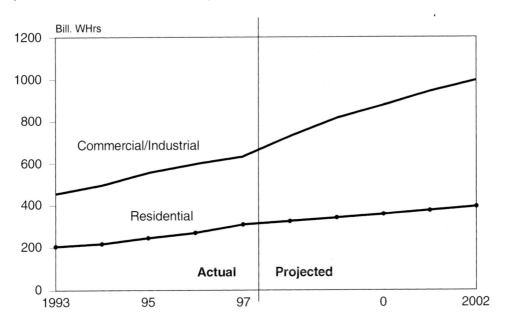

use of wood for cooking also poses other environmental problems. It contributes to general air pollution, and can be especially unhealthy in the household itself, where concentrated levels of suspended particulate matters can contribute significantly to respiratory diseases.

QUALITY OF LIFE

The patchy nature of the data makes it difficult to assess either the quality of life or the intricate dynamics of population-environment relationships in Cebu City in any systematic or comprehensive manner. If it is difficult for the analyst, it is worse for the city leadership, who must plan and lead the city with little systematic information. We rely on impressions, supplemented occasionally with some firm evidence.

Cebu City's population has certainly grown since the Spaniards first encountered it in 1521. Then an active port in the trading network of east and Southeast Asia, it may have contained 2000 people. Established by the Spaniards as the capital of the colony in 1565, it soon lost out to Manila, and became a quiet backwater until the 19th century. Then growth took hold again as the port was opened to the rest of the world and Cebu City became a centre of trade for the central Philippines. The American war and annexation at the turn of the century only furthered this involvement in a large trading network. From less that 50,000 in the first U.S sponsored census of 1903, the city grew rapidly until the Japanese war and occupation caused a major slowdown. After the war, the growth took on again, with three to four percent annual rates until 1980. At that time, with almost 500,000 people, the city had become overcrowded and smaller nearby towns took on rapid growth while Cebu's expansion slowed to a crawl. Today, the city, with some 650,000 people, is part of a large metropolitan area of 1.7 million. The larger area is growing both by natural increase and migration, but the picture for Cebu City itself is less clear. It appears that fertility is declining, and that contraceptive use is on the rise, but neither the city nor the country as a whole has yet completed the demographic transition.

Past population growth has brought severe environmental stresses. The steep slopes behind the city have been shorn of trees and the scrub-filled area is still under substantial pressure from the majority of households and many commercial establishments who use wood and charcoal for cooking fuel. Poverty contributes to this combined pressure, since it is the poorer families who continue to use wood for fuel.

The death rate is low, indicating a fairly good level of health. As a further indication, some infectious diseases, such as gastrointestinal diseases, are no longer major causes of death. Still, respiratory diseases remain important hazards, and new outbreaks of mosquito-born dengue fever are a cause for concern. The majority of the population receives its medical care from the government health system, but the ratio of both facilities and doctors to population is deteriorating.

Water now constitutes an important problem, and the future of both quantity and quality remain in doubt. The coastal aquifer supplying the city is being drawn down too rapidly and the underground fresh-salt water boundary is moving inland with considerable speed. Future water supplies will have to come from rivers above the city, but investments in this infrastructure are not yet being made. Not all households are connected to protected water supplies or to a sewage system, but specific data are lacking. Water quality monitoring is not done systematically, but sample measurements find ground water and beaches polluted with heavy metals, toxic substances and fecal coliform.

Air quality appears to be another serious problem, though systematic data are again lacking. Sporadic, sample measurements show that suspended particulate matter is sometimes far above recommended levels, even reaching levels considered hazardous. Wood fires, vehicle emissions and dust rising from unpaved roads all contribute to what might be a substantial health hazard.

There is a large number of vehicles registered in the city, and an even larger number using the main roads as part of the larger north-south traffic. The city has no mass transit system, but a flourishing fleet of private Jeepneys moves people effectively. This does little, however, to ameliorate the problems of congestion, air quality and vehicle emissions. Good data are lacking on the growth of vehicles, and there are no data on vehicle emissions.

One bright picture is found in education. For much of this century the Philippines has been well served with a system that gives the country an educated and skilled labour force. The strength of this past human capital investment can be seen in the export of skilled and professional workers to the rest of the world. Educated, English speaking domestic servants from the Philippines serve in Singapore, Malaysia and Hong Kong. Skilled, English-speaking labourers are found throughout the oil rich states in the Middle East. Cebu City is a major educational centre for all of Southern Philippines. Its primary education system appears to provide places for all the city's children. Its secondary schools serve the city well, and also attract students from outside. It is a major centre for college and university education, with 35 college and universities, including seven universities and four medical schools serving about 100,000 students.

The future holds many problems for population, environment and their intricate interactions. It appears that growth will continue, and relatively high fertility will contribute to that growth. Though the country experienced a severe economic downturn in 1997, there seems to be a return to economic growth. Together, population and economic growth will produce pressures on land cover, water sources and air quality. While some private groups attempt to pressure the government for more effective public services and environmental protection, government capacities to plan and carry out effective infrastructure development are not encouraging. In the past the country has been plagued with excessive administration centralization in Manila. Many administrations have attempted to devolve authority to give local units more authority and responsibility for their own development. A new move towards devolution is only the most recent of these. Unfortunately, such attempts have not been very successful in the past, and even today the fear is that devolution will merely mean that the central government withdraws services and leadership that local governments are incapable of supplying.

Notes

1. Much of the information presented in the Cebu report was collected from local government units, university departments or individuals in the form of unpublished materials or personal communications. The City Health Officer made available information on predominant diseases and government health services in the city and granted the Office of Population Studies (OPS) staff access to death certificates. Information on private hospitals and practitioners was secured from the Cebu Medical Society. School enrolment figures were collected at the city office of the Department of Education, Culture and Sports. The Cebu City GIS Office made data on roads and parks available, and information on water is largely based on materials obtained from the Water Resources Center of the University of San Carlos. Air pollution information comes from the Chemistry Department of the same university. The Visayan Electric Company, a private organization, provided information on electricity. The Cebu District Office of the Land Transportation Agency provided information on car registration. Finally, road accident data were secured from the Traffic Group Division of the Cebu City Police Office.

3. Dr Franz Seidenschwarz, Botany Research Group, University of San Carlos.

5. The following is based on Fenner, 1985 and Wernstedt & Spencer, 1968.

7. The National Statistics Office prepares population projections after every census. In the past, these projections were for the nation as a whole and for regional and provincial subdivisions only. In late 1998, NSO released preliminary municipal/city projections. The projected population figure for Cebu City by the year 2020 is given as 875,000, which is slightly below the medium projection of 900,000 shown in Figure 6.3 (NSO, 1998).

9. This required a detailed examination to identify persons by residence, eliminating records of persons living outside of the city. Official publications of births or deaths provide them by place of occurrence rather than residence. Thus, the birth rate would be inflated by women coming from outlying rural areas to give birth in Cebu City; the death rate would be similarly inflated by people coming to the city for medical treatment.

10. Based on an unpublished 1997 paper of the Water Resources Center (WRC) of the University of San Carlos.

11. A coastal road bypassing the central city is now under construction, but it is moving very slowly.

Chapter 7

Pusan: Promises and Challenges Rapid Growth

Jung-Duk Lim

THE URBAN SETTING

The Korean peninsula juts down from Manchuria, separating the Japan Sea on the East from the Yellow Sea on the West. It is a mountainous barrier; down its spine runs a range of mountains rising a thousand metres out of the sea close to the shore. On the South-East, the coast is cut with deep inlets penetrating into the land. They provide good shelter from the sea, and promise good harbours. Pusan occupies one of the most favourable of these natural ports.

Across the peninsula to the west of Pusan is a broad low-lying plain, rich in rice with a coast dotted with thousands of low-lying islands. Here, too, there are good natural port locations. A favoured one in recent history was Mokpo. The difference between the East and West ports is the story of colonial domination, war, independence and the modern thrust to urban industrial society that has made South Korea one of Asia's four tigers. As a port to the industrialized world, Pusan grew rapidly while Mokpo languished (Lim & Kim, 1992).

The peninsula is old, home to a rich civilization that stretches back more than 2000 years. But the cities of the peninsula today are the new manifestations of modern urban industrial society. Pusan is one of the most remarkable of these manifestations. Less than a century ago it was a very different place, no more than a small fishing village. Korea, like Japan, opened its ports to the world late in the last century and Pusan began to grow. Soon after, the Japanese colonial expansion began, pushing into Korea through Pusan in the early part of this century. The Japanese reclaimed land at the waterfront, and built piers and warehouses. Since their aim was to push through to Manchuria, the Japanese built a railroad from Pusan to Shinuiju in the north-west in order to move troops and supplies for its colonial conquests.

With newly reclaimed land, piers and a railroad, Pusan still covered only 85 square kilometres of land, hemmed in by the mountains. In 1925, the city was upgraded to a major administrative centre by the Japanese colonial government, and its development as a port city was further promoted. Although Japan's colonial interests dominated the city, its location ultimately proved favourable for a much deeper independent national development.

The end of World War II in 1945 brought independence to Korea, though it was divided at the 38th parallel between Russian troops in the North and US troops in the South. The North Korean attack on the South in 1950 brought North Korean troops down to Pusan, where a staunch defence was mounted at what was known as the 'Pusan Perimeter'. Massive assistance came through Pusan port, permitting the UN forces to hold the port and push the North Korean forces back to the 38th parallel and beyond. As the major staging area for the UN forces, Pusan grew rapidly.

Following the Korean War and considerable internal political turmoil, South Korea came to be headed by a military government, which began a major push for economic development in 1962. The government decided to focus development along the Seoul-Pusan axis, making major investments to promote industrialization. With the early shift to export-oriented industrialization, Pusan again found itself in a central position as the major port for growing export industries. It became the country's largest and busiest port.

The growth of Pusan has, however, been subject to the control of the central government. In the Second National Land Development Plan (1982–91), for example, Pusan and Seoul were both designated as 'growth restrained' cities. Pusan's expansion was blocked by central government policy. The constraints continue to be reflected in the road to area ratio. Pusan had then, and still has today, the worst road ratio of all South Korean cities. Moreover, central government policy led industries to move out of Pusan.

Other developments, however, were designed to ease congestion and expand port facilities. A new port facility is being constructed on Gaduk Island, southwest of the city, scheduled for completion in 2011. This will be exclusively a container port, with 25 berths capable of handling 4.6 million tons per year.

Pusan's geographic condition provides great benefits as well as many challenges. Its sharply rising mountains mean deep waters for the port, which is capable of accommodating ships of 50,000 tons without dredging or construction. But it also means that the city has only a small shelf of land for building. At the mouth of the Nakdong River, which drains a large mountainous area, Pusan has a good supply of water. But industrial development activities upstream, especially at Taegu City, have severely polluted the river water and forced Pusan to invest heavily in water treatment. The city has expanded in area over time, giving it better capacities to plan its development. Central government policy intruded again, however, in establishing 'Green Belts' around all cities. Although this helps to keep Pusan green and the air clean, it further constrains the city's growth. This series of advantages and challenges provide a rich backdrop for examining the city's population-environment dynamics.

POPULATION HISTORY

Population Growth

At the turn of the 20th century, Pusan was still just a small fishing port. By 1925, however, when it became an important administrative centre under Japanese colonial rule, it had grown to just over 100,000 inhabitants. It doubled in the next 15 years, reaching a population of 240,000 by 1940.

Pusan's real growth occurred only after World War II and the Korean War. With the cessation of hostilities in 1945, many Koreans returned from abroad, especially from Japan and China. Pusan was the main port of entrance for those returnees. At the beginning of the Korean War, Pusan was the only large city that was not occupied by the North Korean army, and was flooded with refugees. Some refugees, especially from North Korea, did not return to their homes after the war, further adding to the population.

The second and most rapid phase of post-war growth occurred in the 1960s, spurred by the government's push for rapid economic development. Pusan became a major centre of industrial activities due to its location, port and railroad facilities. Up to the early 1980s, the annual increase rate remained at the five-percent level.

The third phase of change, marking a slower population increase, began in the early 1980s. Though the Korean economy continued to experience rapid industrialization, Pusan began to suffer from the country's industrial restructuring; this is discussed in 'The Economy'. The city's growth rate dropped to an average of two percent below in the 1980s and to one percent in the 1990s. From the late 1980s and to the mid 1990s, there were even periods of population decline. In effect, the population has stabilized in the 1990s.

The United Nations typically makes population projections for the near future, estimating high, medium and low variants, based on different assumptions of the future course of birth and death rates. We have done the same for

Pusan, by estimating what the migration stream might be like under different assumptions. For the projection, we assume that the crude birth rate will not change much and is assumed to be at 14 through 2020. The mortality rate is likely to decrease only slightly to 4.2 in 2020 from 4.3 in 1996. The ageing of the population would normally cause an increase in the death rate, but this will be counteracted by improved medical care for the aged, which reduces mortality. Since Pusan City has been showing a stable migration pattern, both out- and in-migration rates are expected to remain almost same. Under these assumptions, the medium variant projected population in 2020 is about 3,715,000 persons, with low to high variants ranging from 3.20 to 4.45 million. These projections, together with the past growth from 1925, are shown in Figure 7.1. Note that both medium and low variants project some decline in the population for the next quarter century.

Sources of Growth: Natural Increase and Migration

In the years up to about 1970, Pusan grew from both natural increase and in-migration. Through 1960, Pusan, like the rest of the country, experienced rela-

Figure 7.1
Pusan's Population Growth, 1925–97
(With High, Medium and Low Projections to 2020)

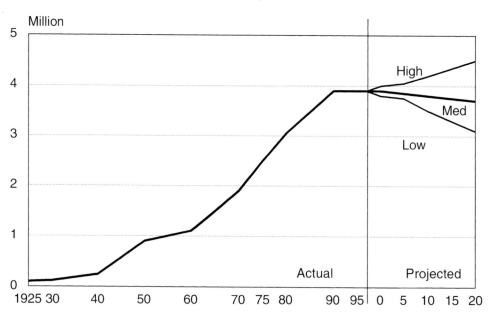

tively high, 'natural' fertility. At that time, the total fertility rate for South Korea was usually above six, and the crude birth rate varied between 30 and 40. As late as 1950, the country's crude death rate was very high, 32, in large part due to the Korean War. By 1955, mortality had fallen to less than 15 and it was below ten by 1970. With continued high fertility, the rapid fall in mortality brought a very high rate of natural increase of approximately three percent per year. In response to this rapid population growth, South Korea embarked on one of the world's earliest and most successful national family planning programmemes, bringing the total fertility rate from six to less than two in a mere 20 years. (UN, 1996)

In our study, we examine Pusan's trends only from 1970 onwards. This presents a picture of the closing of the modern demographic transition that describes population dynamics in both the country as a whole and Pusan itself. The apparent rise in Pusan's birth rate around 1975 is not easily explained. It may be the result of previous in-migration of people in their reproductive ages, or some change in record keeping. In any event, the general pattern fits that of Korea as a whole, with rapid fertility decline after 1960, and the closing of the modern demographic transition. Figure 7.2 shows the course of both birth and

Figure 7.2
Crude Birth and Death Rates, 1970–97
(Republic of Korea and Pusan)

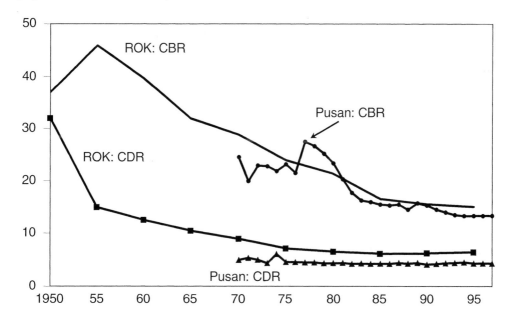

death rates for the city from 1970 through 1998, against the longer backdrop of birth and death rates for South Korea as a whole.

Migration has also played a large role in Pusan's growth. Like natural increase, that role has changed dramatically over time. From 1970 through 1985, Pusan received large numbers of in-migrants from both contiguous and more distant areas, as workers came to share in the high employment and good wages. This initial in-migration has shifted to out-migration, even into adjacent regions, as Pusan became crowded and other urban areas began to participate in the rapid national economic development. Pusan has continually lost population to Seoul. After 1990, however, out-migration streams to other areas have grown rapidly. Pusan still loses population to Seoul, but since 1990, migrants are moving to other metropolitan areas, as well as to areas outside Pusan. The broad outlines of this change are shown in Table 7.1.

Table 7.1
Migration into and out of Pusan

Region	1971	1975	1980	1985	1990	1995
Out-mig. to:						
Seoul	>30,000	>30,000	>30,000	>30,000	>30,000	>30,000
Other Metro.	–	–	<1,000	–	1–5,000	>30,000
Contig. Reg.	–	–	–	–	10–30,000	>30,000
In-mig. from:						
Contig. Reg.	>30,000	>30,000	10–30,000	10–30,000	–	–
Other Reg.	10–30,000	>30,000	10–30,000	5–10,000	5–10,000	–

Households and Household Size

As expected, the average size of households has diminished over the past quarter century, and is expected to decline further. In 1971, there were 5.05 persons per household, and this dropped to 3.6 in 1996. This was in part a consequence of Pusan's fertility decline. The TFR was 4.9 in 1971, but dropped to 1.6 in 1996.

At the same time, the number of households increased more rapidly than population. During the period of 1971 to 1996, the population size doubled, while households grew by a factor of three. This reflects a number of social changes that typically come with economic development. First, in the past, a household typically accommodated two or three generations, including grandparents, parents and children. As income levels rose, sons moved out to establish new households after marriage. Second, as the social security and pension system expanded, aged parents became financially capable of living separately from their children (mostly sons). Third, as the number and proportion of unmarried young adults increased, their higher incomes allowed them to establish independent households.

As family size declines, the number of households may increase in the near future even though the population size declines continuously. However, it is not expected that average household size will decline below three persons in the next 25 years, and the number of households is expected to stabilize, as Figure 7.3 shows.

Figure 7.3
Households and Household Size, 1971–2020

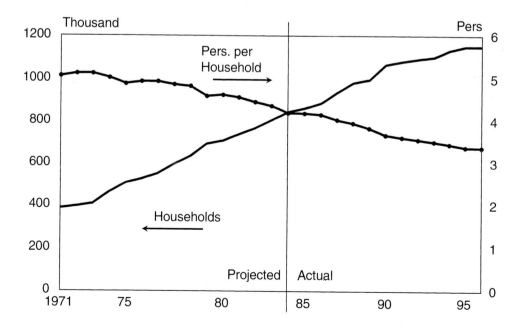

SOCIAL SERVICES

Health and Family Planning

The Republic of Korea embarked on a massive programme to provide primary health care to its entire population in the early 1960s. By 1970, primary health care centres were available in all urban and rural communities. Vaccination programmes had been established, providing protection against infectious diseases throughout the country. This was what lay behind South Korea's rapid decline in mortality after 1955. In Pusan, this meant a substantial increase in clinics and medical facilities and in the ratio of medical personnel to the population. The rapid progress of the past is expected to continue into the near future. Figure 7.4 shows the growth of both medical facilities and medical personnel per 10,000 population in Pusan, and their projected developments to 2020.

The impact of these past developments on disease and death rates is easy to see. Overall death rates declined dramatically even before our period of examination. By 1970, the crude death rate had declined from over 30 in 1950 to about six, which was even a few points below the national average. As would be

Figure 7.4
Health Facilities and Staff per 10,000 Population, 1971–2020

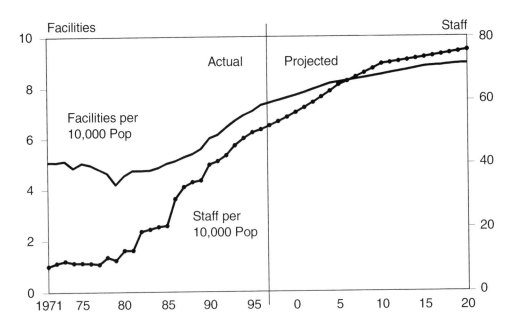

expected from this development, deaths from infectious diseases fell precipitously, to be replaced by deaths from degenerative diseases. Cause of death data for Pusan become available only from 1983, by which time infectious diseases, including gastrointestinal and respiratory, had fallen to below a fifth of all deaths. On the other hand, deaths from circulatory diseases and neoplasm had risen to almost half of all deaths. Such statistics would be expected of an ageing population even if provided with extensive health care.

Education

Data for Pusan's educational system are not available. In their place, we used national level data. It is generally considered, however, that city level experiences, especially for major cities like Pusan, are substantially above the achievement levels of the nation as a whole.

Many studies attribute the cause of South Korea's rapid economic development to high educational achievement. National level data do indeed a show rapid expansion of educational services and attainment. In 1970, for example, the enrolment rate of primary school already exceeded 100 percent[1]; that of middle school was 51.2 percent in 1970, and it grew to 102.9 percent in 1996. The high school enrolment rate was 28.1 percent in 1970 and rose to 89.8 percent in 1996. About 27 percent of high school graduates went to colleges and universities in 1970; by 1996 the rate had reached 55 percent.

The sex structure of education has also changed dramatically during the same short time period. For example, the secondary school enrolment rate of females was substantially lower than males in 1970. From the 1980s, however, the enrolment rate for females had increased much more rapidly than that for males, and by 1990 there was virtually no difference between the two. The same thing happened in the case of college entrance: females now equal males. Evidently, Pusan's figures and numbers are likely to be higher than the national average. Table 7.2 provides the national level data.

WATER

A major portion of the progress in human health and the quality of life was also due to the extension of safe water to the population. In 1971 about two-thirds of Pusan's population was served with approximately 200 litres per day of protected water. By the mid-1980s, virtually all Pusan's population had access to about

Table 7.2
South Korean School Enrolment Ratios (%)

Year	Primary School			Middle School			High School			% HS going to Univ.
	All	Male	Fem.	All	Male	Fem.	All	Male	Fem.	All
1970	101	101	100	51	61	41	28	34	22	27
1975	105	105	105	72	80	63	41	49	33	26
1980	103	102	104	95	98	93	64	70	56	27
1985	100	100	100	100	101	100	80	83	76	36
1990	101	100	101	99	99	99	87	89	84	33
1992	102	101	101	97	97	97	89	91	88	34
1993	101	101	102	96	96	97	90	91	89	38
1994	101	1001	101	99	99	99	89	89	88	45
1995	99	99	99	101	100	101	90	90	89	51
1996	97	97	98	103	103	103	90	90	90	55

Source: Social Indicators in Korea

400 litres per day of safe water. Water quantity and quality had increased together.

Since Pusan is a metropolitan area, there is little water consumption by the agricultural sector. Moreover, as industrial activities have been declining in Pusan, it is estimated that water consumption by households has increased more rapidly than in any other sector. Figure 7.5 shows the rising per capita consumption of water, which is expected to grow only slowly in the near future.

Pusan's real problem lies not in the quantity but quality of water. The main source of Pusan's water supply is the Nakdong River that flows through the Southeast of the Korean peninsula. Pusan is located at the month of the river, downstream from a major industrial centre, Taegu, which discharges much untreated waste directly into the river. This places Pusan in a vulnerable position. Two major measures of water quality are available. Neither is reassuring. Biological oxygen demand declined slightly from 1982 to 1990 but has been increasing steadily since then. Chemical oxygen demand has more than doubled in the past decade and more. Moreover, some environment related NGOs insist that the number of ingredients being monitored is not sufficient to guarantee the quality of drinking water. The measures are shown in Table 7.3.

Figure 7.5
Water Consumption

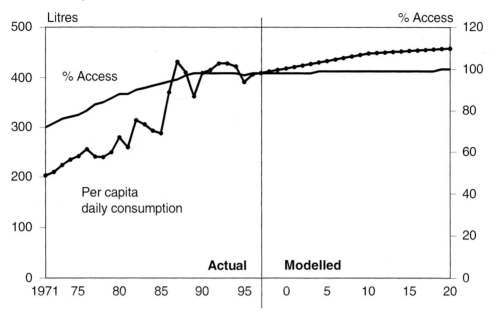

Table 7.3
Pusan: Nakdong River Water Quality Measures

Year	The Quality of Water in Nakdong River	
	BOD(μg/l)	COD(μg/l)
1982	4.3	–
1983	4.0	–
1984	3.0	4.9
1985	4.2	3.9
1986	4.0	5.1
1987	3.7	4.7
1988	4.4	7.0
1989	3.7	5.9
1990	3.3	5.1
1991	3.7	6.5
1992	3.5	6.3
1993	3.9	6.5
1994	4.6	8.8
1995	4.7	8.9

The Korean government categories the quality of water into four classes: first: 'suitable' for drinking; second: 'appropriate' for drinking; third: inappropriate for drinking but suitable for industry use; and fourth: inappropriate for both drinking and industry use. In the past, the quality of Nakdong River was labelled first class. Due to the rapid industrialization in cities like Taegu, however, the quality rapidly declined to third class. Since mid-1980s, both public and private sectors paid more attention to environmental problems and tried to prevent pollution of the river. As a result, the condition of the upper and middle reaches of the river improved somewhat, but the situation in the lower stream, especially in Pusan, remains unchanged. The municipal drinking water authority uses more and more chemical ingredients to purify water.

An environmental controversy now rages between the Pusan area and Taegu, the third largest city in Korea located in the middle reaches of the Nakdong River. Taegu plans to construct the Weechon Industrial Complex beside the river to move industries, such as dying factories, out of the central city. The residents living on the lower reaches of the river vehemently oppose the construction. The controversy has developed to a major political issue, with residents, politicians and local governments taking opposing sides. This controversy was the most sensitive issue of the recent presidential and general elections. The governments and ruling party proposed that measures to prevent water pollution be created at the same time that the industrial complex is constructed. However, the residents of Pusan area did not trust the promise and asked that anti-pollution infrastructure be developed before the industrial complex is constructed. As a solution, recycling was suggested. This measure would require the complex to set up a recycling system that uses all water and emits no wastewater into the river. That method, however, was judged too expensive and technically difficult to implement.

One result of the increased river pollution is that citizens are relying on the underground water in the mountains surrounding the city. The spring water is thought to be both medicinal and superior in quality to the city's piped water. Unfortunately, some of this water has been contaminated by surface pollution, and has hence caused minor outbreaks of gastrointestinal disease. The local government now periodically monitors the quality of these springs and closes them when it finds indications of pollution.

As the quality of water deteriorates and income levels increase, more people purchase bottled water, including mineral water produced by both domestic and foreign firms. Many foreign brands, even from North Korea, now compete in

Korean market. Compared to the past, when water quality was good, the deterioration of water quality can be considered a real economic cost of development.

Pusan discharges its treated waste water down river and into the sea; thus the quality of drinking water is not affected. For the past 25 years at least, there have been no reports of disease outbreaks due to the piped water supply. Sewage discharge could, however, be the source of stream and ocean pollution and bad odours.

The city government claims that it will improve the quality of Nakdong river, bringing it to second class level in the near future. However, as explained earlier, unless other regions cooperate, Pusan will be able to do no more than maintain the quality of pipe water for the time being.

One solution for clean water is construct a canal or pipe connecting Pusan's water source to a distant dam located about 200 kilometres inland; this would bring cleaner water to Pusan. Since construction works will require a huge investment, the city government has not made any decision yet. Furthermore, it is not yet clear that the project is technically feasible.

In projecting water quality, we follow the predictions of city officials, who believe the quality will remain roughly constant, with some improvement in the levels of COD, and no increase in BOD levels. As we shall see later, these projections also take into account the impact of industrial growth on water quality. The projections are shown in Figure 7.6.

AIR QUALITY

Air pollution in Korea over the past 40 years shows an interesting history. Up through the early 1960s, the bulk of air pollution came from toxic gases emitted largely from domestic coal use. The thrust for industrialization in 1970s and 1980s made smoke from factories the main cause of air pollution. Since the mid-1980s, vehicle exhaust has become the most serious problem.

Korea's rapid economic development had a deleterious impact on air quality up until the late 1980s. This was in part because government policy in the 1960s emphasized growth and showed little concern for environmental degradation. In addition, Korea's main source of energy in this period was coal. Factories and electric power plants were powered by coal, and homes used stove heaters that burned a cylinder of pressed coal dust. The extensive use of this high sulphur-content coal produced heavy emissions of sulphur dioxide.

Figure 7.6
Water Quality: Past and Projected Measures

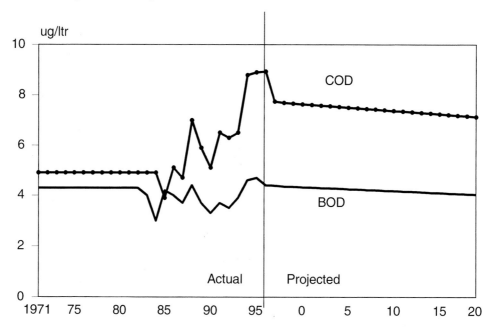

This situation began to change in the late 1960s when low international oil prices led the Korean government to switch from coal to oil for its energy needs. Power plants, factories and homes changed from coal to oil, a habit which, while greatly reducing coal-induced air pollution, added oil as an additional source.

This situation was reversed in the oil shocks of the 1970s. As oil prices rose, the country switched back again to coal. Throughout these changes, however, the government had been enacting environmental protection laws, but they were not effectively implemented. Operating anti-pollution devices in factories imposed a real cost on owners, and often such devices were turned on only when government inspectors were present. Since the 1980s, however, wealth brought by rapid economic development has enabled government to take environmental interests more seriously. Laws have been extended and more effectively enforced, and the increased wealth has meant that cleaner technologies could be adopted in a variety of industries.

Another major problem arose after 1970, however. The city's growing wealth brought an explosive rise in the number of automobiles. As shown below, in the section on transportation, vehicle congestion became one of the most serious of urban problems. Polluting emissions were most severe in the case of buses and trucks. Both were produced extensively with diesel engines, in part because of the substantially lower cost of diesel fuel. The bus system in Korea is private, but central and local governments indirectly control bus fares. Thus, bus companies are neither willing nor able to undertake the heavy investment needed for cleaner engines. In effect, mass transportation costs are substantially weighted by the price index. With such external pressures, it is very difficult to impose any law mandating a change of the gasoline engine.

A more fundamental problem, however, lies in the rapid growth of passenger cars. In Pusan, as in most cities, cars are the main cause of urban air pollution. Moreover, urban traffic, with its frequent stops, increases pollution, as idling engines produce more emissions than do engines running more quickly and thus more efficiently.

Current emphasis in government policy is on reducing emissions from cars and factories. The government has begun to intensify monitoring activities. The Pusan City government now randomly checks the exhaust of cars on the street, and regulations are slowly being tightened. Cost is the most important barrier to better emission control. It will take some time to change to cleaner vehicles. In the case of auto manufacturing, there is neither systematic monitoring nor imposition of cleaner manufacturing standards. Again cost is a major factor. Since auto manufacturing is a major industry in Korea, macro-economic calculations will play a large role in policy formation.

Air pollution is produced not only domestically but also internationally. Polluted air from Chinese industry and vehicles moves across the Yellow Sea. Chemical pollutants and yellow dust from China are carried by strong westerly winds and produce smog, acid rain and increased particulate matter in South Korea. International cooperation is needed to solve these problems. Recently, meetings of Yellow Sea rim or East Sea (Sea of Japan) rim cities, including delegates from Pusan and cities in China and Japan, have been held. The air pollution problem is included on the agenda of some of these meetings, but it is necessary to develop specific international agreements to reduce it.

Despite the economic development and difficulty of reducing air pollution, Korea has made substantial progress since it began serious monitoring in the mid-1980s, and projects a future of relatively clean air. Levels of sulphur dioxide and suspended particulate matter have declined steadily over the past decade. Nitrogen oxides, however, have shown a slight increase, reflecting the growth of automobiles. At the same time, nitrogen oxides have not grown as rapidly as the number of cars, indicating important progress in producing cleaner and more efficient cars.

Actual measurements of air quality were only made in the period 1985 to 1996. Our modelling uses assumptions for 1971 to 1984, and for the future. The modelling of future air quality takes into account the impact of both vehicles and manufacturing. It assumes that the government will implement stronger protection measures, and that both vehicle and manufacturing technologies will become more efficient and cleaner. Figure 7.7 shows levels of sulphur dioxide, suspended particulate mater and nitrogen oxides from 1971 to 2020.

ENERGY

As a rapidly industrializing economy, South Korea has shown an expected rise in energy consumption, in which the entire country has taken part. The per capita consumption in Pusan has risen from about half a ton oil equivalent in 1971 to over 3.5 tons today; it is expected to rise to 6.4 tons by 2020. There has also been an increasing decentralization of the industrializing process, in which provinces outside the two major centres around Seoul and Pusan have shown increasing vitality, and therefore higher energy consumption. Over the past 15

Figure 7.7
Air Quality, 1971–2020

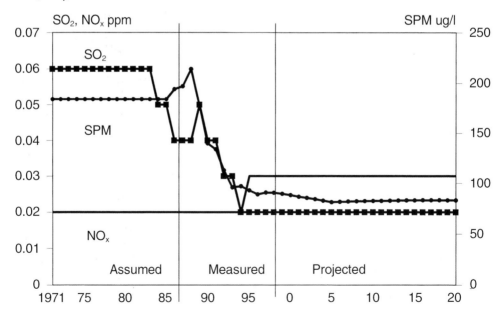

years, for which we have detailed measures, Seoul and Pusan have shown declines in the proportion of total energy consumed, while the provinces have
shown a corresponding increase.

As late as 1971, coal, largely from Korean mines, provided almost a third of
all energy used in Pusan. It continued to grow, reaching nearly 40 percent of all
energy used in 1985. Still, by 1971, petroleum had come to provide the greatest
share of energy, accounting for just over half. It continued to grow despite the oil
shocks, largely because of the very rapid rate of industrialization. Petroleum use
dropped precipitously in the 1980s, but returned to its previous level of about
60 percent. Nuclear power and liquid natural gas have together increased to
about one-eighth. The 'Others' category includes fuel wood, charcoal and straw,
which are all traditionally used for cooking and home heating, and which have
now almost disappeared from use. The changing source of energy, discussed in
the previous section is shown clearly in Table 7.4.

Table 7.4
Changing Sources of Energy (%)

Year	Coal	Petrol	LNG	Hydro	Nuclear	Others
1971	28.1	50.6	–	1.6	–	19.7
1975	29.3	56.8	–	1.5	–	12.4
1980	30.1	61.1	–	1.1	2.0	5.7
1985	39.1	48.2	–	1.6	7.4	3.6
1990	26.2	53.8	3.2	1.7	14.2	0.9
1995	18.7	62.5	6.1	0.9	11.1	0.7
1996	19.4	60.5	7.4	0.8	11.2	0.7

Energy use will continue to pose a major problem for the central government, where the basic policy is set. Individual provinces and cities can do little
on their own to affect energy consumption or sources of energy. Korea has coal,
but it is high in sulphur content and thus its use is costly to the environment.
Oil is the country's major source of energy, but it must be imported and thus
poses serious cost and security problems. Liquid natural gas can be produced
locally from imported gas and is environmentally friendly, but is still quite
expensive. Nuclear power is effective and relatively efficient but it too poses
both environmental and security problems. There have as yet been no leaks of
radioactive material from the plants, but this is a constant source of concern.

Nuclear plants also raise coastal water temperatures considerably in the areas where they are located. Since seawater is used for cooling, these temperature rises can have detrimental effects on the local ecology.

TRANSPORTATION

Nowhere is Pusan's rapid growth more dramatic than in the transportation sector. As in most cities of the world, it has seen a recent explosion in the number of passenger cars. Since it is a major seaport, there has also been a rapid growth of trucks moving cargo in and out of the port. There has also been a growth in buses for the public transportation system that still carries the majority of all passengers. This growth is expected to continue into the future, though at a slower rate. The basic components of the transportation system are seen in Figure 7.8.

As elsewhere, passenger car ownership and operation are expected by all families. In 1971, there was one passenger car for every 64 households. By 1996, there was one car per 2.3 households; it is expected that by 2020, there will be

Figure 7.8
Past and Projected Vehicle Growth

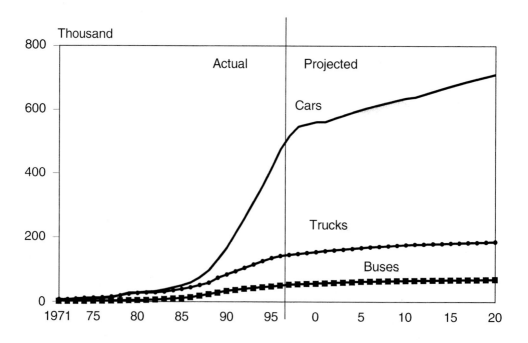

a car for every 1.5 households. This has three major implications: congestion, accidents and pollution.

Congestion

The issue of congestion is dramatically seen in the ratio of vehicles to kilometres of road length. In 1971, there were just over 1000 kilometres of road in Pusan, or about 15 vehicles per kilometre. Cars and trucks each made up about 45 percent; buses made up the rest. Road lengths have doubled in the past 25 years, but the number of vehicles has increased much more rapidly. By 1996, there were over 300 vehicles per kilometre, of which some 70 percent were cars and 20 percent were trucks. This situation is not expected to improve, as the projected road length increase is only 500 kilometres, while vehicles are expected to grow by some 50 percent. By 2020, it is expected that there will be over 370 vehicles per kilometre of road length.

The city has made a number of attempts to reduce passenger car use. One policy forbade owners from using their vehicles when the last digit of the day matched the last digit on the license plate. This should have reduced traffic volume by 10 percent each day, but it did not, and it proved very expensive to enforce. A voluntary 'rainbow plan' asks owners to refrain from using their car one day a week. The days are designated by the seven colours of the rainbow. This voluntary programme has also failed. License fees are already very high, but they do not seem to deter automobile purchase and ownership.

Efforts to relieve congestion by constructing roads for a more efficient flow of port traffic have been hampered by cost and the lack of local autonomy. The one main highway connecting the port to the city and major arteries cannot bear the port traffic. The city received permission from the central government to charge US$14 per container moved in the port. Since Pusan handles about 95 percent of the country's container traffic, this tax does provide some resources for road building. Still, road building constantly lags behind the growth of vehicles.

Public transportation is another solution that has eluded the city. There is an extensive bus system, which now carries about 40 percent of daily traffic. This has declined from 60 percent in 1971, and almost this entire decline has been taken up by passenger cars, which carry just over 20 percent of daily traffic. Taxis carry another 20 percent. The city has built one subway line, which has grown to take up 10 percent of the daily traffic. It has planned another two lines for the near future, which may ease congestion somewhat.

Accidents

The second implication is traffic accidents, and the deaths and personal injuries they cause. The case is mixed. As might be expected, the increase in vehicles has brought an increase in traffic accidents, injuries and deaths. In 1971, there were some 4800 accidents which caused 290 deaths and 4700 personal injuries. In 1996, there were 16,000 accidents, causing 550 deaths and 19,000 personal injuries. Though these deaths and injuries represent a serious cost, they have grown much more slowly than vehicle traffic. This indicates a substantial progress in developing safe and efficient traffic flow patterns. It may also indicate some increase in skill of drivers. In 1971, there were over 300 accidents per 1000 vehicles. This declined to only 24 in 1996. Deaths and injuries per 1000 vehicles in 1971 were 18 and 304 respectively; the figures declined to 0.8 and 29 in 1996. In fact, the peak of all total figures – accidents, deaths and injuries – was reached in 1991. Since then there has been a precipitous decline. The 16,000 accidents in 1996 were down from 23,000 at the peak in 1991; the 19,000 personal injuries were down from 27,000. It is expected that this improvement in safety and efficiency of traffic flows will continue. By the year 2020, accidents are expected to be down to 8000, even with the 50 percent increase in the total number of vehicles. Traffic deaths are thus expected to remain steady at about 500 per year, while personal injuries are expected to decline further to some 17,000 per year. These complicated statistics can be seen more easily in graphic form, as presented in Figure 7.9.

Pollution

The final implication is air pollution. However, as we saw earlier, air quality has improved and is not expected to deteriorate further in the near future. All levels are expected to remain low, largely because of progress in environmental protection, and in engine and emissions technology.

LAND USE: PARKS AND HOUSING

Three inter-connected conditions mark Pusan's land use. First, the city expanded over time with the addition of new areas, though the planning has been hampered by the timing of the central government's land use policies. Second, Pusan is surrounded by a large green belt, which both enhances the quality of

Figure 7.9
Pusan Traffic Accidents, Injuries and Deaths, Per 1000 Vehicles

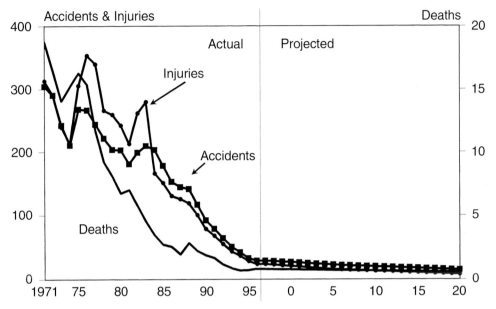

urban life and limits planning options. Third, both conditions have led to a rapid growth in apartment construction, which makes the city very well housed.

Expansion

From a small area facing Yong Do Island in 1914, the city grew to the north and east. In 1942, it expanded westward to the Nakdong River and eastward along the sea. In 1963, Pusan became the first city in Korea to be designated a Municipality, and its boundaries moved northward along the east bank of the river. Three more expansions occurred, in 1978, 1990 and 1995, which together almost doubled the area under municipal administration.

Green Belt

Although there were some advantages of being designated a Municipal City in 1963, which permitted more local autonomy for planning, there was also a distinct disadvantage. This became evident when the government created the Urban Planning Act in the late 1960s. Urban areas were able to plan for territory that could include an entire province, or the Municipal City area. Since Pusan was already a Municipal area, its planning scope was limited to the relatively small area it already occupied.

Another policy that has greatly affected urban planning in Pusan is the central government's establishment of 'Green Belts' around all cities. These are designed to provide cities with undeveloped areas of forests and open lands. In Pusan's case, the green belt now occupies more than half (55 percent) its metropolitan area. Although this measure enhances the quality of urban life, it also severely restricts planning. Moreover, the limited land available for development has driven up land prices in the city. As a result, factories have moved out of the city in search of lower land costs. Even the major areal expansions in 1978, 1990 and 1995 did not alleviate these problems, because most of the newly incorporated areas had been designated Green Belt areas. The map in Figure 7.10 shows both the large Green Belt around the city in heavy lines, and the expansion of Pusan's administrative territory from 1914 to the last major increase in 1995.

Figure 7.10
Map of Pusan's Green Belt and Expansion

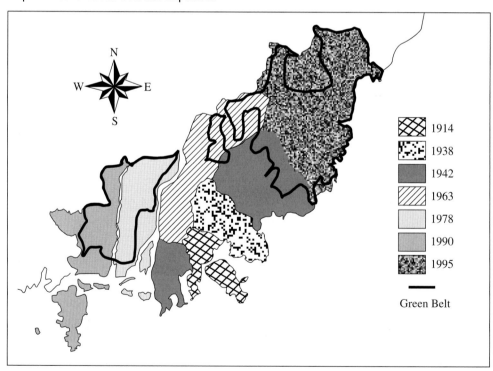

Housing

The movement of factories out of the city left substantial empty tracts of land. Since prices were very high, land use would depend on both profitability and liquidity. Apartment and condominium construction were strongly favoured because units could be sold for cash when they were built. Factory sites were thus rapidly transformed into high rise apartments or condominiums. The result has been a remarkable transformation of Pusan's housing scene. As late as 1960, apartments were almost unknown in Pusan. The great majority of people lived in detached houses, with a substantial minority in row houses. By 1970, there were still only 5000 apartment units, housing less than three percent of the population. Today, there are almost 300,000 apartment units, accounting for just over 40 percent of all dwellings. Figure 7.11 shows this change from the dominance of single family detached housing to a near equality of apartments with detached houses.

This movement was facilitated by the Korean preference for home ownership, which was especially enhanced by the economic conditions of the post war period. Rapid industrialization and high employment provided people with good

Figure 7.11
Pusan's Housing Transformation

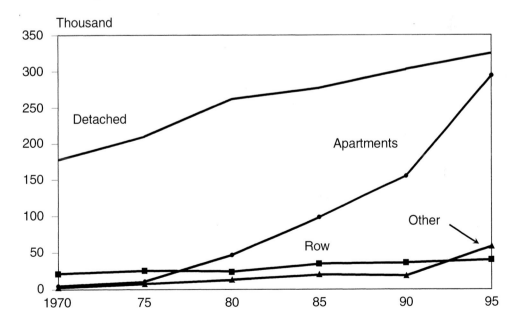

incomes. Inflation and rising land prices made home ownership a good way to protect wealth.

The high demand for housing was met by a vigorous construction industry. The result has been substantial progress in Pusan's housing. The housing supply rate was under 50 percent in 1970. At that time, only approximately 200,000 dwellings accommodated 400,000 households. By 1995, one million households shared almost 720,000 dwellings, raising the housing supply rate to over 70 percent. Considering the population increase and rising number of households, this is a tremendous achievement. Over the period 1971 to 1996, the population of Pusan doubled and the number of households tripled; the number of housing units, however, increased by 4.7 times.

The future of housing appears to be good. The Korean economy has entered a period of low inflation, and long-term credit for house mortgages is more common. Land for housing is limited, however, and since family size is declining, we can expect innovations in space-saving construction. There has also recently been a substantial de-regulation of housing, with the government removing restrictions it had previously placed on rental costs. It is expected that more open market forces will now dominate the housing industry. Government will still take responsibility for low-income housing, however, using public, subsidized apartment construction in slum-clearing programmes. While it is expected that housing overall will improve, it is not expected that future growth will be as rapid as in the past. The projected slight decline in total population (medium variant) will likely be offset by a declining household size; thus a slight increase in households is expected until about 2011. From that point, we expect households and dwellings to begin to decline slightly. It is also expected that the housing supply rate will ascend slowly to about 85 percent by the year 2020. Figure 7.12 shows the results of our modelling exercise, projecting housing growth.

THE ECONOMY

South Korea's major thrust to economic development by way of export-oriented industrialization began in the early 1960s. At this time, Pusan was well placed to lead the way. It had a well-educated and industrious labour force and a well-functioning port. Export manufacturing industries were established in what have historically been leading industries for early industrialization – textiles and

Figure 7.12
Past and Projected Total Housing

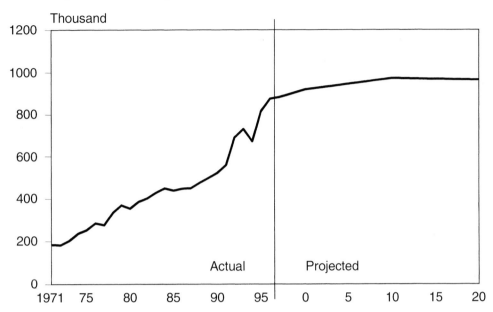

clothing. Pusan became a major centre for clothing and shoe production. In addition, plywood manufacturing played a major role. Compared to the rest of the country, Pusan was already an industrial centre in 1970. Pusan's strong industrial structure can be seen in Table 7.5.

Throughout the 1970s and 1980s, the footwear industry employed about one-third of workers in firms with five or more workers. The value added of the industry accounted for one-fourth of all value added in Pusan's manufacturing sector. Footwear products remained among the top five or six Korean exports up to the 1980s, and Pusan produced more than 80 percent of the total footwear products in the nation. In addition to footwear, garment manufacturing was also an important industry in Pusan. In short, Pusan became a major industrial centre on the basis of these two labour-intensive industries. It also became quite wealthy.

Table 7.5 reflects another pattern of change, however, in which Pusan showed early advantage and later disadvantage. The change of industrial structure in South Korea as a whole shows a pattern common among other rapidly industrializing countries. There has been a steady decline in agriculture along with a rise in manufacturing, and an even greater rise in the tertiary or service sector (including transportation, finance, commerce, entertainment and other service industries). The country showed a steady rise in the manufacturing labour force until 1990, when it registered a slight downturn. The tertiary sector grew steadily, and took a substantial leap upwards after 1990. Pusan, on the other hand, showed remarkable stability in its industrial structure throughout most of the period, showing a sharp downturn of manufacturing and equally sharp upturn of services only after 1990.

Table 7.5
Industrial Structure of South Korea and Pusan
(% Labour Force Distribution)

Year	Korea			Pusan		
	Agri. Forestry & Frisheries	Mining & Manufacturing	SOC & Others	Agri. Forestry & Fisheries	Mining & Manufacturing	SOC & Others
1970	50.4	14.3	35.3	4.4	32.7	63.0
1975	45.7	19.1	35.2	3.5	37.5	59.0
1980	34.0	22.5	43.5	4.8	40.4	54.8
1985	24.9	24.4	50.6	4.0	38.3	57.7
1990	18.3	27.3	54.4	2.2	38.6	59.3
1995	12.5	23.6	64.0	2.3	26.5	71.2

The pattern is not unfamiliar and is easy to explain. Development in Korea brought rising individual wealth, which eventually pushed up the price of labour and made labour intensive industries less competitive. This process was given a rapid push by political events in 1987, when an authoritarian government gave way to a more open and democratic one. Unions gained the freedom to demand higher wages, which employers granted as the country remained in the middle of a substantial economic boom. But Pusan's labour-intensive garment and footwear industries fell victim to the rising labour costs, and to Korean entrepreneurs who were moving out into the global market. Garment and footwear plants relocated to lower wage countries in Southeast and South Asia.

These problems were exacerbated by central government policy, which directed new capital intensive industries to other cities and provinces, depriving Pusan of the opportunity to restructure its own industrial system. This has been in part the reason for Pusan's continuing out-migration stream, which keeps the city from growing and signals its gradual decline in population.

Pusan still has its large and efficient port, however, and a good pool of skilled labour and entrepreneurial talent. The city is making a major shift to service industries. It has made real progress in the past in per capita income, and that progress is expected to continue for at least the next 25 years. Manufacturing is expected to continue its decline as a proportion of income or employment. At the same time, new service industries are coming on line, and more are expected in the near future. Pusan's physical and social conditions will continue to attract both foreign and domestic capital. Thus, we expect the growth rate to continue for the next generation. In our modelling exercises, we have used both the futures of economic production and population numbers to drive other aspects of the environment, especially water and air quality, transportation growth and all its correlates. The results of the modelling exercise are seen in Figure 7.13.

QUALITY OF LIFE

Rapid growth under beneficial and challenging geographic conditions has brought a real and pervasive improvement in the quality of life to Pusan's citizens. Today, the city is much better fed, housed and schooled, and more healthy and far

Figure 7.13
Per Capita Income

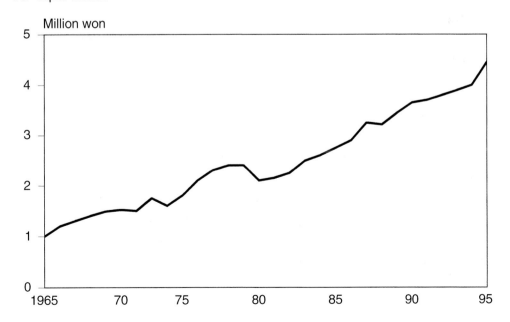

wealthier than it was even two decades ago. Compared with four decades ago, when the city was crammed with refugees, the transformation is little short of miraculous.

Despite rapid industrialization and the explosion in the number of cars, the air has become cleaner, cleansed of sulphur dioxide and particulate matter by a change in energy source, better environmental protection, and cleaner engines. Still, the number of cars continues to present a problem in nitrogen oxides. That may continue to be a problem, or it may be largely mitigated by the coming revolution in automotive power systems. Air quality is threatened from another direction, over which Pusan will have little control. China's industrialization fuelled by high sulphur-content coal, and wind erosion of the light loess soils north and west of Beijing poses a serious threat to Pusan's air quality. Addressing this problem calls for international agreements, which must be directed by South Korea's central government.

Though people own more cars and have gained the freedom of individual travel, traffic congestion has become a major problem, and it does not appear that substantial mitigation will come in the near future. More and better roads are required, but these call for heavy investments and greater local autonomy from the central government. Improvements are being made in the public transportation system, especially as the subway line is to be expanded, but again the demand for investment capital will prove something of a burden. Unfortunately, the central government retains a great deal of control over the city, denying it the capacity to address its own transportation problems. Transportation is likely to continue to pose a problem in congestion, increased travel time, and a decline in parking space.

In the social sector, the city has made immense progress, and this is expected to continue. Educational and health facilities, and staff and services, have improved widely and quickly. All of this has raised the quality of human capital, which will continue to be one of Pusan's major resources.

There is no doubt that the progress made in health, education and economic development have been greatly facilitated by the rapid reduction of fertility in the three decades following independence in 1945. The Republic of Korea established one of the world's first full scale family planning programmes, which brought high-quality contraceptive services to even the most remote rural areas in less than two decades. The decline of fertility improved maternal and child health and helped to bring down infant and maternal death rates. It also freed women to enter the labour force, and greatly extended the provision of social services without massive increases in cost.

There are, however, problems ahead, and unfortunately the city will have little control over some of them. Water quality may be one of the most intractable. In its downstream position, Pusan's water supply is polluted by upstream industrialization, especially from the rapid growth city of Taegu. This is a problem for the central government. It might also be solved by a larger regional scope of planning, but it seems unlikely that the central government will devolve authority to a regional body.

Pusan, as all South Korea, is also affected by the larger economic currents of the global market. The recent rapid downturn of the value of the won and the collapse of much speculative financing demonstrated how destructive that external impact could be. While there is little Korea itself can do about such external shocks, it can increase its own internal financial strength, as it is now doing, through a series of financial reforms. It is clear that these are being strongly assisted by the country's recent move to a more open, democratic form of government. This bodes well for the country and for Pusan in the future.

Notes

1. Enrolment ratios can exceed 100 percent because the rate is in effect the ratio of school enrolments to the number of children of appropriate age. For example, primary school enrolment can exceed 100 percent when the number of primary school children exceeds the number of children six to 11 years of age. If children begin in school before age six and continue beyond age 12, they will be in excess of the number of children six to 11 years. It is not uncommon for countries that are rapidly expanding educational services to show ratios in excess of 100 percent in the early stages of expansion.

Chapter 8

Kobe City: Well-Managed Population-Environment Dynamics

Kiyoyuki Kanemitsu
Kyogi Ueda
Tsukasa Hashimoto
Miho Koike
Gayl D. Ness
Michael M. Low

THE URBAN SETTING

Until Japan was opened to the world in 1868, Kobe was no more than a tiny fishing village hugging the eastern portion of Cape Wada. By the time the city was formally established in 1889, the population was already at 135,000; nearly a million tons of goods moved through its port[1]. The city continued to grow rapidly, reaching almost 250,000 people and handling 1.6 million tons of cargo by the turn of the century. By 1940, the population had reached one million and the port handled 5.5 million tons of cargo. Today, Kobe is Japan's largest port, and one of the country's most cosmopolitan cities.

Geography: Advantage, Challenge and Response

Kobe's geographic location offers both advantages and challenges. The deep, sheltered waters of Osaka Bay give Kobe an excellent port location for world-wide trade centred on the Pacific Ocean. The core of the city occupies a narrow ledge running 30 kilometres East to West along the northern shore of Osaka Bay. Its north-south width is a mere two to four kilometres. To the south, the land drops off sharply into the bay, providing a fine, deep-water harbour. On the north, the weathered granite Rokko Mountains rise sharply to about 1000 metres, hemming the city in and making physical expansion difficult.

These conditions led to Kobe's famous 'Mountains to the Sea' project to expand its port facilities. Beginning in the mid-1960s, the city began removing the tops of some of the Rokko Mountains, using the fill to create an artificial island just off the city's centre. Port Island rose in the late 1960s, with over 430 hectares comprising port facilities, housing, commercial space, parks and a large sports complex. New towns were built on the flattened mountain tops, linked to the centre by bus, subway and rail. The project was so successful that work on a second Rokko Island began in 1972. Now, Port Island is being expanded substantially. Planned for the next phase is the development of another island off Port Island to accommodate a domestic airport. In Figure 8.1, the development of the port area over time is shown.

Figure 8.1
Kobe's Development, 1872–1991

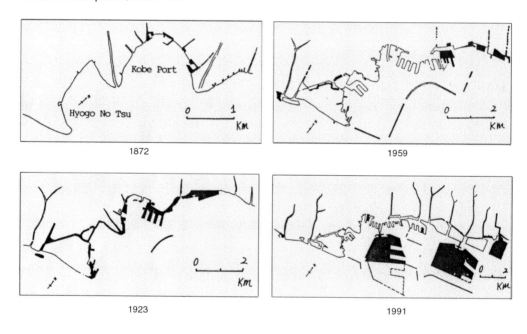

1872

1959

1923

1991

Fresh Water

From the Rokko Mountains, 52 small streams and rivers cut through Kobe to the Bay. Their total discharge is 73 million cubic metres per year; they provide the city with about 22 percent of its water. Seventy-five percent of the city's water, however, is drawn from Lake Biwa, whose waters flow into Osaka Bay through the Yodo River. Just under three percent of the water supply is derived from two prefectural dams. Thus, three water authorities supply the city. The Hanshin Water Supply Authority manages the largest amount: that from Lake Biwa and the Yodo River. The Hyogo prefecture manages the dams, and Kobe City manages its three main reservoirs and a few small springs and rivers.

Favourable Wind and Water Currents

Winds and water currents favour Kobe. Prevailing winds come from the west and the north to north-east; there is on average only one calm day per year and almost 90 days in which the winds are at their maximum for the city. The winds are not strong, but they are consistent. Thus, they carry any air pollution southward, out to sea, or to a lesser extent eastward toward Osaka. There are occasional winds from the south and west, which could drive urban pollution up against the mountains, producing the kind of poor urban air quality that distinguishes Los Angeles. Fortunately, the southerly and easterly winds are quite rare, and weaker than the prevailing winds.

Ocean currents are equally helpful. The Japanese Current, or *Kuroshio*, rises around Taiwan and moves northward. Near Japan's southern islands, it splits. A minor stream runs north, then east into the Japan Sea, between Japan and Korea. The main current, however, first runs easterly, then north-easterly, brushing the length of Kyushu and Honshu islands. The current is powerful, running on the surface at two to four knots per hour. Passing the narrow inlet to the great Bay of Osaka, it draws currents out of the Bay into the Pacific. Thus, any pollution that flows into Osaka Bay is drawn out to sea.

Port and Population Growth

Kobe's population growth has, until recently, been closely associated with its port development (Yamasaki, 1992). The numbers of people and ships grew rapidly in its first half century, hitting a million people and about 3500 ocean-going ships per year by 1940. The great destruction of World War II forced the evacuation of school children and many families; the mere 400,000 left behind endured the almost total destruction of the city in 1945. That year, the port recorded the arrival of only 26 ocean-going ships.

Reconstruction came quickly, however. By 1956, the population was back to its pre-war level of one million people, from which it continued to grow slowly to its current 1.4 million. In 1956, the port recorded the entry of over 4000 ships carrying seven million tons. While population growth slowed, the port continued to expand, recording over 10,000 ocean going vessels carrying more than 55 million tons of freight in 1994[2].

Socio-Economic Transformation

As a major port, Kobe has experienced the development of heavy industry from its earliest days. At first, there were basic steel, iron, shipbuilding, machinery and chemical industries, as well as food processing and sake brewing. More recently, the city has developed as a centre for fashion, tourism and other service industries. Heavy industries have been relocated, some overseas, and the city is now experiencing a classic transformation from manufacturing to service industries. This transformation will substantially impact the population-environment relationship, as service industries tend to be more environmentally benign.

Environmental Monitoring and Management

Starting around 1960, Kobe, like other Japanese cities[3], experienced growing concern for the environmental impact of industrial development. As early as 1964, it installed monitoring stations to begin automatic, continuous measurements of air quality. First, sulphur dioxide (SO_2) was tracked, with other major pollutants following closely behind. For at least the past 25 years, data on nitrogen oxides (NO_x), carbon monoxide (CO) and suspended particulate matter (SPM) have been recorded. There are 13 general air pollution-monitoring stations placed in key locations throughout the city. Six are positioned at roadside locations for assessing the specific impact of vehicular traffic on air quality. For source pollution-monitoring, there are 19 stations in factories. In addition, there are three water pollution-monitoring stations: two at mouth of rivers and one in a river. To top it, the city has two meteorological monitoring stations.

All the monitoring stations, except the six air observatories, are electronically linked: the data flow into a central collecting and processing unit. This system enables city officials to monitor environmental conditions and, when necessary, send out pollution and flood alerts. It also provides the public with visual displays of environmental conditions where they can learn about environmental monitoring and management.

Although the central government now establishes environmental standards under various national air and water quality laws, Kobe City government continues to be responsible for and have authority over a wide range of environmental conditions. Along with the rising interest in environmental quality in the 1960s, the City government established its own extensive list of minimum standards for Kobe's quality of life. In 1970, it published 'The Kobe City Principle of Civil Minimums'. This document established the criteria for 27 conditions for a high quality of life, grouped under four major headings: Living Environment, Working Environment, Educational Environment, and Environmental Protection and Welfare Services. The various arms of City government have been given explicit responsibilities for achieving the goals of this document.

Earthquake

At 5:46 a.m. on 17 January 1995, Kobe and the areas in its vicinity were hit by an earthquake measuring 7.2 on the Richter scale and lasting twenty seconds. This seismic event was a catastrophe unprecedented in postwar Japan, challenging not only the city, but also the country and its disaster management systems and services.

The destruction was massive. In Kobe, 4320 people were killed and 14,679 injured. The houses and buildings destroyed numbered 67,000, or one percent of all residential houses in the city. A further 55,000 houses were partially destroyed and declared unsafe to live in. In the ten days following the earthquake, 175 fires broke out, destroying about 7000 houses and other buildings.

Vital utilities, such as electricity and water supplies, were almost completely cut off, and roughly 80 percent of the city was cut from its gas supply. The transportation network also sustained heavy damage: an elevated expressway collapsed, roads were blocked, and train services were disrupted; severe congestion resulted in affected areas. Kobe Port, where 30 percent of the nation's marine transportation network is concentrated, was severely damaged and came to a complete standstill: almost all port-facilities, including wharves and container cranes, were affected.

While immediate intensive efforts went into responding to the catastrophic situation, plans to begin a long-term recovery process were also quickly laid. A reconstruction plan incorporating goals and measures to restore the lives of Kobe's citizens and the city's industries was drawn up by the end of June 1995. The plan sought to establish the city as a model anti-disaster city by drawing upon its harsh experience to establish an explicit set of 'Standards for a Safe City'.

Four and a half years have passed since the enormous environmental destruction took place. More than eight million tons of rubble and debris have been cleared. All utilities and services have been restored, renovated, and reinforced with quake-resistant devices. The transportation systems also re-opened much sooner than expected. The reconstruction of damaged roads, bridges and elevated freeways was completed ahead of schedule. The combined efforts of all parties concerned made Kobe Port's full restoration possible in March of 1997. More than 110,000 building permits have been issued since the earthquake, far exceeding the 67,000 buildings lost. Now a superficial tour of Kobe reveals little evidence of the crisis.

This does not mean, however, that the city has fully recovered from the impact of the disaster. Among major challenges the city faces, the revitalization of the local economy is of crucial importance. Given the continued slowdown of the Japanese economy, coupled with significant physical and social disruption, the city could suffer a permanent reduction in economic activity and demand, unless new strategies are developed. Such ambitious attempts include a large-scale theme park, a new city centre in eastern Kobe, a new location of the World Health Organization Center for Health Development, a new domestic airport, additional infrastructure to attract new industries, a new business-development zone with expanded port facilities, and an array of commercial enterprises for new business ventures. Whether everything will materialize as planned remains to be seen.

Kobe continues its efforts to turn the destruction of the Great Hanshin-Awaji Earthquake into an opportunity to build a safe, comfortable and viable city.

POPULATION HISTORY

Kobe opened to the world as a new port in 1868. By the time it officially formed as a city in 1889, its population had reached 134,700[4]. The population continued to grow rapidly, reaching 245,000 by 1900, and one million in 1939. The great destruction of the war years saw a major decline in the population, as children and families were evacuated to safer locations. The population fell to a low of about 400,000 in 1945. After the war, the population rebounded quickly, reaching its pre-war level of one million in a single decade. Its growth rate began to slow after 1970, by which time it had reached 1.3 million people. Today, the rate shows only a very slight increase. In the following population charts, we shall see the various impacts of the earthquake and the process of recovery. Figure 8.2 also shows the impact of the war and the earthquake, from which the population total is making only a slow recovery.

Figure 8.2
Kobe's Population, 1927–97

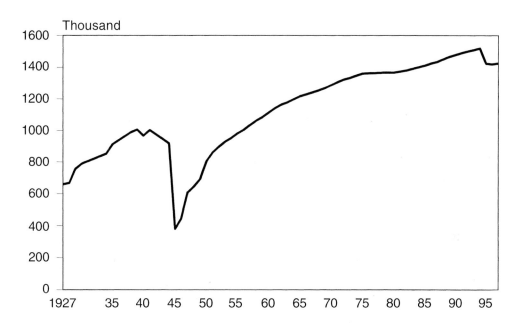

Migration

Past population growth was the result of both natural increase and migration. Natural increase was positive throughout the study period, with births always exceeding deaths. Until the war, there were always more in-migrants than out-migrants. Through the 1960s and 70s, after the immediate reconstruction following the war, out-migration was greater than in-migration. Since about 1980, however, the trends seem to have levelled, with about 65,000 in-migrants and 60,000 out-migrants per year. We note that the 1995 earthquake forced substantial out-migration: almost 100,000 left the city, while only about 55,000 migrated in. In the next year, however, there was a return to the net in-migration of the recent past. Migration has varied considerably, as seen in Figures 8.3 and 8.4.

Households and Household Size

Along with the pattern of natural increase and net migration, there has been substantial change in the composition and size of the average household. House-

Figure 8.3
In- and Out-Migration, 1970–97

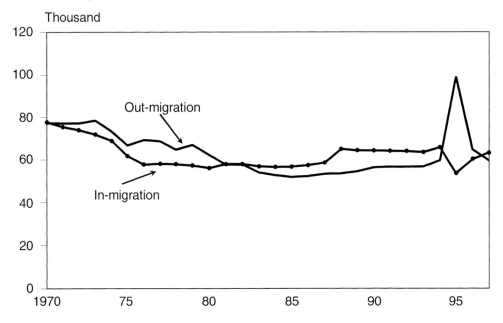

Figure 8.4
Net Migration, 1970–97

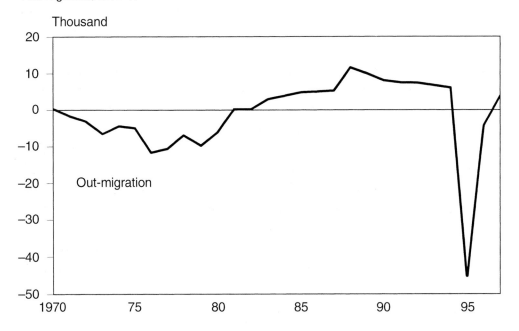

holds have been growing in number, but shrinking in size. The 100,000 households of the prewar period have increased steadily, numbering almost 600,000
today. The prewar period saw households averaging 4.5 persons. The average size
held steady at about four during the 1950s but has since declined steadily to
about 2.5 today. With continued ageing of the population, it is likely that this
trend will continue. This is all readily apparent in Figure 8.5.

The relationship between population and household growth shows an identifiable trend as well. From 1945 to 1960, the population grew more rapidly than
households. In the 1960s, however, this began to change, and today the number
of households is growing more rapidly than the total population. This occurred
for a number of reasons. First, as the population ages, women tend to outlive
their husbands, creating an increase in single person households occupied by
older, widowed women. Second, the birth rate has been declining, resulting in
more households with one or no children, rather than two or three. In addition,
the age of marriage has been rising throughout Japan for many years. In urban
areas, this means an increase in single, young-person households.

Age Structure

Kobe is experiencing a major problem that all of Japan faces. With very low
levels of fertility, the population is ageing substantially and quickly. For Japan as
a whole, the portion of the population under 15 years old makes up 16.2 percent,
while the portion that is over 65 makes up 14.2 percent. By the year 2020, the
UN's medium variant estimate shows the younger age group shrinking to 14.2
percent, while the older group will grow to 25.4 percent. As the Figure 8.6
shows, Kobe's experience will be very close to that of the nation as a whole.

When we extend the view to the future, using standard projections, 1998 was
the last year in which the younger population was slightly larger in number (0.5
percentage points) than the elder. In 1999, the elder population is expected to
be 0.5 percentage point larger. From then on, the numerical dominance of the
elderly is likely to continue rising, because of advances in health. However, that
people are living longer poses a problem for Kobe and for Japan: the need for
schools will decline, but that for services for the elderly will increase. A more
serious implication is the prospect of an overall decline in total population. The
UN median variant estimates that this decline will occur around 2005 to 2010.
This prospect is unprecedented for Japan and poses a major challenge; it forces
the country to plan for a very new type of future.

Figure 8.5
Households and Persons per Household, 1970–97

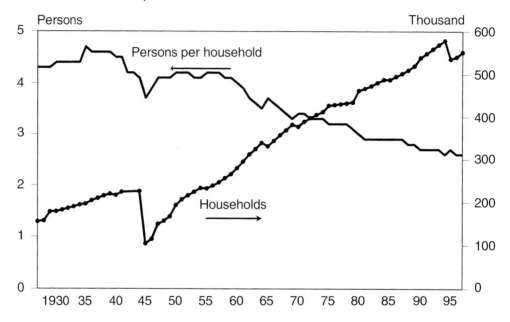

Figure 8.6
Changing Age Structure

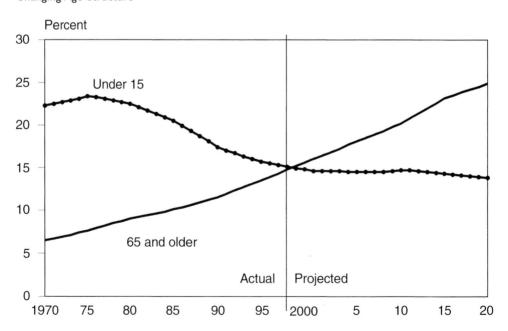

A Population Projection

Using STELLA, we produced a three-variant model of Kobe's population for the future. In the high variant model, it was assumed that Kobe would experience an economic boom; that in-migration will rise and stabilize at 4.6 percent per year; and that out-migration will decline to 3.9 percent. We further assumed that most in-migrants would be young, productive and reproductive, causing the birth rate to rise to 11 per 1000 and the death rate to decline to six per 1000.

For the low estimate, we assumed an economic slump in the city, with out-migration and in-migration stabilizing at 4.4 and 3.9 percent respectively. This implies a rapid ageing of Kobe's population, resulting in an increase in the death rate, which we assumed will stabilize at nine per 1000. We assumed the birth rate would fall to eight per 1000.

The medium estimate assumed a levelling-off of all rates at their current levels, taking into account that the rate for 1995 is an aberration due to the earthquake and assuming that all rates would quickly return to 1994 levels.

These results can be seen in Figure 8.7.

Figure 8.7
Kobe Population Projection II
(With High, Medium and Low Variants)

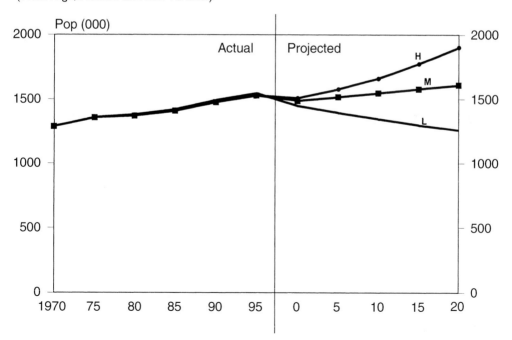

Although these assumptions were only for modest differences in rates of natural increase and net migration, they still produced substantial differences in the total population. Between the High and Low variants, there is a difference of over half a million people. By 2020, the high variant projected 1.902 million; the low variant, 1.257 million. These numbers would have a substantial impact on the city's character.

At this point the high variant seems more probable than the low, but the median projection is the most likely. This is due to observations of continued population and economic growth in Kobe over the past decade, despite the general economic slowdown that Japan has experienced. This growth has, however, been quite modest.

SOCIAL SERVICES

Kobe is well served with medical and educational facilities, providing high levels of health and education.

Health Services and Health

The physical infrastructure for health care – hospitals and clinics – was largely in place by the beginning of our study period, increasing only slightly since then.

- In 1970, there were 1244 clinics with 1670 beds, and 93 hospitals with a total of 14,991 beds; by 1995 clinics had increased to 1367 with 1376 beds; hospitals had grown to 109 with 20,072 beds.
- The ratio of beds per 1000 population stood at 12.9 in 1970 and by 1995 had increased to 15.1, about a 17-percent increase.

The medical personnel of these facilities were already numerous in 1970, with 2.2 medical doctors and 3.3 paramedical personnel[5] to every 1000 people. By 1995, the ratio for medical doctors had increased to 2.8 doctors per 1000 people, and the ratio of paramedics had more than doubled, to 7.4.

For measures of health, we begin with the most general and sensitive measure: the infant mortality rate. In 1970, Japan's rate was already one of the lowest in the world at 10.6. Only Sweden had a lower rate, at ten. Like the rest of Japan, Kobe's infant mortality rate continued to decline steadily to only three in 1994, making it the lowest in the world. In 1995, the trauma of the earthquake temporarily increased the rate to 5.1.

Other diseases have shown a trend expected by the high standard of living and increasing age of the population. The incidence of gastrointestinal infectious diseases has been low, and continues to decline, while that of respiratory infectious diseases (pneumonia and bronchitis) has begun rising. Gastrointestinal cancer has been an important cause of death throughout the study period, with respiratory cancer showing a steady increase as well.

The steady increase of respiratory infections and cancer as causes of death are likely related to the ageing of the population. As we shall see later, this coincides with dramatic reductions in air pollution. If the population was not ageing, we should expect the reductions in air pollution to be linked to reductions in respiratory diseases as a cause of death.

Education

Educational facilities in Kobe are extensive, and schooling is widely available. The figures for students have shown trends expected by the relatively slow growth and ageing of the population. All show growth to peaks in the late 1970s and beyond, with each peak coming in waves of three or four years.

- Kindergarten students numbered 25,431 in 1970, peaked at 32,265 in 1978, and declined steadily thereafter to 21,930 in 1995.
- Primary school students numbered 106,467 in 1970, and peaked at 134,904 in 1981 (three years later than the kindergarten peak).
- Junior high school students numbered 46,783 in 1970, peaked at 70,977 in 1986 (five years after the primary peak). Thereafter, their numbers have declined, to 52,601 in 1995.
- High school students numbered 49,069 in 1970, peaked at 71,799 in 1989 (three years after the Junior high peak).
- Junior college students doubled from 5171 in 1970 to 10,754 in 1995.
- University students more than doubled in the same period, increasing from 27,067 to 61,044.

The number of junior college and university students has continued to increase throughout the 1990s and will probably continue to do so through the first quarter of the 21st century. This represents a general trend of extending the years of education, preparing young people for higher levels of skills needed in modern society.

Fertility Control

Japan has a somewhat distinctive pattern of fertility limitation, due in part to the historical conditions under which the major fertility decline took place. Like all other industrialized nations, Japan has passed through the demographic transition, moving from high to low birth and death rates. The mortality decline came gradually, starting at the end of the 19th century and sinking to low levels, as urbanization and industrialization increased the standard of living. Fertility began to fall in the 1920s, but moved rather slowly up to the period of great disruptions that followed World War II (Muramatsu, 1984). With the cessation of hostilities and massive return of troops from overseas, Japan experienced a brief baby boom, as did many other nations. But Japan was devastated and under extremely harsh economic and physical conditions, leading Japanese women to resort to extensive abortions. At the time illegal and unsafe, these abortions resulted in high levels of maternal mortality. It must be remembered that virtually no effective and inexpensive contraceptive methods were available then; those would come only in the late 1960s, when Japan's fertility had already declined to modern levels.

The economic and health pressures of the immediate postwar period led to major government policy changes in the late 1940s and early 50s. The new policies made abortions for the most part legal and safe. This led to a rapid decline in fertility and also dramatically reduced maternal and infant mortality.

Abortion has remained one of the major methods of fertility limitation in Japan even to the present. Kobe follows this general pattern, having a relatively high abortion rate. With 40 abortions per 100 births in 1970, approximately 29 percent of all pregnancies ended in induced abortion. The rate has declined steadily in the last 15 years; at present about 22 percent of pregnancies end in induced abortion. Since abortions are now legal and safe in Japan, maternal mortality rates associated with the procedure are extremely low.

The Welfare Safety Net

Like all of Japan and most wealthy nations, Kobe has a welfare policy that provides individuals with a safety net of assistance for emergencies, such as when unemployment or injury make it impossible to earn an adequate income. For the past 25 years, only a small number of households and individuals have received such assistance. The proportion of all households on welfare grew slowly from 2.4 percent in 1970 to 3.5 percent in 1985, then declined to three percent in 1989. The number of individuals covered amounted to only about 1.8 percent of the population; this figure has remained relatively constant since. These households, often with just one member, usually consisted of older persons. The average number of persons per household on welfare was 1.80 in 1970, 1.65 in 1985, and 1.80 in 1989. Overall, households on welfare are smaller than the average of all households by one-half to one person.

WATER, SEWAGE AND WASTES

Water and Sewage

Water supplies in Kobe were well developed by 1970, and have not expanded much since then. All residents have direct access to high quality city-supplied water. Average annual consumption has grown slowly from about 125 cubic metres per person in 1970, to 145 in 1984; it declined to 140 in 1987, finally rose slightly to 143 by 1989, and then remained steady. For the future, we assumed a mild increase to 150 cubic metres per person.

Sewage flows grew more rapidly when Kobe's sewage system was expanded dramatically after 1970, when only 35 percent of the households were connected to the main sewer system (Yamasaki, 1992, p. 183). Houses without sewer connections used septic holding tanks that were periodically cleaned by city services. In the past 25 years the sewer system has been greatly expanded, so that now 99 percent of all households are connected to it. Only a few rural households continue to use local septic systems. This expansion implied a great increase in the volume of sewage flow. The cubic metre of flow per person grew from only 37 in 1970 to 144 by 1995. By that time, 100 percent of residences had flush toilets, and all but a very few were connected to the sewage system. For the future, we assumed a slight increase to 150 cubic metres per person.

Thus, the data depict a gradual increase in total water consumption and a larger growth in sewage flows over the past 25 years. For the future, projected population growth will produce a rise from about 220 to 241 million cubic metres for both water and sewage flows. This projection can be viewed in Figure 8.8.

Figure 8.8
Water and Sewage Flows

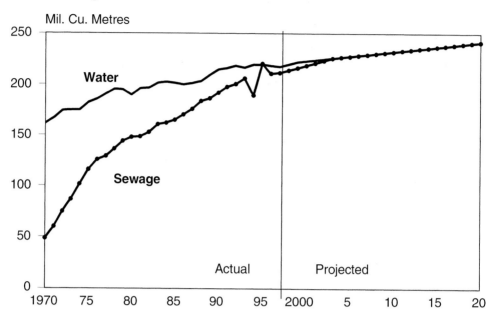

Wastes

Wastes produced by urban systems constitute a major problem for all societies. Like most cities, Kobe has witnessed a rapid growth of solid wastes from households, public services and businesses. This growth has been more rapid than population itself.

Data on wastes in Kobe make distinctions between household, bulky and business wastes. Household wastes include common kitchen garbage, paper and vegetation, as well as light, burnable, discarded items; these are collected twice weekly and incinerated at one of Kobe's five incinerating plants. Bulky wastes include discarded furniture, appliances and other large objects, which are collected twice monthly. Business wastes are created and disposed of by the establishments themselves. Used plastic bottles, aluminium and steel cans, meant for recycling, are collected twice monthly.

From 1970 to 1997, household wastes grew from 247,000 to 441,000 tons; bulky wastes from 13,000 to 131,000 tons; and business wastes from 68,000 to 304,000 tons. Despite an active campaign to 'reduce, reuse, and recycle', wastes continued to grow rapidly, with recycling accounting for just over 1000 tons per year.

Business wastes also increased, but not more rapidly than the value of total output. Adding together the output of primary, secondary and tertiary industries provides an indicator of the total output of Kobe's industries. But total output is expressed in yen, and there are two measures of value: in constant and current prices. In current value, business wastes are increasing more rapidly than total output, at about 0.5 tons of waste for every additional 100,000 yen of output. But at constant 1985 prices, wastes per output are declining, by about 0.5 tons for every 100,000 yen.

In effect, the volume of household wastes in Kobe has been growing more rapidly than population and households, but the value of business wastes has been declining with the real value of industrial output.

Modelling the future requires assumptions about the growth of wastes per household or per industrial output. We do not currently have sufficient information to project future industrial output, but can make projections about future households. Thus our projections deal only with household wastes, including both common and bulky wastes.

Since 1981, when household wastes were at a low point of a decline from 1970, they have grown to approximately 32 pounds per household per year. Bulky wastes have grown steadily throughout the period, without decline, at about 15 pounds per year per household. Projecting these rates to the future along with the projected rise in the number of households suggests that household wastes could reach over 800,000 tons; bulky wastes near half that. In effect, each could double in volume. All this can be seen in Figure 8.9.

It is important to remember our assumption that wastes per household will continue to grow at past rates. If these growth rates are not reduced, Kobe may face a large increase in household wastes over the next quarter century. Recent legal changes, such as the 1995 Container and Package Recycling Law and the 1997 enhanced enforcement of the law concerning glass and plastic bottles, may reduce this rate of growth. Our projection simply states that if past trends continue and new laws do not reduce the rate of growth in household wastes, wastes could more than double over the next generation.

AIR QUALITY

The story of air quality in Kobe over the past quarter century is one of progress. It began with a reduction in pollution, which lead to cleaner air despite a

Figure 8.9
Modelled Growth of Household and Bulky Wastes

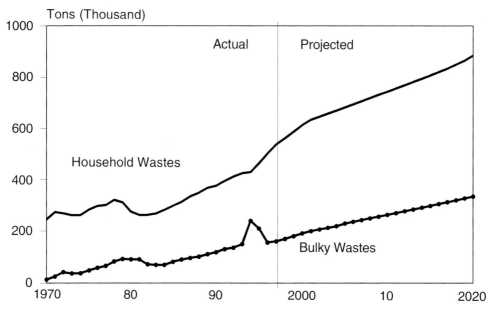

dramatic rise in the number of vehicles. This implies progressively cleaner vehicles and rapidly rising use of public transportation. The future, however, is less certain.

Cleaner Air

The quality of air in Kobe has increased over the past quarter century, although not all gasses showed the same amount of change. The three major automobile emissions, nitrogen oxides (NO_x), Carbon Monoxide (CO), and Suspended Particulate Matter (SPM), all declined precipitously from 1970 to the mid-1980s. NO_x is measured both at dispersed monitoring stations and roadside stations; the former giving a general level for the city as a whole, the latter measuring vehicle impact more specifically. The overall city measure shows the same general trend, though with lower levels.

SPM showed a similar pattern, though with a less dramatic rise after 1985.

The greatest improvement has been in the levels of CO, which fell sharply from 1973 to the end of that decade and have declined very slowly since then.

Figure 8.10
Nitrogen Oxides: Roadside and Overall City Monitoring

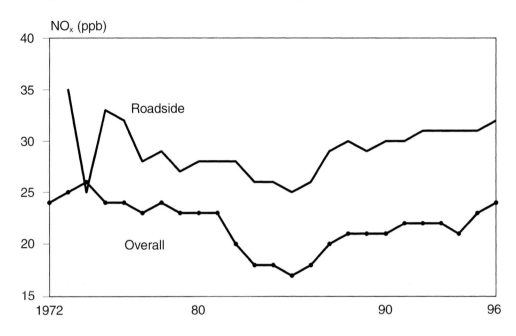

Figure 8.11
Suspended Particulate Matter

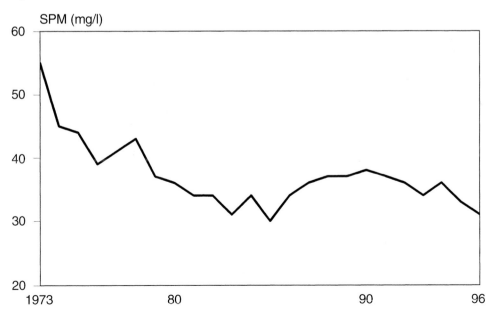

Figure 8.12
Carbon Monoxide

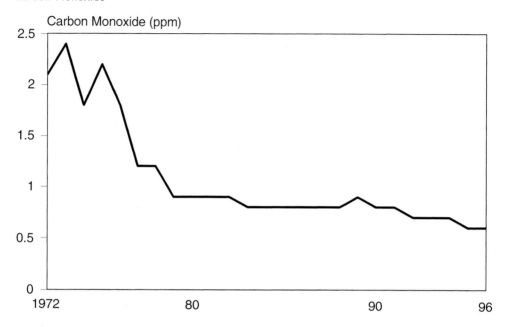

During this same period, the number of vehicles in Kobe increased dramatically, as the Table 8.1 shows.

Table 8.1
Vehicles in Kobe 1960–95

Year	Automobiles	Small Vehicles	Mopeds (<50cc)	Buses	Trucks	Total
1960	8717	26953	23277	539	16675	76161
1965	22831	41323	38479	948	24573	128154
1970	60582	57966	42637	1404	45889	208478
1975	120617	57751	54262	2164	69733	304527
1980	171348	59374	106678	1980	75832	415212
1985	218869	91701	184407	1979	73342	570298
1990	292134	128520	171330	2128	77406	671518
1995	356532	149076	181059	2160	74079	762906

* Upper limit of displacement of small vehicles was 360cc from April 1955 to January 1976, 550cc from February 1976 to January 1990, and 660cc from February 1990 up to 1995.

During the period when air quality was improving, automobiles grew by a factor of almost six, mopeds by four, and other small vehicles by 2.4. Total vehicles grew by a factor of 3.6. Quite obviously, vehicles were getting cleaner. We obtained a rough view of the emissions per vehicle by examining the ratio of air quality measurement to numbers of vehicles.

It is apparent that vehicles must have been improving dramatically in terms of emission control. For this analysis we simply divided the ambient levels of each emission by the total number of vehicles. Here we examine NO_x in parts per billion and CO in parts per million, and SPM in milligrams per litre. These are ambient, not direct measures of emissions, though roadside monitors took the NO_x values. In each case we show air quality measures per 100,000 vehicles.

NO_x per vehicle showed the expected dramatic decline, then a decided levelling off at about five ppb per 100,000 vehicles in 1983. SPM ended its dramatic decline in 1983 as well, but then continued a very gradual downslide with a slight rise in the late 1980s. CO levels ended their dramatic decline about 1980, but have continued to decline slowly since then. This makes the trajectories of air quality shown in Figures 8.10 to 8.12 more understandable. The rise in NO_x after 1985 came primarily from a dramatic increase in vehicles, while levels per vehicle remained roughly stable. Continued low levels of CO come from the continuing decline of CO per vehicle, which was sufficient to counteract the rise in vehicles. SPM measures stand between these two, with continued low ratios of per vehicle overcome by the large rise in vehicles.

The Future

How will vehicle numbers grow in the future, and what impact will this have on air quality? First, let us look at past growth in the five different categories of vehicles:

- Mopeds grew rapidly from about 42,000 in 1970 to about 190,000 in 1985, then seem to have levelled off.
- Other small vehicles grew rapidly from 1960, dipped briefly in the mid-1970s, then continued their rapid growth to the present.
- Automobiles have shown the steadiest growth from 1960 through the present, reaching a level of around 350,000 in 1995 then continuing an upward trend.

- Buses increased rapidly from a few hundred in 1960 to 2000 in the early 1970s, and have remained at that level since.
- Finally, trucks showed a pattern similar to that of busses, rising rapidly then levelling off, though at a much higher level: around 80,000.

To project the overall increase in vehicles by the year 2020, we used STELLA to model their numbers. For three types of vehicles – automobiles, other small vehicles and mopeds – a ratio of vehicles per person was used, since primarily individuals and families make such purchases. These ratios all grew over the past 25 years, though with slightly different trajectories.

Automobiles rose from 0.008 per person in 1960 to 0.25 in 1995. Other small vehicles also rose, growing from 0.02 to 0.10 per person. Mopeds rose from 0.02 to 0.13 in 1984, declined slightly, then rose to 0.13 again in 1995. In modelling the future, we assumed that automobiles would increase to 0.4 per person, or roughly one per household. We assumed other small vehicles would rise to 0.17 per person, and that mopeds would remain at about 0.13 per person. Finally, we assumed that the number of trucks and buses would remain roughly constant. Our projected numbers of vehicles from this modelling exercise are shown in Table 8.2.

Table 8.2
Projected Vehicles in Kobe, 1995–2020

Year	Total	Automobiles	Other Sm. Veh.	Mopeds	Trucks	Buses
1995	761,376	328,115	171,756	184,534	74,808	2163
2000	908,828	410,219	234,000	187,637	74,808	2163
2005	1,024,165	482,469	276,289	188,435	74,808	2163
2010	1,124,232	546,277	188,026	188,026	74,808	2163
2015	1,226,880	619,324	186,578	186,578	74,808	2163
2020	1,325,085	689,250	374,649	184,214	74,808	2163

Our calculations project a dramatic rise in the number of vehicles in the next quarter century. To link this rise in vehicles to air quality, we took a simple ratio of ambient air quality per vehicle, using measures for N_2O, CO and SPM. For N_2O, we used roadside measures; for CO and SPM, the ambient levels for the city as a whole. We made two projections, each with different assumptions about future emission control technology and regulation.

Projection A: Constant 1995 Emissions

For this model, we used past ratios of vehicles to emissions and simply assumed that the low levels currently in place would continue into the future, that is, that vehicle emissions technology and laws will remain the same for the next 25 years. With this assumption the model produced the results shown in Figure 8.13.

Levels of CO are projected to remain well below the high levels of the early 1970s, despite the projected rise in vehicle numbers. SPM could rise almost to the high level of 1973. The most serious rise projected is that for NO_x, which could reach 53 ppb, substantially above the high levels of the early 1970s.

Thus, if emission control technology and regulation remain the same as in 1995 and the number of vehicles grow as our model projects, air quality might decline to the point where it would pose a major health hazard, especially for the aged[6].

These projections were modelled on past experience with rising vehicle numbers and the decline of the ratio of ambient emissions to vehicles. The

Figure 8.13
Kobe Air Quality Model, 1970–2020
(Assuming 1995 Emissions Technology)

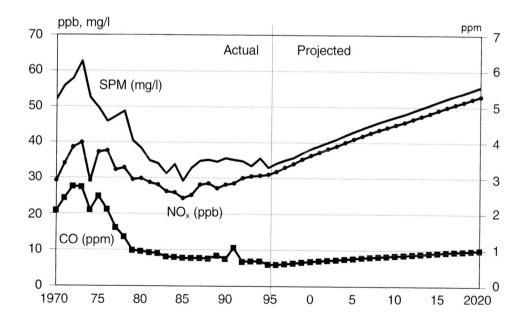

projected emissions, however, will depend very much on the technology affect-ing vehicle emissions. This may be especially important for NO_x and SPM.

Projection B: Improving Emissions Control

We also modelled future air quality with assumptions about cleaner vehicle emissions. In 1998, the Japanese Environment Agency set new standards to reduce NO_x emissions by 70 percent for gasoline engines by the year 2000, and 25 percent for diesel engines by the year 1999. At that time, gasoline vehicles constituted 82 percent of all vehicles, with 18 percent consisting of diesel; however, 25 percent of annual emissions of NO_x came from gasoline and 75 percent from diesel vehicles. These ratios are considered accurate for Kobe as well. Given the new standards and the ratio of proportions of diesel and gasoline vehicles, we modelled future air quality under future standards.

If emission goals are reached, NO_x emissions will decline by a total of 36.25 percent:

$$[(0.25 \times 0.70) + (0.75 \times 0.25) = 0.175 + 0.1875 = 36.25\% \text{ decline.}]$$

The 1994 N_2O emission per 100,000 vehicles in Kobe was 4.190 ppb, imply-ing a decline to 2.671 by 2000. If this level remained constant after the year 2000, there would still be growth of NO_x due to increase in vehicles, but the levels would be much lower. In discussion with Kobe City environmental offic-ers, however, we found that emissions technology and regulations are expected to continue to improve, to the extent that current low levels of the three pollutants will remain roughly constant. If our expectations for vehicle growth are correct, SPM emissions must decline by a further 47 percent and NO_x by a further 75 percent. We modelled this future steady level of emissions, shown in Figure 8.14.

Vehicle manufacturers, especially in Japan, have shown remarkable abilities to produce cleaner and cleaner engines. Emission standards keep rising, and manufacturers appear to be able to meet and even surpass them. Thus, it is probably not unrealistic to expect a more environmentally benign scenario to be realized.

Manufacturing and Air Quality

One of the major emissions from manufacturing is sulphur dioxide. The story of this emission is much like that of others. It has declined drastically from an

Figure 8.14
Kobe Air Quality Model, 1970–2020
(Assuming Improved Emissions Technology)

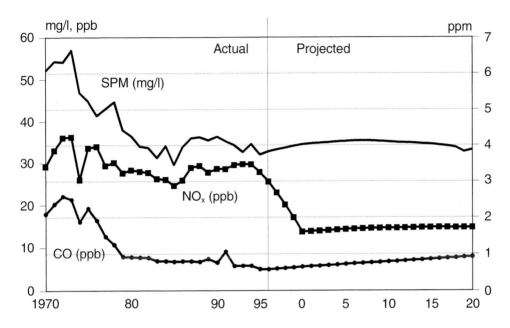

average of about 45 ppb per year in 1970 to about ten in 1980. From there it continued to decline, though at a slower rate. It now remains at very low levels. At the same time, the value of manufacturing output has increased substantially, from about one trillion yen in 1970 to three trillion in 1990, followed by a slight decline to 1995.

This improvement came in part from a relocation of more polluting industries to other locations, and in part from investments in pollution control. Thus the rise in output has not brought with it a rise in emissions.

TRANSPORTATION

Public Transportation

The use of public transportation has increased dramatically in the past two decades, and this increase can be associated with cleaner air. The cleaner electric train system has grown to claim the great majority of passengers, while the number of bus and taxi passengers have declined.

- Bus passenger trips declined steadily from 1970 to 1987, and may be levelling off. Buses claimed 24 percent of all passengers in 1970, and now show about 17 percent.
- Taxi passenger trips declined to about 1975, where they hovered between 70 and 80 million. Taxis lost the largest share of passengers, declining from 20 percent in 1970 to only 11 percent in 1989.
- Train passenger trips have shown steady growth throughout the period. Now almost 75 percent of all passenger trips are accounted for by the public rail system, up from 56 percent in 1970.

The train system is electric powered, and taxis use low-emitting LPG fuels. Only buses use the more polluting gasoline and diesel fuels, and they now account for just a sixth of public transportation users. Thus, Kobe's public transportation system can be counted as a force for cleaner air.

The Future of Public Transportation

Next, we looked to the future of the public transportation system, modelling it by making three simple assumptions. We assumed that the passenger trips per population for trains would continue to rise as they have in the past. In effect, we extended the trend of the past 25 years into the next 25. The ratio of passenger trips to the total population has grown from 237 per person in 1970, to 294 in 1989. We assumed the ratio would continue to grow steadily, rising to 356 in 2020.

For buses and taxis, we assumed a continuation of the 1995 ratio. In both cases, the steady decline of the past halted in 1987, and the ratio has been constant since. Thus, we felt it reasonable to assume a constant ratio for the next 25 years. We summarize both past trends and our projected assumptions in Table 8.3.

Table 8.3
Passenger Trips Per Capita

	Actual		Assumed
Year	1970	1989	2020
Trains	237	294	356
Buses	100.5	81	81
Taxis	84.3	48	48

With these assumptions, our model for the past and future shows the trends in Figure 8.15. We foresee a growth of train passenger trips to over 500 million by 2020. Buses may carry just over 100 million passengers, and taxis just under 100 million.

Figure 8.15
Trends in Passenger Trips by Pubic Transportation Type

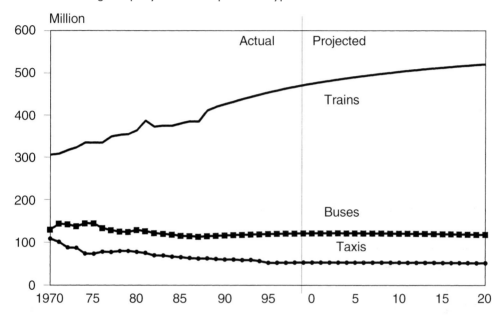

Vehicle Density

Next, we examined vehicle density. Kobe's road length has grown substantially over the past 25 years. Two measures of road were available: length in kilometres and area in 1000 square metres. In 1970, there were 3708 kilometres of road, and by 1990 that distance had grown to 5085 kilometres. Road area grew along with this, from 17,027 square metres in 1970 to 26,679 in 1995. The two measures are closely associated[7]. Essentially, for every 223 metres of road length added during this period, 1000 square metres were added to the area. In other words, it does not matter which measure we use to assess vehicle density.

Although road length grew rapidly over the past 25 years, the number of vehicles grew more rapidly. Thus, the vehicles per kilometre of road grew substantially, from 56 vehicles per kilometre of road in 1970, to 146 in 1995. Vehicles per 1000 square metre of road grew from 12 in 1970 to 29 in 1995. For a future projection, assuming no growth in road length or area, vehicle density will grow to just over 50 per 1000 square metres, as Figure 8.16 shows.

Figure 8.16
Growth of Vehicle Density

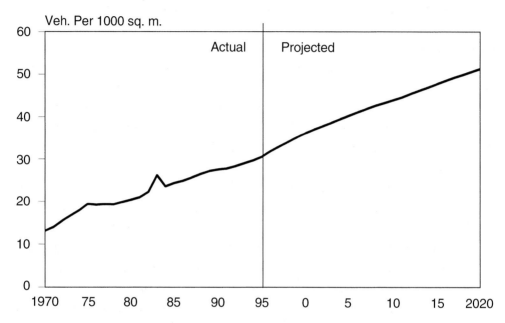

It is not easy at this time to say what this projected rise in density implies. It is, of course, an average figure, making no distinction between a potentially highly congested central city, and less densely travelled roads in the suburbs or the more rural areas. In a comparative analysis of Kobe and Niigata (Yamasaki, 1992), we found that traffic flows moved more rapidly in Kobe than in Niigata, despite the larger number of vehicles in Kobe.

LAND USE

Although many aspects of land use can be examined, we limited our study to two issues: housing and open spaces. This kept the study more manageable, but it was also based on the argument that these two aspects of land use are among the most important contributors to a city's quality of life.

Housing

Virtually all residential housing in Kobe was destroyed during World War II. Reconstruction began quickly; the evacuated population moved back and the city began to rebuild itself. By 1958, in just over a decade, there were a quarter of a million residences, and from that point thousands of new units were added yearly. Figure 8.17 shows the overall growth of residential housing up to 1992.

The first units were rather simple and crude, devoid of some basic amenities. They were also relatively crowded. But as building progressed the quality increased, as did the size of the new units. In the 1960s, the thousands of new units being built were averaging about 53 square metres each. By the 1980s, however, new units were averaging 80 to 100 square metres each. But quality was improving in another way as well. In 1958, almost no residences had flush toilets. By 1990, virtually all residences had been so equipped. Figure 8.18 shows the percent of residences that had flush toilets and connections to the central sewer system.

The size of households has declined in Kobe, as has already been noted. In 1958, a typical household had just over four persons, and the average size of new dwellings was about 60 square metres. This implies less than 15 square metres per person. By 1990, the average household had declined to just over two persons, while average size of new residences was near 90 square metres. Thus, the average area per person rose to over 30 square metres.

Housing was one of the major areas to be affected by the earthquake. To recapitulate from Section 1, the Great Hanshin-Awaji Earthquake struck Kobe on 17 January 1995, causing massive destruction. Over 67,000 buildings totally collapsed, 55,000 were partially destroyed, almost 4000 were completely destroyed by fire, and 350 were partially burned. The heaviest hit areas were in the central wards, where there were many older, one- and two-storey wooden buildings.

The city immediately established temporary shelters in schools, public buildings, tents in the parks and open spaces. At the peak on 26 January, there were some 599 of these shelters housing 236,899 evacuees.

The city also set about providing more adequate temporary housing. Prefabricated rectangular modules of about ten by five metres were placed in rows in city parks and other open spaces. These provided comfortable homes with living and bedrooms, kitchen, toilet and washing facilities for households of one to four persons. By August, all temporary evacuation centres were closed; the 32,346 module homes were providing liveable space for almost 40,000 people. There was an exodus of near 100,000 form the city, and others found accommodation with friends and relatives.

Figure 8.17
Growth of Total and New Residences

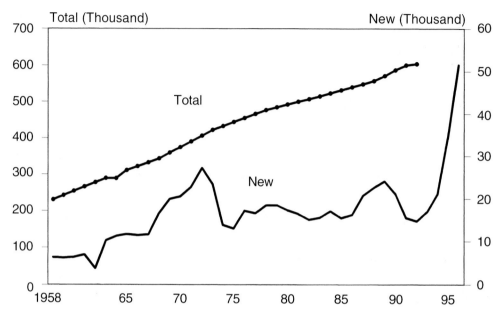

Figure 8.18
Indices of Housing Quality

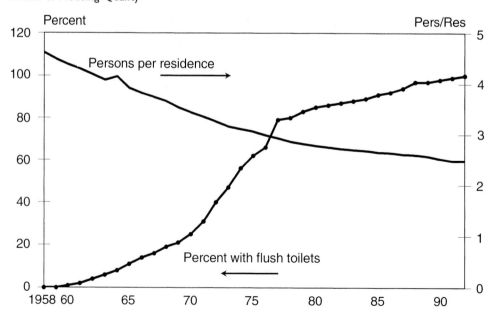

In addition, the city and its citizens began rebuilding the residential stock almost immediately. New housing had hovered around 15,000 to 20,000 units per year since 1970. In 1995, it jumped to 34,000, and to 51,000 the next year. The destruction of residences was massive, but the city recovered quickly, maintaining a high quality of residential housing for the citizens.

The Future of Housing

The future demand for housing depends on both the growth of population and the change in the size of households. As shown in the section on population history, the average size of households has declined from 4.2 in 1950 to 2.5 today. We assumed that the average size would continue to decline, especially as the population of aged and the sex ratio shifted to greater female dominance among the aged. We expected that this ageing would increase the number of one-person households, causing the overall average persons per household to decline to about two. With those assumptions, Figure 8.19 shows that the projected future requirements for residences could rise to about 805,000 by the year 2020.

Figure 8.19
Housing: Modelling Past Trends and Future Needs

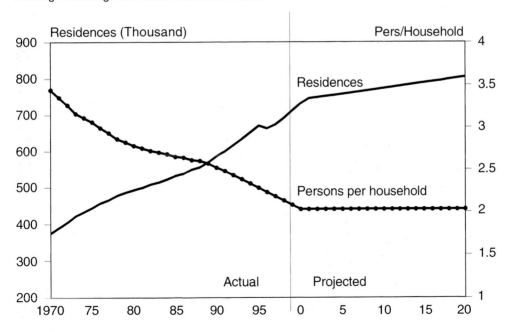

Open Spaces

In addition to the issue of housing, we considered that of open spaces. The parks and open spaces a city provides allow its citizens to take refuge from the high pace of the city life.

Kobe experienced two major periods of expansion. Just after the war, it grew from about 100 to 400 square kilometres. Then from 1950 to 1958, it added roughly 100 square kilometres, absorbing smaller towns around it. Today the city extends over almost 550 square kilometres.

Built-up areas for housing, industry and commerce took up 50.6 square kilometres in 1970 and expanded to 85.8 square kilometres by 1995. Specifically designated parks in the city took up only 3.4 square kilometres in 1970, growing to 22.9 in 1995. As of 1995, these built up areas and parks extended over 108.7 square kilometres.

This implies open spaces of 439.3 square kilometres within the city's boundaries. This includes the extensive, forested slopes of the Rokko Mountains, which provide trails for hiking. It also includes the rolling landscape to the north of the Rokko Mountains, some of which is taken up by farms and rice fields. This amounts to a third of a square kilometre of open area per 1000 inhabitants, or approximately 315 square metres per person. Thus Kobe is well supplied with open spaces for its citizens.

THE ECONOMY

Port and Shipping

Established as an open seaport for the outside world that was forcing itself on Japan, Kobe came to be dominated by shipping, which encouraged the emergence of a wide range of related activities. Steel and shipbuilding soon became major industries. Together, they created demand for other goods and services, which stimulated growth of agriculture, food processing, textiles, shoemaking and sake brewing among others.

The war destroyed virtually the entire physical infrastructure, including port facilities, rail lines, and factories, as well as housing and commercial establishments. These were quickly rebuilt, however, especially under the stimulus of the Korean War, which created a large demand for Japanese goods and services. Japan declared the 1960s the decade of development, and aimed to double its per capita GNP in that period. The country succeeded wildly, surpassing its targets many times over. This decade was one in which Kobe reached a critical juncture. The national economy was taking off, world trade was growing rapidly and Japan was becoming a major player in that trade. Kobe's seaport was overwhelmed, and became something of a bottleneck on growth.

These were the pressures that led Kobe, under Mayor Miyazaki, to envision, plan and execute its formidable 'Mountains to the Sea' project. The story is an exciting one, which has been told elsewhere in great detail (Takayose, 1985). Kobe made handsome profits from the island's construction, and launched the building of a second island, Rokko Island. This broke the bottleneck in trade, making Kobe a highly successful port. The long-term movements of ships and tonnage can be seen in Figure 8.19.

The devastation of the war and rapid growth of both ships and tonnage in the 1960s through 1975 can be clearly seen. One can also see the destruction of the 1995 earthquake and the quick recovery in a single year. By 1985, the container port had been operating for almost a decade, and the number of container ships began to grow. Ships became larger, so numbers declined while tonnage continued to grow.

Figure 8.20
The Growth of Shipping: Ships and Tonnage, 1927–95

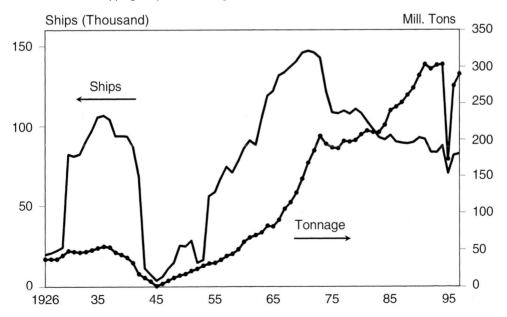

Manufacturing and Services

While shipping remains dominant, it does not account for all of Kobe's productive capacity. Moreover, city leaders have for some time recognized the dangers of excessive specialization, and have worked to draw in different industries to diversify the productive system. In this they have been quite successful. The manufacturing sector has long been an integral part of Kobe's economy, though there has been a considerable change in its character over the past half century. Steel and shipbuilding have been relocated out of the city and country; their place has being taken by more high technology forms of industry: chemicals, electronics, and fashion. For example, manufacturing output has grown steadily over the past 25 years from one to three trillion yen, while manufacturing workers have declined from 150,000 to 90,000. Kobe also has an active wholesale and retail industry, with 65,000 and 86,000 workers respectively, and almost 10,000 restaurants with 45,000 workers.

Income and Consumption

All these industries provide Kobe's citizens with a high standard of living and a steadily growing level of income and consumption, though available information is not specific. Mean monthly wage and salary data are available, but are drawn from sample surveys of the entire prefecture, including more than just the city. The average wages in Kobe are thought to be higher than that in the prefecture on the whole, but the trend over time should be roughly similar.

Along with the increase in salaries and consumption, however, prices have increased, dampening the apparent growth in standard of living. For example, the consumer price index, set at one for 1985, was .365 in 1970, and rose steadily to 1.14 in 1995. Thus, although the mean monthly salary in current prices grew from 80,000 yen in 1970 to 352,000 in 1989, an increase of about 17 percent per year, the real or deflated average salary grew from 220,000 to 340,000, a growth of only about 2.8 percent per year, as seen in Figure 8.21.

Similarly, consumption in current prices grew by about 10 percent per year, from 90,000 to 284,000, but in real or deflated terms, this was only a growth of about 0.5 percent per year, from 249,000 to 274,000 yen.

One additional complication should be added to this set of figures. Consumption figures effectively point to the household or family as the basic unit of action. It is households that consume food, housing and durable goods, like cars and appliances. We have seen that the average size of the household has de-

Figure 8.21
Average Salaries
(In Constant (1985) and Current Prices)

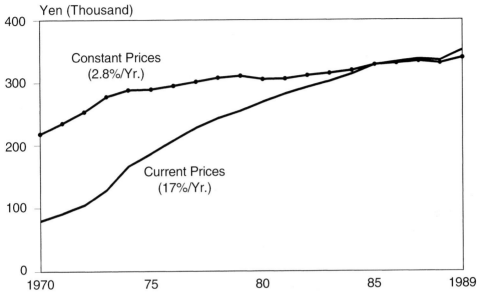

clined from near five persons in 1950, to about 3.5 in 1970 and to 2.5 in 1995. This means that the level of consumption per capita has risen in real terms, considerably more than the 0.5 percent per year that the figures show. The same can be said of income, with one more complicating twist. As the number of women increase in the labour force, there is a rise in two-income families. While precise data are not available, this indicates that in both consumption and income, Kobe's citizens have enjoyed a substantial economic improvement over the past half century, and certainly over the past 25 years.

Officially, Kobe continues to show low levels of unemployment, but there has been a steady change in the ratio of job openings to job applicants. In the early 1970s, there were far more openings than applicants; this indicates a brief period of labour shortage. By 1975, applicants outnumbered openings by more than two to one, but toward the end of the 1980s, the two sets of figures came into closer balance.

QUALITY OF LIFE

Overall, this data set indicates a city with a high and rising standard of living. From the perspective of our basic model, all environmental measures indicate a high quality of life. There is sufficient water of high quality; air quality has improved and is of now very high standard; housing is adequate and has improved in amount and quality; and there is much open space, including built-up parks and natural areas. Energy is also unproblematic: it appears more than sufficient for domestic and commercial needs, with little prospect of future shortages. Energy is, however, quite outside of the purview of the urban administration, so we have little ability to discuss its condition.

All the institutional sectors examined here – transportation, production and social services – appear to be highly productive and environmentally clean. Transportation has improved greatly; there is both a large increase in private vehicles and in passenger-trips by clean forms of public transportation, such as electric trains. All of this substantial growth in transportation has been accompanied not by a decline but an increase in air quality. The productive sector has provided increasing real incomes for individuals and households, along with an increase rather than a decrease in air quality.

The social sector provides high quality schools and medical services for all the population. Infectious diseases have declined dramatically as a result of high quality medical and environmental services.

The one problematic issue for Kobe, and even more so for all Japan, is the low fertility level and pronounced ageing of the population. The country's total population is expected to continue to grow up to 2005 and then to begin a slow absolute decline. As a vibrant urban area, Kobe can be expected to continue growing through the period of our analysis, 2020, but its growth will be very slow. The implications of slow growth and ageing are deep and serious. They are now the subject of considerable discussion and analysis, but the future is not at all clear.

The population-environment relationship in Kobe has been a benign and productive one. The population has grown substantially while the environment has become healthier. This accords to what the IUCN-World Conservation Union calls sustainable development: promoting the welfare of people and ecosystems now and into the future.

In 1970, the City of Kobe adopted a set of targets on the minimum level of life quality measures to be achieved. This move indicates a visionary leadership and an actively participating citizenry. But there is another condition, which we have observed in previous comparative analyses of the Asian urban scene. Kobe's civil service has a very low turnover rate and a very high level of tenure. For most, the city administration is a lifetime commitment. Civil servants know the city well. They have worked through its problems and are committed to making Kobe a better city for the citizens and their own families. This life-time tendency to tenure has two very powerful advantages: knowledge and commitment. It makes the city administration well qualified to promote the welfare of both the citizens and their urban environment.

The Great Hanshin-Awaji Earthquake provided a dramatic illustration of the quality of both civil administration and civil society in Kobe. The recovery from the earthquake came quickly, more quickly than anticipated or scheduled. This quick recovery was accomplished not by national government support alone, but more importantly by an effective city government working with an energetic citizenry.

Kobe demonstrates that urban population-environment dynamics can lead to positive outcomes for the great majority, producing a high and rising quality of life.

Notes

1. These data are from *A Centennial Tribute of Kobe*, 1989. Data on shipping include only ocean-going vessels and tonnage.
2. In 1995, Kobe experienced the Great Hanshin-Awaji Earthquake that destroyed much of the port and the elevated highways serving it. Thus, 1994 is the last year for which comparable figures are available.
3. Nishimura (1989) reviews the many local city governments and citizen groups that began monitoring environmental impacts in the late 1950s and early 1960s under the impetus of the great move for industrial development.
4. City of Kobe, *A Centennial Tribute to Kobe*, Kobe, 1989.
5. Registered Nurses, Licensed Practical Nurses and Midwives. All these ratios use population in 1994 as the base, since the earthquake diminished the 1995 population. Staff figures for 1995 are actually combined hospital staff for 1994 and clinic staff for 1993, the last year for which clinic data are available.
6. It would be a simple matter to connect the rise in air pollutants to the death rate. We note in Chapter 10 that there is much evidence now that for every ten-microgram rise in SPM, the death rate will increase by one percent. With the crude death rate for Kobe already very low, however, at less than 10 per 1000, the rise in SPM would not cause a perceptible rise in the death rate. But there is a more important problem. We noted above that deaths from respiratory infections and cancers have risen over the past two decades, despite the decline we have seen in air pollutants. We speculated above that this was due to the ageing of the population. Thus, to connect projections of air pollutants to the death rate, we should know age-specific death rates, and propose that rising pollutants would have an especially pronounced impact on the rising aged population. At present, we do not have data for this type of analysis, but will return to this point in Chapter 10 in suggesting next steps in the research.
7. The linear regression equation for the two is $Y = -1.3 + 0.233x$, with an R squared of 0.958.

Part III

Comparisons, Lessons and Implications

Chapter 9

Five Cities:
Lessons of Matter and Method

Gayl D. Ness

Here, then, have been systematic attempts to examine the population-environment dynamics in five Asian cities. What can we learn from the studies? What do they tell us about the course of this relationship, its causes and consequences? And what can the studies tell us about this specific strategy of enquiry? A comparative treatment of the five studies provides the first step in answering these questions. Let us look at the studies together to see what we can learn from them. But first, we must also look back to Chapter 3, with its model and the lessons AUICK has learnt from a decade of urban studies in Asia.

The first observation is that there are lessons of both *matter* and *method*. We can learn much about the *matter*, or the substance of population-environment dynamics. Here, we shall organize the discussion according to the order of the presentations in Part II, beginning with The Urban Setting and moving through the Quality of Life. However, there are additional lessons to be learnt about the *method* of enquiry. These lessons concern both the model we began with, and the use of dynamic modelling to link past to future. We can also learn something about that part of the model with the inelegant and cumbersome title, social-political-economic-cultural system (SPECS). We shall try to glean from these studies some insights into the governance of the urban system, how it varies, and how this variance affects the population-environment dynamics.

We must begin with a caveat. The lessons we seek to learn here are from the five case studies reported in the chapters above. But what we find in an individual city, especially with our closed system model that looks only at the city, might not be consistent with what we can see by taking a larger view. In effect, there are the not uncommon problems here of linking micro and macro views of any social conditions. More specifically in this case, we encounter the problem of linking city conditions with global conditions. We shall draw attention to these problems as we go along. In the next chapter we shall return to the question of scale, and closed and open systems approaches. There we shall identify what now appears to be an intractable problem: deciding on the units of analysis to be used when we move from the closed city system to the more open system.

LESSONS OF MATTER

The Urban Setting

Three of our cities are port cities located on deepwater bays with mountains rising sharply behind, restricting expansion. The other two are inland cities, stretched out on plains that offer little or no physical constraints to growth. One of the first observations to be made from these differences is something we have often seen: population-environment dynamics are highly location-specific (Ness & Golay, 1997; UNFPA, 1997). Consider the following:

- Khon Kaen's air quality is strongly affected by seasonal rains. The air is clean in rainy season; its quality deteriorates in dry season.
- Kobe's air quality is enhanced by prevailing winds that blow away much pollution.
- Kobe is somewhat protected, by a mountain barrier, from air pollution and acid rain carried by prevailing westerly winds, from rapidly industrializing China.
- Pusan is far less protected by its mountains and suffers considerable air pollution blown in from rapidly industrializing China
- Pusan's water quality is affected by its position at the mouth of a river. Upstream pollution from rapidly industrializing areas is its main water problem.

Thus, location affects air and water quality quite apart from what a city may do in the way of burning fossil fuels for transportation or dumping wastes into its water system.

But these observations also speak to some of the limitations of this type of study, which focuses on individual cities as more or less closed systems. There is little Pusan can do by itself about the upstream pollution; the central government will have to act. To be sure, Pusan can try to persuade the central government to provide stronger overall environmental protection. But in Kobe, we do not observe, nor do we ask, where its air pollution goes as it is blown away from the city. This surely counts as a limitation.

Cebu City also shows an aspect of this location-specific condition. Sitting on a rich coastal aquifer, it can draw water from the ground and has not had to rely on rivers. Population growth and economic development, however, are eating away at its aquifer, and will force the city to turn to river waters in the future. Then the seasonality of the run-off and the potential for upstream pollution will present a new set of problems.

> **Population-environment dynamics are highly location-specific. Thus any attempt to examine issues or address problems must begin with the conditions of a specific location.**

Population Dynamics

Our five cities provide illustrations of populations at almost all stages of the demographic transition. Kobe is a city that has completed the earlier (see chapter 2) version of the demographic transition. Mortality and fertility fell rather slowly in the past, and without the use of much of the modern technology to control mortality or fertility. Now mortality and fertility are very low and the population is ageing rapidly. At the other end of the spectrum is Faisalabad, which is just beginning the modern version of the transition. Mortality has been brought down rapidly by the use of the full panoply of modern mortality controlling technology. But fertility has yet to show much change. This implies current rapid population growth and a very young population with the potential for significant continued growth.

In between are three cities ranged along path of the modern transition. Pusan is furthest along, having experienced very rapid declines first in mortality and then in infertility. The full range of modern technology and new government programmes for health and family planning were extensively used and highly successful. Khon Kaen is close to Pusan, with its rapid fertility transition coming just a decade later, but both transitions were very much a product of modern government health and family planning policies and programmes. Both cities now benefit from lower levels of fertility, which reduce growth pressures and provide a higher level of individual and family health. But neither is as advanced in the transition as Kobe and thus the problems of dealing with an ageing population lie considerably in their futures. Finally, Cebu has experienced rapid mortality decline from the new medical and public health technology. It has begun to experience some fertility decline, and is more advanced than Faisalabad but less advanced than Khon Kaen or Pusan. Thus the city still faces pressures of growth from natural increase, and the health problems that accompany high fertility.

All the five cities have grown rapidly in the recent past. Regardless of how old the city is, whether it can trace its history to five centuries back, as in Cebu, or just a century, as in Faisalabad, all are manifestations of the new, powerful and universal wave of the urban-industrial growth discussed in Chapter 2. Kobe is the earliest and oldest growth. It rose from virtually nothing in 1850 to a million people by 1940. The war brought destruction and mass exodus, but post war reconstruction brought it back to a million and more in a few decades. The other four cities all grew very rapidly in just the past half-century, with rates that were often as high as five percent per year. All were part of rapidly growing national populations, but all grew at rates considerably above those of the nation as a whole.

Three of the cities – Kobe, Pusan and Cebu City – appear to have stopped growing. Cebu City may be losing population now; Pusan – and possibly Kobe – may decline slightly in the near future. Khon Kaen appears destined to continue growing, though at a moderate rate. Faisalabad may be threatened with extremely rapid growth if projections of agricultural collapse due to increasing salinization prove accurate. But all these cities are also a part of increasing urbanization. Even if they cease to grow, they are becoming parts of larger metropolitan systems that continue to grow.

The sources of growth vary considerably, however. All have grown through expansion of their physical areas, pushing through their boundaries to include rural areas and smaller adjacent towns and villages. For the most part, however, this growth from areal expansion has not been systematically tracked in analyses of growth. Nor have people asked what the implications, costs and benefits are of this type of growth. For the most part it appears to have been beneficial, extending the revenue base and giving urban administrators larger areas of jurisdiction, which makes for more effective urban planning. Indeed the problems of planning in Cebu City and Pusan appear to be exacerbated by their inability to expand their administrative boundaries any farther.

More effective urban planning often requires an expansion of the city's boundaries to include areas that directly affect its conditions. This confirms one of the lessons AUICK has learnt from its studies.

We can also see from these cases that growth need not imply environmental degradation. Pusan is surrounded by a lush green belt that helps the city breathe and provides a pleasant environment for its citizens. Not long ago the Rokko Mountains behind Kobe were bare of vegetation: they had been stripped of wood for fuel and building. Today the mountains are green and protected, providing the citizens with excellent parks and protecting the soil from erosion and the city from flooding. But urban growth can be environmentally destructive. Cebu's bare hills and polluted waters and Faisalabad's water and sewage problems illustrate how growth can degrade the environment.

Finally slowing population growth appears to have substantial advantages for all cities. Kobe, Pusan and Khon Kaen now reap the benefits of past declines in fertility. The demands on health and educational services from a young population have been considerably mitigated, giving all three cities more resources to spend per individual. The result has been a healthier society. Though data are lacking, it appears that Cebu might suffer from the high abortion rates that are common in the Philippines, which derive from the weakness of health and family planning programmes. Faisalabad feels the pressure from high fertility in educational costs and in declining health and educational services from the government.

Slowing population growth by reducing fertility has been shown to be advantageous for a city's residents and for the management of its population-environment relationship.

Health and Family Planning

Health provides an important tracer to indicate the quality of the population-environment relationship. High levels of human health, implying low levels of morbidity and mortality, signify a positive relationship; low levels of health imply some form of stress in the relationship. In the modern urban-industrial transformation, governments have taken on a major responsibility for providing services and resources to promote human health. Primary health care is a major government mechanism for dealing with the infectious diseases associated with stresses in the population-environment relationship. Family planning services, public and private, represent the major mechanism for promoting reproductive health and the transition from high to low fertility. Our five cities illustrate stages in the provision of government health and family planning services and their impact on human health. They also illustrate the variation in government strength and capacity in providing these services.

Faisalabad is the least developed, or the furthest behind, in providing health services and promoting health. The infant mortality rate (91) is relatively high, but the maternal mortality rate (62) is relatively low for an LDR. Infectious diseases, such as typhoid and dysentery, are still the major causes of death and indicate weak environmental health services. Though government medical services have grown, they have been dwarfed by the parallel growth of private medical services. This reflects a common trend in Pakistan, where people have often given up on government social services and have increasingly turned to the private sector for assistance. In family planing, Faisalabad shows substantially higher levels of contraceptive use (42 percent) than the country as a whole, probably reflecting the level of wealth and urban development that have made fertility control more popular and possible.

Khon Kaen and Cebu are relatively similar in their lower levels of infant and maternal mortality and declines in infectious diseases as the major cause of death. But their data also raise questions. The rapid rise of *treatments* for gastrointestinal diseases in Khon Kaen does not fit well with the apparent increase in water quality, and suggests merely better treatment. Cebu may be experiencing erosion of government medical services as the ratio of medical staff to population deteriorates. Khon Kaen shares with the rest of Thailand very high levels of contraceptive use and fertility decline; Cebu's contraceptive use is higher than the national average, but remains only about half that in Khon Kaen.

Pusan and Kobe show the advantages of wealth. Both have developed extensive primary health and medical services and have populations with very high levels of health. Both also have very low levels of fertility, though these are from different sources. An extensive and very effective national family planning programme that made contraceptives readily available throughout the country gave Pusan control of its fertility rates. Kobe's fertility was brought down and kept low primarily by abortion, which became a major mechanism for fertility control in Japan, because the process began under the great economic stress of the immediate post war period, and more than a decade before modern contraceptives became available.

Primary health care and family planning programmes have worked together to promote urban quality of life; where they have lagged, quality of life suffers. This accords well with the findings of previous AUICK urban surveys.

Education

All five cities reflect one of the major avenues of progress experienced throughout Asia in the past half-century. Education has improved for all. Primary education is now nearly universal throughout Asia, and major gains have been made in gender equality. Everywhere, girls are going to school in increasing numbers. Secondary and tertiary education are advancing rapidly, also with increasing gender equality. Our five cities clearly reflect this progress, but they show other interesting differences as well.

Again, national wealth matters. Faisalabad is not as advanced in education as the other four cities. Primary education has become almost universal for boys in Faisalabad; girls lag behind but the gap is narrowing. Secondary education has advanced but is far from universal. There is a major agricultural university with a large component of women students, though the proportion of the population in tertiary education remains rather small. Khon Kaen and Cebu both show universal primary education for both boys and girls, with major progress in secondary education as well. Gender equality is common in Southeast Asia, which has historically shown far less sequestering of women, far greater gender equality, and far lower male child preference than either South or East Asia.

Khon Kaen and Cebu also show another dimension of urbanization and education, one common to many developing regions. Primary and secondary enrolment figures are inflated, but the cause of this inflation differs considerably. In Thailand, it is common for rural families to send their children to live with friends and relatives so that they can take advantage of the better urban educational services. This practice inflates Khon Kaen school enrolment to levels three to five times what would be expected from the size of the city alone. In the Philippines, primary education is widespread in the rural areas. There is not so much rural-to-urban movement for schooling. It is common, however, for primary schools to have students beyond primary school age; the same is true for the secondary schools. Thus, the inflation in the Philippines is much smaller than in Thailand, and results from urban structural conditions.

Pusan and Kobe have long had universal education at both primary and secondary levels. Both national wealth and a high cultural value placed upon education lie behind these achievements. Neither city shows the inflated primary and secondary rolls that we see in Khon Kaen or Cebu, since educational services at these levels are fully developed for each country as a whole.

Education has advanced throughout Asia, with advancements in gender equality as well. Both national wealth and culture affect the advance of gender equality. Southeast Asia leads East and South Asia in cultural support for gender equality. This, too, accords well with findings of previous AUICK urban surveys.

In all of these areas, the experience of our five cities closely follows the course of Asia as a whole, both in its overall progress, and in the differences within the region.

Water: Quantity and Quality

Water is one of the most critical points of intersection between population and the environment. People need water, and population growth inevitably increases demand for it. But people also need clean water, and the activities that people engage in to improve their quality of life often threaten the cleanliness of their water and also other life forms, whose viability is necessary for human life. Our five cities illustrate both the complex nature of the water connection and what cities can do to promote a sustainable people-water relationship. There are problems of both quantity and quality; for our five cities, the problem of quality appears more severe than that of quantity.

We noted in Chapter 2 that Asia shows exceptionally high levels of population density, comparable to those in Western and Southern Europe, and far above the levels in Africa and the Americas. Water is a major reason for these high population densities. Asia is a well-watered land and our five cities share in this general benefit.

Even Faisalabad, set on an arid plain with little precipitation, is rich in water from the great Indus River system and the modern canals that spread its waters throughout the valley. Supplied by the snows of the Himalayas, the system seems to provide an unending supply of waters. The city may be plagued by a different type of water problem, however. The canal waters that brought rich agricultural output to this once arid and barren land now leave behind salts as they evaporate before seeping into the soils. Canal irrigated agriculture may prove to be unsustainable, as it has in other ancient civilizations. The waters that once brought life may as easily take it away.

Khon Kaen is served by the south-west monsoon winds that bring vast amounts of rainwater to Thailand from the Indian Ocean. In the dry season, waters come from three rivers that drain the large north-east plateau into the Mekong River. Cebu, too, benefits from water-laden south-west monsoon winds, but the schedule is slightly altered by the fragmented land and sea masses that surround it. It is also blessed with a rich aquifer, charged by eons of rains that built massive storage tanks in the porous limestone that lies under the city. Population growth and development are overdrawing the aquifer, however, shifting the fresh-to-salt-water boundary inland and threatening this basic water supply. Soon, the city will have to turn to the weaker, seasonal rivers that drain its mountain range, leaving Cebu with an uncertain future. Pusan lies at the mouth of a large river flowing out of the mountains of South Korea. Supplies for the future are relatively secure. Kobe could initially draw on the many small rivers and streams that flow out of the Rokko Mountains into the bay. With growth and development, however, it has had to draw on the waters of Lake Biwa, and the Yodo River that flows from the lake into Osaka Bay. Demands may increase and problems may appear on the horizon, but water quantity is not one of the most pressing for these cities, except for Cebu, where the future of the aquifer is very uncertain.

Water *quality*, however, is a problem for all of these cities. The most serious is in Faisalabad, where human and industrial wastes pose a serious threat to water quality. The flat terrain exacerbates the problem, as wastewater must be pumped out of the area. In-migration and natural increase have added to the population and increased the level of human wastes. Industrial development, which gives jobs to the citizens, adds to the pollution. The past rates of population and industrial growth have apparently overwhelmed the city's and the central government's capacities for infrastructure development, especially as the government seems increasingly incapable of mounting effective public infrastructure projects. Water at the source in Faisalabad is deemed safe for drinking, but is of questionable quality at the point of use by the population. In the short rainy seasons, wastewater pumping is inadequate, and the city is flooded with sewage. This problem is reflected in the rates of gastrointestinal diseases. It is also a problem beyond the city's capacity, and today the World Bank has been called upon by the Central government to lend support. The future is not a secure one.

Khon Kaen's water quality appears to be improving, though there are questions about the validity of the measurements. The rise of *treatments* for gastrointestinal diseases raises more questions. It is not compatible with the apparent increase in water quality and may reflect simply an improvement in treatment rather than an increase in incidence. Cebu is decidedly troubled with human and industrial wastes in its rivers and beaches, though, unlike Khon Kaen, this is not reflected in data on disease. In both cases, better information is needed.

Pusan's water quality is constantly threatened by upstream industrial development, which is a high priority of the central government, and desired by most citizens for the jobs and income it brings. For the near future, however, Pusan has sufficient wealth to increase its investments in water purification.

Kobe is relatively secure. Its water remains of high quality, benefiting both from its own investments in purification and from the industrial restructuring that has taken heavy industry out of the city, replacing it with far less polluting service industries. There may be trouble in the longer future, but for the near future, adequate water quality seems assured.

Water *quantity* depends on local conditions, but everywhere water *quality* is threatened by modern industrial activity and population growth.

Air Quality

Unlike water, air quality is far less affected by the number of people than by what they do. Clearly, one of the most important ways in which humans reduce air quality is burn fossil fuel in automotive vehicles. In our five cities, it appears that vehicular traffic is a, or *the*, major source of air pollution. This is a condition shared with most of the world, as gas-fuelled vehicles have grown at rapid rates everywhere. The process seems inevitable and inexorable. And, everywhere, vehicles imply higher levels of nitrogen oxides, carbon monoxide, suspended particulate matter, and – where it is not removed from gasoline by law – lead. All these pollutants are known to affect the level of respiratory diseases, and lead is especially damaging to the neurological development of young children.

But our cities also show something else that is slightly more complicated: wealth, both individual and societal, affects air quality. Wealth affects what types of fuels are used, and it also affects how much city managers know about the conditions, causes and effects of air quality, and thus, what they can do about it.

We know little about air quality in Faisalabad: it is not measured. People complain of dust and pollution from vehicles, but there is little beyond individual impressions to tell us about air quality. Cebu City has taken a few sporadic measures of air quality. The radical fluctuations of the measures and their sparse coverage make it impossible to tell whether conditions are getting better or worse. But there is another observation we can make about Cebu. The great majority of households and business establishments use wood or charcoal for cooking. This habit strips the surrounding hills of vegetation and fills the air with heavy amounts of smoke, or suspended particulate matter. The three measures taken in the downtown area in May 1997 all showed very high levels of suspended particulate matter; one was above the level considered 'hazardous', the other two were between 'alert' and 'hazardous'. Moreover, it is clear that the use of wood for cooking is largely a matter of economic class: the poor use wood; the middle class use liquid petroleum gas or kerosene; the very wealthy use electricity. Together, these account for a third of the city's population. Thus, societal poverty, together with the rapid increase in vehicles, appears to have a negative impact on air quality, but we are uncertain of the magnitude and the direction of change because there is no systematic monitoring.

Khon Kaen has recently begun measuring air quality, but there are as yet insufficient data to determine if air quality is changing. From one year of data, a clear seasonal trend is apparent. The air is cleansed by the seasonal monsoon rains, but we do not know if overall air quality is changing or in which direction it is changing. As with water quality and gastrointestinal diseases, the rise of *treatments* for respiratory diseases leaves more questions than answers. Has there been a real rise in the incidence of the diseases, or merely better treatment for the diseases?

Pusan provides details of the dynamic picture to be expected when a society increases its wealth over time. Since 1970, petroleum has provided half or more of the city's energy. But in the 1970s, coal, and especially pressed blocks of coal dust for home heating, pumped great amounts of particulate matter into the air. Since 1985, coal use has declined and cleaner forms of energy have taken its place: liquid natural gas, nuclear and hydroelectric power. Together with cleaner automobiles, this has greatly increased air quality in the city.

Kobe's condition shows the great advantage of wealth. The city has been measuring air quality for two decades and more, and the measures show surprisingly positive results. Despite the great growth in the number of automobiles, air quality has actually increased. Future projections show a more complex picture, however. If emission technology remains as it is today, the expected increase in automobiles could raise air pollutants to levels seen before 1970, when they were very high. To project a constant level of air quality for the city, it is necessary to assume a continued decline in auto-emissions. Given the emergence of hybrid and hydrogen engines, however, it is not difficult to defend these assumptions. A wealthy city like Kobe can have a high quality of personal vehicular transportation and also clean air.

> **Air quality is everywhere threatened by increased automotive traffic. But poverty also increases pollution while wealth protects air quality[1]. These observations refer to the individual cities and the situation may be quite different at the global level, where air pollution from fossil fuel consumption is much greater in wealthy than in poor countries.**

This is a highly contentious issue. The conflict over who causes the most pollution surfaced early in the environmental movement at the 1972 Stockholm Conference, and it has not subsided. There is no doubt that carbon emissions, both total and per capita, are much higher in the rich than in the poor countries (World Resources, 1992–92). The 24 industrial countries of the Organization for European Cooperation and Development (OECD) consume 40 percent to 50 percent of the world's fossil fuels, and other resources as well. Their demand for timber products and meat is responsible for much forest clearing both through logging and burning. But poor countries and poor people also contribute substantially to environmental degradation. China and India are increasing coal consumption very rapidly and will soon approach US levels of total, though not per capita, carbon emissions. The two countries already outstrip the US in methane emissions. Moreover, poor farmers in poor countries are also responsible for substantial amounts of forest burning. As the World Resources review (1992–93, p. 30) stated: "The evidence of human poverty and deprivation in the world is unmistakable, as is the evidence of the worsening environmental conditions caused by and contributing to poverty."

For our analysis, however, the issue is the problem of linking case studies with global conditions. With the city as the unit of analysis, the link between poverty and air pollution is clear: poverty means more pollution. At a global level, however, the link is often reversed; the rich pollute more than the poor. We shall try to deal with this issue more fully in the final chapter.

Energy

Only three cities provide information and discussions of energy usage. Pusan is the most wealthy, and has shown a dramatic transformation to cleaner forms of energy. Coal was still extensively used as late as 1970 for home heating. Cylinders of pressed coal dust were used in small space heaters, which were inefficient and seriously polluted the city's air. Wealth enabled the city to move to more efficient and cleaner energy for home heating. Electricity, supplied by oil burning and nuclear plants, has taken the place of coal, bringing about more comfort and cleaner air.

Faisalabad and Cebu also provide data and show an interesting paradox. Though Pakistan is considered less wealthy than the Philippines, with an estimated per capita GNP of US$490 versus US$1220 (World Bank, 1999), far fewer of its households use wood or charcoal for heating and cooking. Some 80 percent of Faisalabad's households have electrical connections and 65 percent are served by natural gas. In Cebu, more than 60 percent of households (i.e. the poorer) still use wood and charcoal for heating and cooking. The negative effect on Cebu's air quality has already been noted.

Poverty, the use of wood for cooking, and deforestation combine to link population growth and energy use to environmental degradation. The specific impact of human behaviour on the environment, however, is always location-specific. In other areas, wealth, rather than poverty, is associated with greater environmental degradation.

Transportation

Transportation systems in our five cities run the gamut from the most modern to that rich mix of ancient and modern found in many cities in the LDRs. These systems' impact on the environment and quality of life are not difficult to discern. While all cities are alike in that they have experienced a very rapid increase of automobiles and motorcycles, their differences are dramatic and closely related to wealth.

Faisalabad's road system is limited and varies from broad, well-paved avenues to gutted dirt roads. The rapidly growing numbers of cars and motorcycles compete with slow-moving horse, donkey and camel carts. Bicycles have also exploded in number, providing clean transportation for a large portion of the city's population. The flat land of the city makes the bicycle a useful form of transportation. But motorcycles have also increased rapidly in number, greatly contributing to both air and noise pollution. Public transportation is limited, but large diesel-burning buses ply between the city and the surrounding country-side. In appearance, the flow is chaotic and undisciplined, and marred by substantial numbers of accidents and injuries.

Cebu is not far ahead, though it has seen the disappearance of the traditional horse-drawn carriages of the Philippines. Cars and motorcycles have increased rapidly; most roads are unpaved; the lack of peripheral roads means that the island's north-south traffic must all pass through the heart of the city[2]. Road dust adds to the polluted air, already heavily laden with wood smoke from cooking fires. There is no real mass transit system, but private Jeepneys provide an efficient, if not environmentally benign, form of cheap public transportation. The hilly nature of the land precludes the extensive use of bicycles.

Khon Kaen is more developed with a good system of paved roads that easily accommodates the rapid rise of cars, motorcycles and pick-up trucks, of which Thailand is alleged to have more than any other country, with the exception of the United States.

Pusan and Kobe share the same terrain problems; they are crowded onto narrow coastal shelves that make road construction costly. Kobe has considerable advantages over Pusan, however, in having greater control over its own transportation planning. It has constructed an efficient road system that moves goods into and out of the port without clogging city streets. And its excellent mass transit system uses efficient and clean electric trains to carry a very large portion of daily population movement. Pusan's mass transit system has been slower to develop, and the city has been constrained by central government restrictions that keep it from developing the roads it needs, to move both city and port traffic more smoothly.

Wealth affects the impact of a transportation system on the environment. Everywhere, vehicles are growing exponentially; poor cities find it more difficult to mitigate the impact of this growth on environmental degradation, but rich cities show more rapid growth of vehicles, possibly offsetting the positive impacts of cleaner emissions technology.

Land Use

All the five cities have extended their boundaries over the past half-century and more, in some cases facilitating urban planning and administration. This move accords with one of the early lessons AUICK learned from its studies of urban development: cities often need control over larger areas to improve their planning and administration.

Kobe's earlier expansion greatly facilitated its planning. Faisalabad and Khon Kaen expanded their boundaries in the past as the population outgrew earlier bounds. Conversely, Pusan now finds itself constrained in space, and this seems to obstruct more effective urban planning. It earlier extension and its designation as a Metropolitan City unfortunately came before the country's urban planning act; this essentially limited Pusan's planning to its existing boundaries, while other cities could extend planning to their entire province. Cebu's boundaries extend high into its surrounding hills, though this does not seem to help planning as the hills are primarily used by wealthy citizens to build houses above the city's noise and pollution. Cebu may overcome its areal limit on planning through collaboration with adjacent municipalities to form larger urban development areas. At present, it appears that all cities are roughly tied to their current boundaries, and little further change is foreseen.

Parks or open spaces, and housing, the two specific areas dealt with in this examination of land use, show the impact of wealth and geography. Extensive green belts and parks serve Kobe and Pusan, including pleasant waterfront developments that add considerably to those cities' quality of life. Much poorer, Cebu's waterfront is contaminated with human wastes and its city parks are few, small and offer little respite from the dust and heat of the city. Slightly wealthier Khon Kaen is better served, with a large centrally located man-made lake, an extensive park-like university campus, and a green agricultural hinterland. Faisalabad is also well supplied with open spaces, including some city parks and the agricultural hinterland, despite its lower level of wealth; here geography has played a supporting role.

Housing also varies by wealth, with Kobe and Pusan leading by far with increasingly well-housed populations. Recently constructed apartments are especially important in both cases; individual single family houses have always dominated in Pusan and are becoming more common in Kobe.

Cities require a large area for effective planning. This can be obtained through expansion of the city boundaries, or development of integrated planning activities with other administrative units. Housing is a critical component of the quality of life, and is very much affected by levels of individual and national wealth.

The Productive System

Here is a paradox. All five countries of our cities have experienced serious economic difficulties in the past two years. Pakistan is the poorest and has seen considerable erosion of its wealth due to world monetary and trade pressures, as well as to a weak political system and extensive corruption. Japan has allegedly been mired in recession for the past decade. Thailand and South Korea experienced the highly publicized great collapses of Asian economies in late 1997. The Philippines was less severely hit, but only because it had been deeper in recession when the collapse came. Yet all of these cities appear to have relatively high levels of employment with strong, productive industries, and little obvious grinding poverty. Faisalabad is a major textile exporter whose cottons are prized on the world market for their quality. Khon Kaen is the centre of an increasingly productive agricultural and industrial system. Cebu, Pusan and Kobe have well developed and productive ports. Kobe and Pusan also have other, newer, service-type industries that are more environmentally benign than their earlier heavy and textile industries. Kobe's earthquake of January 1995 was very costly to the city and the national government, but recovery has been quick and strong. The port has lost international business to nearby competitors, but it is still a strong revenue earner for the city.

The environmental impact of these productive systems is mixed. Only in Faisalabad are the industries important contributors to environmental pollution. Khon Kaen's industries are not known to be heavy polluters. In Cebu, it is primarily the service industry – restaurants in particular – that pollutes the air by their use of wood for cooking. Where sulphur dioxide emissions are measured, as in Pusan and Kobe, levels have declined while manufacturing output has increased.

> **In these five cities, the productive system seems to contribute to the citizen's welfare through providing employment, and (except in Faisalabad) is not associated with severe environmental pollution: all this despite the severe economic problems that have beset the entire region.**

Quality of Life

Health, educational opportunities, the quality of government services, available housing, ease of transportation, and the cleanliness of air and water are the components of quality of life as we conceive it. On these conditions, it is not difficult to rank our five cities. Kobe is clearly at the top, followed closely by Pusan. Khon Kaen follows, while even further down the hierarchy are Cebu and Faisalabad.

Four of the five cities have clear problems in the future. Khon Kaen is the one that shows little danger on the near horizon, as population growth has been reduced and the environmental conditions appear favourable. Faisalabad may be overrun with migrants from a collapsing agricultural hinterland. Cebu's water and air do not now appear to be improving, and the signs of future deterioration are ominous. Pusan and Kobe may face problems of slowed growth, which pose something of a paradox.

Rapid population growth is often associated with environmental degradation and is in any event clearly unsustainable. One of the major problems for Asian cities is that rapid growth from both in-migration and natural increase has tended to overwhelm capacities of the urban infrastructure. Slowing population growth has been beneficial for cities like Khon Kaen and is considered a necessity for most societies, and for the world as a whole (IUCN, 1991).

However, when fertility falls below replacement level and remains low for a generation and more another kind of sustainability problem emerges. Kobe's ageing population and low fertility raise precisely that question. Can the city continue to be a vibrant and productive place if its population does not replace itself? To be sure, the city can maintain a productive population through in-migration, at least until the overall national population growth turns negative and begins to weigh on the city itself. But what happens when the nation begins to decline in numbers? This is a new phenomenon facing many Asian countries, and it has given rise to extensive new demographic studies (Hermalin, 1995, 1998)[3]. How long can a city or society remain viable with fertility so low that growth in numbers turns to decline? For Kobe, the question is somewhat urgent. For Pusan, it lies at least another generation into the future.

Wealth and SPECS

What underlies the differences in the population-environment nexus that we have summarized above? Why or how have Kobe and Pusan been so much more successful than the other cities in giving their citizens a high quality of life, including higher productivity and a cleaner environment? How and why has Khon Kaen done better than Cebu, or Cebu than Faisalabad? Part of the answer is clear: wealth. Wealthy cities can afford the infrastructure to protect their water supplies and dispose of wastes safely. They can also provide citizens with good housing and open spaces, afford environmental protection that reduces pollution with new, cleaner technology, and provide health and educational services that protect the citizens from disease and help them develop to their full human potential.

Any common measure of wealth provides the same rank order of our five cities that we proposed for their quality of life. The World Bank provides estimates of per capita Gross National Income, and of Real Gross Domestic Product per capita, based on a parity purchasing power calculation. The latter is designed to reflect the local costs of a similar basket of goods that a US dollar would purchase in the United States (World Bank, 1999). Their values are shown in Table 9.1.

Table 9.1
Two Measures of National Wealth (Data for 1997)

Country	GNP per capita US$	Real GNP per capita US$
Japan	37,750	23,400
South Korea	10,500	13,500
Thailand	2800	6590
Philippines	1220	3670
Pakistan	490	1590

Japan is the richest country in Asia and one of the richest in the world. South Korea ranks only behind Japan, Singapore and Hong Kong in Asia. Thailand compares well with its South-East Asian neighbours, ranking only behind Singapore and Malaysia, but ahead of the Philippines, Indonesia, Vietnam, Laos and Cambodia (there is no estimate for Myanmar or Burma). Though Pakistan is the poorest of our five, it has a higher level of wealth than India, Nepal and Bangladesh, and lags behind only Sri Lanka in South Asia.

Wealth clearly matters. But that also begs the question of what produces wealth, and how national wealth is translated into individual or urban welfare. In 1950, for example, the Philippines was well ahead of Thailand in wealth and welfare; today Thailand is clearly ahead. The Philippines was even far ahead of South Korea, which was wracked by war in 1950. For some reason, South Korea emerged from the war and embarked on a policy of social and economic development that led it to overtake and bypass the Philippines by a very large margin in both wealth and welfare.

Beyond wealth, we should examine the system of governance, or the social-political-economic-cultural system (SPECS) of a city. To approach this system, we begin first with observations of national governments, then move to the city.

Wealth matters, but there are also conditions beyond wealth that determine the extent to which national wealth is translated into national welfare. These conditions include a complex mix of social, political, economic and cultural forces that we call SPECS.

National political systems, including both the structure and the culture of politics, differ considerably, and there is increasing evidence that this difference affects economic and social development, and by extension the quality of life and the character of the population-environment nexus. The 1997 issue of the World Bank's *World Development Report* was subtitled 'The State in a Changing World'. In drawing attention to the role of the state in promoting economic development, its basic conclusion was that social and economic development requires an *effective state*. The first job of states, the report held (p. 4), encompasses five fundamental tasks:

- Establishing a foundation of law
- Maintaining a non-distortionary policy environment
- Investing in basic social services and infrastructure
- Protecting the vulnerable
- Protecting the environment

We could say much the same about the governance of a city, though the 'non-distortionary' condition requires some adjustment or local adaptation. Attached to this condition for the Bank is the necessity of maintaining macroeconomic stability. The World Bank is by nature primarily concerned with maintaining open international markets, and avoiding policies that distort markets and the discipline they impose. While the international may be less an issue for city governments, non-distortionary can imply an open and accountable government with less room for corruption.

The Bank also makes a series of other observations of effective governance that can be directly applied to our five cities. One concerns staffing the administration on the basis of merit rather than personal selection. It cites studies (e.g.

p. 93) that show the Philippines civil service to be far more deeply penetrated by political appointments than other Asian countries, which more extensively use merit measured by examinations and degrees. Sociologists call these criteria universalistic, since they are applicable to all candidates regardless of personal connections. The Bank also notes that low turnover rates in the civil service produce better government than high rates of turnover. This is a lesson learned by AUICK in its ten years of examining Asian urban administration. All of these suggest criteria against which we can judge the SPECS of the urban system.

In a somewhat parallel analysis of the performance of city governments, John Friedman (1998) comments on the World Bank analysis and makes arguments more specifically directed at cities. His first position is that the Bank errs in maintaining its focus on the nation state as the natural unit for the analysis of economic development. Friedman (p. 15) contends that "the global space of flows is more accurately modelled by articulating it through a network of city-regions that function as the new core areas of the world economy." This speaks to our earlier discussion of the limitations of our study of five cities, to which we shall return shortly. More important at this point, however, is Friedman's identification of the need for a *political community*. By this, he means 'a collective entity whose management is ultimately accountable to its…citizens.' He also identifies the effectiveness of city government as the capacity to do three things: make effective policy decisions, implement those decisions, and produce good outcomes. He refers to these three more simply as good governance, good management and good outcomes.

Elsewhere (Ness & Ando, 1984), we used the same three-part framework to examine the development of population policies in Asia. With that narrow focus, it was easy to identify the date and the strength of the new population *policy*, the extent to which the policy was *implemented*, and the *outcome* of the policy in both contraceptive use and fertility decline. That study also found that the strength of the political-administrative system accounted for the greater capacities of some countries to make the decisions and implement the policies that brought a higher quality of life to their citizens.

For the broad range of issues cities must deal with to provide a high quality of life, a wider range of criteria and observations must be used. Policy decisions are more than decisions to mount a family planning programme, and outcomes involve far more than contraceptive use and fertility decline. Nonetheless, for any specific issue, from health and education to water, waste or environmental protection, the same three-part process can be observed and assessed. Moreover, the strength of the political administrative system can be expected to account for differences in cities' abilities to transform wealth into welfare, or to provide what Friedman calls good governance, good management and good outcomes.

We can now make a series of observations about our five cities, for the most part interpreting, reading between the lines, or relying on interviews with city officials. It must be emphasized that this is a personal assessment. I have not asked the city authors for their concurrence. For purposes of testing validity, that would have been necessary. But since these assessments may be viewed as criticisms of city government, I do not wish to associate the city authors with these remarks. The authors are, indeed, attempting to work with city governments to promote a higher quality of life in the city, and public criticisms could well undermine their capacity to work with the governments. Thus, the following judgements are my own; they come from personal experience in all the cities and countries, from extensive reading, and from some speculation about how a governing system works and what causes it to work the way it does. It is, in effect, a very personal assessment. I shall order each discussion from the best to the worst served by the city's SPECS.

Kobe

It is difficult to find fault with the Kobe government on any of the criteria we identified above. The government is a stable one with low rates of turnover. City officials make a lifetime career of government service. They know the city and appear highly committed to its success in meeting any problems it confronts. Moreover, the city has been blessed with leaders of long vision, one of the elements that John Friedman identified as a critical component of good governance. Past Mayor Miyazaki and the current Mayor Sasayama are clearly leaders who take the long view of the city's development. Additionally, individual capacity and merit appear to be the main criteria for appointment and advancement in the city government. Salaries and benefits are roughly comparable to those in the private sector, and are certainly high enough to preclude extensive corruption. The city has also been sufficiently powerful to wrest control from the central government, giving it the authority to identify and address problems it sees as important.

Kobe's government has followed national standards in collecting data on population and environmental conditions. As we saw in Chapter 8, the city has good data on virtually all components of its quality of life. Air and water quality are intensely monitored. Regular data of high apparent validity are available on all social conditions, from health services and conditions to education and social welfare. The city clearly has a substantial amount of good information regularly available to city officials by which they can monitor conditions, set standards and examine results. Moreover, the city has a citizen's elected council to which the government is closely attuned. The city has a series of offices in each ward, giving citizens a local neighbourhood point where they can take their problems, voice complaints, and obtain information and assistance. In effect, the government is close to the people. In part, this comes from modern democratic processes, but it also comes from deep roots in the Japanese political culture. Government officers feel a strong sense of responsibility for the well-being of their citizens. This is not a new phenomenon arising with democratic structures, as it was in the West; rather, it is a long-standing component of the Japanese political culture, such as that which enjoins people to be loyal to government. This loyalty is not expressed simply in withholding criticism, but in working actively to promote the power and interests of the government. When government makes a decision, citizens feel obliged to carry out that decision in the best possible way. This is a political culture, in short, that produces committed government officers and loyal, hardworking citizens, bound together to promote the common good of society. This implies no fundamental distinction between family, community and nation. All are fused together in one cohesive community.

This is not to say there is no conflict between the government and the citizens. Currently, for example, there is substantial popular opposition to the building of the new airport, which the government strongly favours. Still, in the last City Council election, the pro-airport forces obtained more seats than the anti-forces. There is no doubt that the conflict will continue to be an important one, though it is also possible to predict a continuing dialogue between the city government and the people.

In short, there is strong visionary leadership with good capacity to make policy decisions and an effective bureaucracy that can implement those decisions, producing outcomes that promote the quality of life in the city.

Pusan

Much of what is said about Kobe's government can be said of Pusan's. The city has a well-established civil service, appointed and promoted primarily on the basis of merit, and implying an entire lifetime's devotion to the city. Salary levels are high, thus eliminating a major structural cause of corruption. Turnover rates are low, and the city is staffed with experienced and committed civil servants. It has had political and appointed leaders of long vision, and it is closely attuned to the population and its needs. Its historical and geographical positions have placed both the city and the country at the centre of violent external conflicts, over which the city had little control, and could do little more than endure. But out of each phase of externally induced violence, the country and the city have emerged with the ability to make effective policy decisions and to implement them.

There is also a political culture similar to Japan's that draws all Koreans into a form of consanguineous community. Long experience under repressive colonial and indigenous military governments have recently given way to strong democratic movements. The country now has an open, elected government with increasing accountability. The city also has an elected council, with local units represented. These movements have gone a long way in a relatively short time to build what Friedman calls a political community, where the government is accountable to the citizens. This gives the city a committed, visionary leadership; an effective, meritorious civil service, and a citizenry willing to work together for the common good; conditions that distinguish the Korean political culture and help us to understand how the country has made so much progress in a short time. But that same culture has also exacted a heavy toll on the environment precisely through the industrialization that has raised the standard of living so dramatically (Eder, 1996; Kim, 1997; Koo, 1993).

The one disadvantage that the city seems to endure concerns the central government and its insistence on direct control. Unlike Kobe, Pusan has relatively little control over many aspects of its development. In addition, its boundaries as a Metropolitan City constrain it from the kind of urban planning possible in other cities, that can include an entire province in their plans. This has obstructed urban planning and left the city with less than optimum authority to address its problems.

Khon Kaen

Like Kobe and Pusan, Khon Kaen's city government appears to work well. Public services, including health, education and utilities, are well organized and well staffed. The city is clean, the streets are well paved, and traffic moves smoothly. Education and health illustrate the good capacity of the combined national and local governments to establish and implement long-term visions and policies.

This has not happened overnight. It has taken time, but progress has been steady. On the whole, human health is high, fertility has gone down, and educational attainment has steadily increased, for girls as well as boys.

The city government, as that for the province and the nation, is well staffed, with relatively little political influence. Staff salaries are sufficient to preclude extensive corruption, though this is not true of all national services, such as forestry. Appointment criteria include universalistic ones, education and degrees, and there is at least some merit in considerations for advancement. Turnover seems relatively low, giving the city a competent and committed civil service. While there is a private sector for health and education, it is not as extensive as that we found in Cebu and Faisalabad. In effect, government social services have been extended to the great majority of the population and are sufficiently acceptable to the population to preclude the emergence of a large private sector.

Unlike Kobe and Pusan, however, Khon Kaen's capacity to monitor its conditions is only weakly developed. Population data are quite good, but the rules of counting do not give city managers a good sense of what is happening in the city. Some health measures, such as infant and maternal mortality rates, show a high level of health, but treatments raise questions and need to be validated. Facilities and staff numbers are known, but they seem not to be considered in future planning. Water quality has been monitored for almost two decades, though the quality of the monitoring is suspect. Air quality has only been measured for the past year. Thus, all measures are less than adequate as tools for assessing current conditions or planning for the future. In addition, the central government retains extensive control over many local issues. Khon Kaen is fortunate that the central government has been committed to making the city a major centre for the Northeast Region, but it has had little real influence with the central government.

Thailand lacks the strong sense of political community that we find in Japan and Korea. It has what has been called a 'loosely structured social system', in which ties to family and community are relatively fluid and undemanding[4]. At the same time, Buddhism, the Monarchy and the Thai language provide a deep sense of identity with the nation as a whole[5]. If there is little of the 'active loyalty' demanded of the Japanese, there are still links that bring Thais to help one another. We saw this in the inflation of school enrolment, brought on by the ability of rural people to send their children to both friends and relatives in Khon Kaen for better educational opportunities.

Khon Kaen has an elected city council that is identified by local issues and local leaders. That is, the national party system is not clearly reflected in local elected leaders; conditions and interests in the city are more important mobilizing forces for the electorate. Nor are there the strong family ties that we shall see undermine the formation of a political community in Cebu City and Faisalabad. Though there is still some way to go, it seems clear that a political community is emerging, implying a government accountable to the citizens, a government capable of framing good programmes and achieving good outcomes.

Cebu City

With political appointments going deep into the Philippines' civil service and little basic information about the conditions of the city available to officials, the weakness of the governance system in Cebu is immediately apparent. Further evidence lies in the weakness of the physical infrastructure and the fragmented nature of public services. Most telling is the water situation. The aquifer that gives the city its water is being drawn down radically and the fresh-salt water boundary is moving inland at a rapid rate. Yet there is little concern in city government and no capacity to control the digging of private wells, especially by the wealthy residents who are moving up into the hills to escape the city's pollution. There is no apparent ability to deal with the deteriorating air quality; public transportation rests in the hands of private Jeepney owners; and the city has no capacity to plan for a mass transit system that might reduce some of the degrading emissions. Official salaries are extremely modest, which encourages widespread corruption. At the lowest levels, citizens are asked for 'donations' for educational and health services that should be free. At the upper levels, corruption is a common theme in the unfettered and free-swinging press.

If 'establishing a foundation of law' is a critical component of effective government, as the World Bank proposes, Cebu has some major problems. The wealthy live in enclosed and guarded compounds: high walls, iron gates and guards are a common feature of their homes. The pressure of the police on the poor is commonly remarked upon. A society of laws that provides protection to all is a distant dream. If the bright spot in Cebu City is the education system, it is one where public education is failing, leading to the development of an extensive private system. This only increases the gap between the rich and the poor, undermining the development of a political community that will demand accountability of city officials.

Underlying these problems may be a more fundamental characteristic of the Philippines political culture. Family ties are exceptionally strong. So are the common patron-client ties by which the poor attempt to tie themselves to powerful sponsors with their individual loyalty. While there are advantages to strong family ties, in this case they undermine the development of a political community[6]. There are political parties in the Philippines, but they are weak structures with little capacity to articulate public interests. Individual candidates do not rely on a party for support, but use their own resources to gain election. A change of upper-level elected officers brings mass movements of other representatives from the losing to the wining party. Elected office thus becomes an opportunity to enrich oneself at the public trough, rather than an opportunity to serve and to be accountable to a citizenry.

It is not too much to suggest that the Philippines has fallen far behind South Korea in social and economic development, because its political culture lacks the capacity to provide good government, good management and good outcomes.

Faisalabad

Much of what is said about Cebu applies as well to Faisalabad. The administrative structure is weak. At the upper level, turnover is rapid as city managers seek advancement with either the national or the provincial civil service. Salaries are relatively low, making officials vulnerable to offers that undermine the accountability of the service. City officials complain that elected members of the town council care only about resources for their wards, from which they can also gain privately, than about the condition of the city as a whole. Good data are lacking by which city officials can monitor existing conditions, identify problems and plan for the alleviation of ills. Public services are weak, and their place is extensively being taken by private services, as people lose faith in government.

Again, there is an indication of causes in the political culture, where family ties are strong and may work against the development of a larger political community. As in Cebu, houses of the wealthy are family compounds surrounded with high walls and iron gates. There is little law to give security to the wealthy, nor are the police noted for protection of the poor.

But there are also forces in the national political scene that pose serious problems for the emergence of a political community in the city. Military governments have ruled Pakistan for about half of its independent national life.

They have ruled by fiat, and though they have aimed to bring a clean and accountable government to the country, they have never succeeded, more often than not providing the additional experience of an unaccountable government. They have also intruded into local governments, such as Faisalabad, appointing administrators who are accountable upward, not downward to the citizens. Unfortunately, this has also been true of civilian governments as well. Central intrusion has often precluded the emergence of local political communities where government is accountable to the citizens.

All of these conditions at the city level only mirror the condition at the upper levels of national government. There, stories of corruption are the daily fare, and the magnitudes of wealth moving to foreign bank accounts are staggering. The military coup of October 1999 exemplifies the twin persistent intertwined problems: personal corruption and a non-existent political community. That recent coup was greeted with positive sentiments and hope in Pakistan, but recently reports suggest that once again the hope is fading that the military could clean up a corrupt political system and provide a better government[7]. Pakistan is far wealthier than India, Bangladesh and Nepal, but it has done far less to translate that wealth into welfare than have its three, poorer neighbours.

Note that all the cities have some form of elected council, implying structures and rules that are supposed to make the government accountable to the citizens. These are the formal trappings of a political community; they may be considered necessary conditions. They are not, however, sufficient conditions. These comparisons show the importance of an underlying political culture that determines how those structures and rules will be used and what they will produce. It is at least in part to this level that we must look for explanations of the different paths the countries and cities have taken and the different outcomes they have generated in the quality of life for their citizens. All have faced the overwhelming external forces of 'globalization', but it has been the internal capacities of their national and local governments that appear to determine how those external forces will affect the quality of life.

LESSONS OF METHOD

The Model

We began with a simplified model of urban population-environment relationships. It included four elements of the environment and three institutional conditions that were considered most critical in determining the extent to which the population and environment are related. Moreover, the model posited that the ultimate outcome of the urban population-environment relationship is the quality of life. How has that model worked? Has it posed significant questions and led to any new insights? Has it omitted conditions that should be included?

We believe the model has worked fairly well, though to be sure, it will be more useful for others to make this judgement and suggest alternatives. Still, this model has allowed us to make a coherent comparison of five cities. The environmental elements seem to have covered the subject well, and the institutional components do appear to be those most critically linked to environmental quality and change. But we must still look more closely at the model and the modelling to make a more informed judgement of their utility.

The Modelling

Our method included identification of a 50-year period for the analysis, using data from the past 25 years and dynamic modelling procedures to look a quarter century into the future. This, we believe, is especially useful. Dynamic modelling allowed us to examine a complex set of relationships and to project trends and relationships into the future. In the projection into the future, however, this kind of modelling demands two things: a recognition that these are projections, not predictions, and that they are based on assumptions that must be made explicit. That is, all the assumptions and observations that go into the model must be visible and must admit challenge. We argue that this type of explicit and challengeable modelling is superior to the more common modelling, where assumptions are not made explicit and visible, and thus cannot be challenged.

> **Modelling produces projections, not predictions. Projections are based on assumptions that must be made explicit so they can be challenged and changed.**

The modelling has also provided some insights that might not have been attained without this type of analysis. Kobe's air quality could well deteriorate with the expected rise in the number of automobiles. That is the clear finding when we assume no future changes in emissions technology, and a highly plausible increase of automobiles. Discussions with city technicians, however, show that they foresee major improvements in emissions technology and thus a continued low level of air pollution. It is difficult to quarrel with their projections, especially with the revolution in automotive energy systems that is now breaking upon us. Kobe's urban planers may not, however, have been aware of the potential for substantial increase in solid wastes. Making this possibility explicit could lead to a more aggressive recycling effort that could avert this growth.

Pusan's projected decline in its population provides city planners with information for their internal plans, and arguments to the central government for greater authority and resources for their planning. Projections of increases in both automobile and nitrogen oxides indicate problems in both transportation and air quality that the city will have to address.

Khon Kaen's modelling experience has been perhaps the most interesting. It has pointed clearly to the problem of weak data collection in the city. The data collection system does not now allow city officials to know much about current conditions or to think clearly about the future. The modelling exercises demonstrated what could be done, and thus led to specific recommendations for monitoring that will better serve urban administrators. Modelling has provided what we believe is a more valid view of population dynamics than is available from the city's data collection and recording procedures. It has also provided insights into the dynamics of the school population that should be especially useful for city, provincial and national educational planners.

Even the Cebu City study, where no modelling was possible, provides good lessons. The incapacity to build models because of the poor data collection process shows how city officials really cannot plan for the future if they know so little about the current conditions. Cebu also shows that data are available, as was apparent in the result of the fine effort mounted to construct a life table for the city from the death registration. Air and water quality measures show clear trouble ahead, but they also show that the lack of systematic monitoring deprives city officials of the information they need for effective planning. To be sure, our analysis of the urban governance system raised questions about the interest of city officials in effective planning, but without good data even the weakest interest would be frustrated. Moreover, there is the possibility that better data might themselves lead to greater interest in effective urban planning. We shall turn to this issue in the final chapter.

Finally, the exercise in Faisalabad, as in Cebu, clearly shows the lack of data needed for planning. But it also shows what can be done if more and better data are available. Urban administrators question the projection of such a rapid population growth for the future, but the modelling exercise points to clear and very urgent problems in agricultural decline. Whether city or provincial officials are willing and able to act on these urgent concerns is a more serious question.

> **Data are necessary. Planners and analysts need data on past and current conditions to understand how population and environment are related. Capacities to use data are also necessary, but without data they are impotent.**

> **Dynamic modelling provides an effective tool for identifying data needs for and using data to look into the future to understand possible implications of current patterns of behaviour.**

Limitations

The limitations of dealing with cities as closed systems remain, and are highlighted in these studies. We are led to ignore, or treat as a mere externality, sources of environmental change that arise outside the city. Pusan's water pollution is a good case in point. It must be taken as a given for the city, increasing costs for greater purification costs, or pursuing attempts to move water from more distant, cleaner areas. Nor do we examine the impact of pollutants that flow out of the city. That air pollution is blown out of Kobe may be good for Kobe's citizens, but there is a cost somewhere that should not be ignored. Khon Kaen disposes of wastewater into purifying holding tanks, which also provide a source of livelihood in fishing, but those tanks drain into rivers that find their way into the Mekong River. The city does not ask – nor do we – what the quality of the water is that ultimately flows into that river system.

The limitations may be more important when we consider the urban governance system, though here we are at least led to see some of the impositions presented by the central government. There is much a city government cannot do, because the national government makes the decisions. There is also much a city cannot do because its jurisdiction is cut many ways by different central and provincial agencies that exercise authority over some of its territory or activities. While our studies have produced specific observations of this set of governance problems, they have not been central to our analysis, nor does our model lead us to ask these questions systematically and comprehensively. This is a severe limitation inherent in the closed system model we have adopted for these five city studies.

Addressing these issues presents something of a dilemma. First, the original closed-system model was proposed as a first step. It was deliberately made simple so that its application would be feasible, as a first cut at the problem. We believe the first cut has been sufficiently rewarding to lead to more advanced and more complicated models, some of which we shall attempt to identify in the final chapter. But there is also some utility to a model that focuses specifically on what a city can do by itself. Developing tools by which a city government can examine its conditions and their likely course into the future can provide city officials with information they can use. The AUICK strategy of encouraging teams of social scientists and urban administrators to work together attempts to do just this. It cannot specify what urban administrators should do. It is they who should decide what to do, given their intimate knowledge of how to draw resources both from the local environment as well as from the regional, national or even international environment. Thus, with all its limitations, the strategy and our models have potential for promoting better urban planning. That may be a modest advantage, but it is not without value, especially for urban managers.

A closed-system model for examining urban population-environment dynamics has two major advantages: it focuses attention on conditions over which urban administrators might have some control; and it provides a more simple set of problems for beginning the dynamic modelling that helps us to look ahead.

The major weakness of the closed system approach is that it ignores external sources of urban problems, and the impact the city has on the world outside its boundaries.

Linking city conditions to wider, global conditions represents a major problem for future research and development.

Notes

1. A recent publication of the Population Reference Bureau (De Souza, 1999) provides evidence of the opposite, however. This is a report on a study of the use of automobiles in three cities: Bangkok, Mexico City and Washington DC. Here it is clear that vehicular use and consequently air pollution are directly proportional to family income, education and male-headed households. However, this study did not distinguish the type of vehicle, vehicle age and actual individual pollution by class. If poorer people drive older and more pollution-causing cars, the relationship between income and pollution would be much more complicated.

2. Note again, that a peripheral road is now being built to divert north-south traffic around Cebu City, though the slow pace of construction raises concerns.

3. Albert A. Hermalin, University of Michigan Population Studies Center, is principal investigator of a major study of ageing, "Rapid Demographic Change and the Welfare of the Elderly". This is a collaborative project including the Philippines, Singapore and Thailand, with work as well on the other countries of East, Southeast and South Asia.

4. Lucian Hanks (1975) was one of the earliest to propose this formulation. It was contested by Rabibhadana (1976), who saw rather a patron-client system, and Suvanajata (1976), who questioned the basic observation. Still, there is a fluid nature of society with kinship relations that are, for example, far more open than those in the Philippines.

5. The Siam Society (1989) organized a conference on Thai society culture and the environment in 1988. The published proceedings provide a broad and deep view of Thai society and polity and how this view is related to urbanization and the population-environment dynamics. See also Charles F. Keyes' (1987) important analysis of the Buddhist kingdom as a modern nation state.

6. This is not a new idea. Max Weber (1930; 1958) proposed that Christianity "broke the fetters of the sib", breaking with earlier "tribal" religions, thus making way for the emergence of a new type of urban community in Europe after the tenth century. Edward Banfield (1958) made the case again in a study of Southern Italy. Peter Berger (1972) made the point once again by showing the distinct differences between US and Latin American family structures.

7. See the New York Times article of Monday, 6 March 2000, "Pakistanis, Eager for Change, Are Left Frustrated After Coup", p. A10.

Chapter 10

What is to be Done?

Gayl D. Ness with Michael M. Low

A classic question that typically comes at the end of studies such as this. We have examined population-environment relationships in five cities. What does that examination tell us to do next? What are the policy implications for urban and national governments, or for the international agencies that now abound and aim to help promote sustainable living, a higher quality of life, better urban planning and other good things? What are the research questions? What do these studies tell us about what we do not know, and what questions should be asked in the future? Finally, what can the studies tell us about the strategies of combining inquiry and action, or about policy research?

To begin, we focus on the five cities, and we must first ask about their representativeness. Are they representative of Asian cities? Yes and no, and both in a statistical sense. They can be said to represent the *size distribution* of Asia's medium-sized cities. The five cities have between 100,000 and four million people, within the range an earlier UNFPA (1987) conference defined as 'medium-sized'. They also represent the range of independence of the medium-sized cities that stand *functionally* between the great metropolises, or capital cities, and the smaller towns and villages. The three poorest of our cities have little independence from their national governments; Pusan has more, and Kobe has much independence. The five cities also represent the *distribution of wealth*, ranging from the most wealthy to one of the poorest. In this sense they represent the range of conditions in medium-sized cities.

But, no, they do not represent medium-sized cities in any sense of *central tendency*. The concept of an *average* for such widely divergent urban conditions would be difficult to defend in any case. Thus, the five cities together can tell us something about the range of conditions and relationships that can be expected. They cannot, however, provide precise guidelines for dealing with urban population-environment dynamics everywhere. Finally, one of our basic observations – the location-specific character of population-environment dynamics stated in Chapter 9 – should caution against simple universal proposals, applicable in all cities.

Thus, we shall begin modestly with suggestions for our five cities themselves, and only after that make some tentative foray into the broader arena. For these five cities, we have something to say about measurements or monitoring, about a model of the urban system, and about modelling population-environment dynamics in overall. Finally, we shall make a modest proposal, for better management of urban population-environment dynamics, which we believe is especially suited to three of the cities, but which may also have some relevance in a broader arena.

MORE AND BETTER MONITORING IS REQUIRED IN THREE CITIES

One of the most striking differences in our five cities, from the perspective of population-environment dynamics, is the amount and quality of the data available and the way those data are used.

Kobe and Pusan provide good models, showing us what we can know if there are extensive, valid data. Such data imply accurate and timely information on important conditions, spanning a number of years. With more than 20 years of data available for Pusan and Kobe, it was reasonable to construct models of critical relationships that lead to defensible projections. It is also clear that Kobe and Pusan have highly developed urban governments with good capacities to use the data at hand for more effective city management.

Khon Kaen, Faisalabad and Cebu show declining amounts and quality of data available to social scientists and urban planners. Quite clearly, all three cities need more and better data. But they also need more developed capacities to use given data for urban management. Specific requirements can be identified for the major elements in our model. While one could go on endlessly with suggestions for more extensive modelling, we shall limit ourselves to six that we feel are especially valuable for these cities.

Population movements

Population movements should be tracked more carefully. Birth and death registration is a first step. The three countries with deficient data all have laws in place for registering vital statistics: those laws should be fully implemented. The Philippines and Thailand have registration procedures that now yield relatively good data at the national level; Pakistan's vital registration lags considerably. Upgrading the vital registration procedure in Pakistan would yield important basic information. For all three, focusing registration processes on local units of government could be especially valuable.

But, as we saw in both Cebu and Khon Kaen, more than simply registering births and deaths is needed. Those data must be organized and presented in a manner that is both timely and useful. They should be reported annually, especially to urban administrators. To make data more useful, births and deaths should note not only the place of occurrence but also the subject's place of residence. Further, regular reports of births and deaths should distinguish urban residents from those residing outside the city. (What that implies in the way of defining city boundaries is dealt with elsewhere.) Cities will always be centres of attraction for such basic services as medicine and health. Thus, we can usually expect that people from outside the city will enter for health services and will add both births and deaths to the city's register. Such movements are easy to track if registration and reporting regularly include the place of residence.

Tracking migration is far more difficult. Few countries have the kind of population register such as that which enables Kobe and Pusan to know the difference even between daytime and night-time populations for different city wards. Even if population registers are mandated by law, they can lag very seriously in implementation. It is difficult to suggest specific steps to track migration when a population is not fully registered. It is possible, however, for local police and other ground level functionaries to make estimates of the level and changes of migrants. There are also ways to validate those estimates against census and survey data, a point to which we shall return in our final proposal.

There is, however, one important thing to be done to examine migration potentials: this is especially relevant for Faisalabad. Recall that the large agricultural families, fragmentation of holdings, and increasing salinization raise the potential of a massive urban in-migration. It would not be difficult for the Faisalabad Agricultural University to undertake an agricultural survey to assess the size of the surrounding rural population, its age structure and patterns of land holding, and recent changes in crop yields. This survey would provide city managers with information on the potential for near future in-migration.

Health

Health is typically measured in ways that have become well standardized and extensively promoted by international organizations, especially by the World Health Organization (WHO). Again, the problem is less of the technical procedures than their actual implementation. We saw that in Khon Kaen, even where reporting appears to be well organized, there can easily be serious questions about data accuracy. For example, does the rapid rise of *treatments* for respiratory and gastrointestinal diseases imply a rise in incidence, or care availability? That these treatment measures have risen so rapidly implies that no one in city government is really assessing the figures or using them for urban planning. Each of the cities can indicate what the leading causes of death are, but they typically do not report them. The three cities need to develop ways to monitor causes of death and incidences of diseases with greater accuracy and to report these in a timely fashion.

Education

Education, too, is typically measured and reported with relatively standard procedures, since schools are usually required to submit reports to higher authorities. Too often, of course, schools report only to these authorities and not to city governments, thus depriving city managers of information that could be important for their work. As with births and deaths, enrolment data should distinguish city dwellers from those from outside the city who come for education.

We saw that Khon Kaen's school enrolment data appear to have problems of validity. The radical changes, reflecting differences of as many as 10,000 to 20,000 students between one year and the next, demand explanation. Are those data accurate? If not, how can accuracy be improved? If they are accurate, what is happening to the school-aged population to cause such wild swings? These are questions that mayors and urban administrators need to ask to discover what is happening in this very critical area of social services.

Water

Water has been monitored in most cities for years. Again, the procedures are standard and the technology fairly simple and inexpensive. For cities that provide water through public utilities to the population, measures of quantity and quality should be available. As we saw in Khon Kaen, however, the monitoring is often done, but it needs to be more carefully supervised and scrutinized. Without real oversight, the figures obtained and written into logs or reports may be suspect or quite useless. For many poor cities, and even some more affluent like Cebu, many people draw water from rivers or their own wells that lie outside of the city's public utilities infrastructure. In such cases, urban planners and administrators need estimates of the proportion of people served by other than public sources, and the quality of the water they use must be assessed regularly. Such estimates can be made relatively easily by sample survey work, for which procedures are well known, simple and relatively inexpensive. This would normally be the responsibility of a city's water department, but other courses of action are available, and will be discussed in this chapter's final section.

Air Quality

Air quality is a condition that has only more recently been subject to extensive monitoring. By this time, however, the monitoring can be done easily with relatively inexpensive machines that take constant or periodic recordings. Kobe provides an excellent model, with air quality measures from automatic machines fed directly into a central computer system so that records can easily be kept and reports easily generated. As in other cases, the technology has been well developed and has become more affordable, allowing poorer countries and cities to leap-frog the longer and slower technological developments of the past. Khon Kaen has begun to monitor air quality sporadically; Cebu City and Faisalabad have yet to start. All three need to put in place and implement a monitoring system that can track both seasonal and yearly changes. Khon Kaen needs to be sure its new monitoring system is properly placed and well maintained in order to know whether air quality is deteriorating with the rise of vehicles. Kobe's use of roadside monitoring stations for assessing vehicular impact on air quality is a good model for others to follow.

Energy

Energy use is also relatively easily measured and can provide useful information to social scientists and urban administrators. Electrical energy provided by central sources is easy to track, as we saw in Faisalabad; use of oil, kerosene or other commercial products may be harder to track accurately. Since they come through a market with organized distributors, however, there are at least known sources from which to obtain the information. More difficult is assessing the numbers using traditional fuels like wood or dung. And, of course, the numbers and proportions that do use these fuels are largest in the poorer cities, which already have the least capacities for monitoring. It required a special, detailed and externally funded study to estimate wood and charcoal usage in Cebu City. Such a study would be a useful starting point for both Khon Kaen and Faisalabad as well. Once the basic study is done, periodic follow-up estimates can be done by relatively simple sample surveys.

Modelling the Data

To make the data most useful for urban administrators, they should be modelled, as was done in four of our cities. Modelled information can provide the administrators with a capacity to see possible future implications of current conditions. Those administrators are in an especially critical position to do two things needed to promote sustainable development. One is planning for the future using good information about the present. The other is bringing together the findings of different scientific disciplines to deal with the complex and multifaceted problems of population environment dynamics. We have argued extensively elsewhere (Ness & Golay, 1997; UNFPA, 1997) that the specialization of sciences is necessary to increase their powers of understanding. But this specialization also produces a kind of blindness that comes from separation. It is necessary, especially for dealing with population environment dynamics and promoting sustainable development, to build bridges between the disciplines. Modelling tools in the hands of urban administrators trying to understand and plan for the real problems of their cities offer a great potential for bridge building.

MODELS OF THE URBAN SYSTEM

A simple model of the urban system guided these studies. We began with a closed system model and discussed its limitations in Chapters 3 and 9. But many things that happen to a city come from outside its boundaries. How should we deal with those external forces? Cities also have an impact on other areas or cities outside of themselves with such aspects as air or water pollution, wastes and even positive assistance. How should we deal with these external 'foot-prints' of the city?

Here lies a dilemma. Focusing on the city itself has the distinct advantage of dealing with conditions over which local urban administrators may have some real control. For example, the modelling of Kobe's solid waste suggests a future problem that the city can address with a strong recycling programme, as it did in the early 1980s. Trying to extend the boundaries of the analysis to gain a more accurate picture of the city in a larger system may lead to areas over which the urban administrator has little or no control, thus greatly lessening the utility of such studies to the city. At the same time, it is quite obvious that there is much more to urban quality of life than we find in the city alone.

To suggest ways in which observations of urban population-environment dynamics can be expanded, we can extend the model in Chapter 3. First, we can return to the model and go to its origins, which saw the city more as an open than a closed system. To this, we can add an identification of both inputs and outputs, as seen in Figure 10.1.

This figure identifies categories of inputs and outputs but does not indicate sources or destinations. Following the location-specific rule, however, sources should be identified for each individual city. For Kobe and Pusan, there will be many, running very far afield: from the Middle East for oil, to the US for car sales and gastronomic influences (seen in the rapid rise of Japanese restaurants).

Figure 10.1
Urban Population-Environment Dynamics: An Open Systems Model

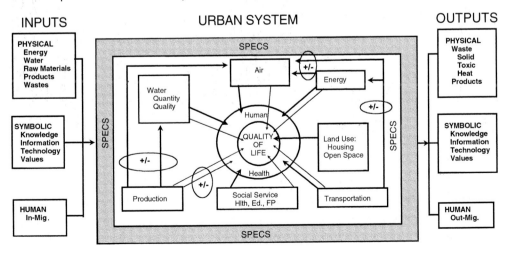

Nearer to home are such places as Taegu City for Pusan's river pollution, and Ashiya as a recipient of Kobe's air pollution. The three less wealthy cities all import oil and export goods. Their imprint, however, would be less pronounced, and nearby sources and destinations more important, than the global arenas affected by the wealthier cities. It is undoubtedly possible to classify cities on the bases of the extent of their imprint, including both the physical distances involved, and the magnitude and diversity of their inputs and outputs.

But this model raises an important question of the unit of analysis. In dealing with a single city as a closed system, we can use the administrative boundaries of the city. This is useful in part because administratively defined areas usually collect the data that we need. But if we wish to include sources and sinks of urban processes, what boundaries can we use? How do we define the area to be examined? And how do we sort out the impact of a specific city, or even a network of cities, on the sources of inputs and the areas of impact? Indonesian forests are being destroyed to provide Kobe and Pusan with timber, but what is the relative weight of these two cities on Indonesian forest destruction? Kobe's emissions may affect Ashiya and Osaka, but how do we assess the weight of Kobe's inputs, relative to those of other areas? We have no answers to these questions, but clearly they must be addressed if we wish to work with open system models of urban areas.

There is more, however, in the way of external forces and consequences than those shown in Figure 10.1. One of the most important is the set of conditions that affects the city's SPECS. A city's political system is very much affected by its parent political systems. Usually the most immediate is the provincial or state government with the national government as the most important determinant of the city's rules and procedures of governance. Typically, national governments define the powers allotted to provinces and cities, and these are often relatively uniform for all or most cities under a national government. Even here, however, there are differences that must be noted. Kobe is much more independent of the Japanese government than is Seoul of the South Korean government. Kobe also has a larger revenue base from its port and related industries, and greater discretion both in mobilizing and using its resources. Khon Kaen, Cebu and Faisalabad are constrained by both provincial and national governments, and are considerably less independent than either Kobe or Pusan. For any city it is necessary to identify and specify the authority and responsibility accorded by its parent government(s). Figure 10.2 suggests one way to think about this set of relationships.

Figure 10.2
Urban Linkages to Larger Systems
(For political, economic, cultural and social systems)

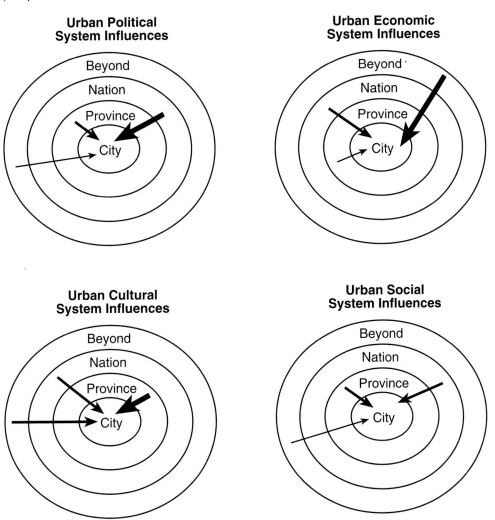

Figure 10.2 uses circles to represent provincial, national and international arenas that affect the city. The different thicknesses of the lines suggests the relative weight of the external system on the city. This figure might reflect the impact of external forces on Faisalabad's, Cebu's or Khon Kaen's political systems, where the national government has the greatest impact, the provincial government somewhat less, and the environment beyond the country only very small, or perhaps none. Economic influences would find the global system dominant. For the city's cultural system, we might expect the provincial area to

be dominant, with national and international arenas sharing a moderate influence. The social system, reflecting family and legal systems, might show a moderate influence from both provincial and national arenas, and a very weak influence from the international arena. These are, to be sure, no more than suggested hypotheses to be tested. What is required is a more precise definition of each of these parts of the system, and operational definitions of external influence. This amounts to a substantial and very serious research agenda.

It is possible at this time, however, to suggest a number of apparent secular trends in this set of relationships. Globalization implies centripetal forces that increasingly draw cities into a single world economic and, to a lesser extent, cultural system with very strong influences. It also suggests that these forces will increase in both complexity and magnitude. Cheap goods from outside produce changes in consumption and production. External investments can move employment in from, or out to, distant economic centres. They can shift production into or away from a city, causing rapid changes in unemployment. There are also messages in movies, the mass media and on the Internet that influence cultures and all manner of behaviour. External technological changes have affected birth and death rates. The rise of international agreements, from postal procedures to environmental protection, draws cities into a larger sphere of influence that can well limit their initiative and independence of action.

In addition to economic globalization, there is another aspect of global change that will be very important for individual cities. Major climate changes are now a distinct possibility for the world, with very different regional patterns to be expected. City managers could be faced with major changes in diseases, in agricultural output, or in water availability due to climate change. There is little they can do about these things, but the prospects are real for massive changes.

There are centrifugal forces as well. As we saw in Cebu City, there is interest in devolving authority and responsibility to lower levels of government. International organizations (World Bank, 1999) now tend to encourage central governments to devolve authority to cities, and in some cases this is happening, however slowly. Giving cities more authority, responsibility and resources will increase their need to develop capacities to manage their environment more effectively.

But the outcomes of the centripetal and centrifugal forces are highly location specific. Kobe and Pusan are different despite their considerable similarities. Cebu City, Khon Kaen and Faisalabad will face very different forces and the way they address those forces will differ considerably. Thus, to understand how a city works in a larger system, it will be necessary to specify those external forces that are operative, what their sources are, what form they are taking, and what impact they have. It is relatively easy to depict these broader connections in pictures of models. It is more difficult, however, to develop the specifics for a given city. But that is precisely what must be done if we are to understand better how cities operate in larger systems[1].

MODELLING

The modelling done on these five cities has barely scratched the surface of population-environment dynamics; this was necessary because the first steps must always be relatively simple ones. Since these steps have now been taken for our five cities, it is easier to suggest ways in which the modelling could be extended to provide better insights into population-environment dynamics and the quality of life. One could go on for many pages with these suggestions, but we shall identify only four issues that we feel would be especially good candidates for extended modelling.

Health, Air and Water Quality

These qualities represent obvious first choices. In no case were we able to draw links between air or water quality, and death rates. The links are there in reality, of course, and it would be most useful to attempt to make them more explicit, since they can provide powerful arguments for promoting environmental quality. The links between water quality or air quality and gastrointestinal and respiratory diseases are quite well known. Thus, we could easily connect air quality to a measure of respiratory diseases and subsequently to the death rate[2]. But the link between diseases and death rates is complex and depends on a variety of other things, such as medical services and the general health of a population. Thus, links to the death rate should come from air and water quality measures and also from measures of medical services available to, or used by, a population. In addition, the crude death rate is affected by fundamental demographic conditions, such as the age structure of a population. We saw evidence of this in Kobe, where declining air pollution was associated in time with a steady increase in respiratory diseases and cancer as the cause of death. We speculated that these disease increases were the result of the ageing of the population, but we did not have the data to test that hypothesis. Thus to model the health impact of air or water quality will require the inclusion of age structure data or a disaggregation of the population by age categories. The deeper we wish to go into precise specification, the more complex the model will become.

Education

Education is another good candidate for extending the modelling. In none of our studies did we attempt to link education to either costs or benefits. For national educational planners, however, such linkages are important. Providing some information on those linkages could give a city considerable powers of persuasion with the national government. Although it is somewhat complex, there is an excellent example of this type of modelling in the IIASA study of Mauritius (Lutz, 1994). Lutz used a multi-state population projection model to include age, sex, educational attainment, and labour force participation. This allowed analysts and administrators to see population as a productive force, with varying levels of capacity and participation. Moreover, the model has the capacity to link population quality and dynamics to the productive sector. Lutz showed, for example, that the fertility decline Mauritius experienced in the 1950s and 60s released a substantial female population into the labour force, thus contributing to the country's rapid economic development. It is difficult to over-emphasize the importance of Lutz' innovation to the world of population-environment modelling. Most models use population as a single figure for the total number of people (Ness, 1994). This tends to define population as primarily a force of consumption and waste production, by definition implying environmental degradation or stress. Lutz's perspective sees people as producers as well as just consumers.

Developing more complex models of population-education-production would allow Kobe and Pusan, for example, to look ahead at possible labour requirements and the capacity of the city to satisfy those demands. This would provide another useful view of the implications of low birth rates and the decline of the young population. Will Kobe's and Pusan's educational institutions be able to satisfy the future demand for workers? The answer to this question would also provide insights into the importance of future streams of migrants into and out of the cities. Khon Kaen could also ask this question, though it might be expected at this time that its educational output would be able to keep well ahead of the demand for labour. This may be true for the next two decades, until the recent decline in the birth rates begins to reduce the numbers of people less than 19 years of age. A comparable analysis for Cebu and Faisalabad would likely point to the increasing pressures on employment that those cities will experience in the near future, due to the lack of rapid fertility decline in the recent past.

Production and Environmental Quality

These qualities represent another linkage that we have not attempted to model. It is easy to suggest that a more complex model should develop the links between production and its benefits in jobs and income on the one hand, and its costs in pollution on the other. To model this information would require highly detailed studies that are probably far beyond the regular capacities of the three poorer cities in our studies. Still, studies of environmental pollution are a rapidly growing industry, and we can expect that they will become more feasible in the near future. Pusan and Kobe are already undertaking such studies, in their well-regulated environmental monitoring of industrial establishments. For the other three cities, one might suggest highly focused studies of specific industries that are important to the city. Textiles in Faisalabad, and the range of relatively new industries in Khon Kaen, would be good candidates. It is unlikely, however, that such studies will be carried out without external assistance.

Housing

The urban administrators surveyed by AUICK have consistently recognized housing as an important issue, but largely confined to poorer cities and countries. For Korea and Japan, the housing problem has not been identified in past surveys as critical, and our modelling exercises also indicated considerable progress and little problem for the future. Even in the poorer countries of the AUICK surveys, however, not all housing was problematic; only that for low-cost housing and, in some cases, the problem of the homeless, proved an issue. Thus we have included housing as an important aspect of land use in its impact on the quality of life, but we have not attempted to model housing; it has merely been used as a condition to be observed and added to our narrative descriptions of the quality of life. But modelling housing would provide urban administrators with some insights into the magnitude of the problem and the ways in which that problem might be addressed. Such modelling would require information about costs, which could then be linked to employment and income as outcomes of the productive sector. The information could also be linked to household size, as was done for Khon Kaen, to produce projections about the future demand for housing. This demand in turn could be linked back to the productive sector to see how housing demand might stimulate activity, leading to rising incomes that would then lead to a greater stock of housing in the city. It would also be necessary to build links to the financial sector to indicate the availability of mortgage capital for house building. Capital requirements could be an especially useful type of study for Khon Kaen, where there is a perceived housing shortage, and where ideas have been promoted for the government to assist by developing some kind of mortgage insurance scheme that would stimulate the housing market.

Much more could be said about future extensions of the kind of modelling used in the city studies, but this will have to suffice for now. Our modelling exercise merely recognizes that much more can be done. How to proceed to extend the modelling presents another problem: that of creating specific programs and organizational strategies to implement the programs. The following modest proposal does precisely that. It suggests a programmatic strategy to improve and increase the modelling of Asian urban population-environment dynamics.

A MODEST PROPOSAL: CITY-UNIVERSITY PARTNERSHIPS

Kobe and Pusan appear to have no problems both in collecting and using data to assess population-environment dynamics or their quality of life. Khon Kaen, Cebu City and Faisalabad, however, face serious problems doing the same, but this does not mean the cities are without resources for monitoring. After all, social scientists at local universities did the work of data collection and analysis for these studies. The data are there. What is lacking is the political organization and the technical capacity to make the data available and useful to urban administrators.

Would it not be possible for those cities to use their local universities to help collect and analyse data on a systematic and sustained basis? San Carlos University in Cebu City provides what could be a useful model. The University has a Water Resources Center that researches water quantity and quality in the city and on the island. Moreover, the University's Department of Chemistry has done some sporadic air quality measurement, and its Office of Population Studies has strong capacities in demography. Cebu is not alone in having a university as an important local resource. Khon Kaen and Faisalabad also have high quality universities with technical departments that could establish regular monitoring of city conditions. To tap this set of resources, we propose the formation of specific **city-university partnerships**.

Two important steps would be required to develop such a city-university partnership. One would be to create a specific and formal ongoing relationship between the city and the university. The other would be to create multi-disciplinary team both within the university and the city government to bring together the necessary specializations into one operating unit. The history of such cross-organizational cooperation is sufficiently weak to suggest that this will not be easy. Leadership, vision and resources would be required[3].

This proposal is for a partnership between a specified group of urban administrators and a collection of university faculty from different departments. For simplicity, we call this the **URBPED** (for urban population-environment dynamics) **Team**. Such a team would include appropriate technical people and some elected representatives from the city. On the university side, it should include people from departments with the technical capacities for monitoring such aspects as water, air, land use, energy, and population and health. It would be most useful to establish an office within the university to provide a secretariat for the Team, and to give that secretariat the resources to bring the team together. The secretariat might be associated with a department of urban and regional planning, which would link the monitoring to training future leaders. The decision on location would have to be made locally, but it would be of the utmost importance to choose a unit and leader with the capacity to bring together different disciplines. This is never an easy task, and special care would have to be taken to select leaders and create structures and processes that would guarantee interdisciplinary participation. Such participation would be a major criterion in judging the success of the unit.

To begin the process, the URBPED Team of urban administrators and university scientists would have to meet to specify what would be measured, and how and by whom. In some cases, this might simply mean providing the Team with copies of data the city already collects; in other cases, such as air monitoring in Faisalabad and Cebu City, establishing new procedures would be required. Sites would have to be selected and equipment obtained, set in place, and maintained regularly. It would be most useful if the monitoring equipment were be automatic and connected to a central computer control at the university. But even in this case, regular observation, calibration and maintenance of the monitoring equipment would have to be part of the normal procedure and training of students.

A partnership of this type would have a number of advantages. One would be reducing city costs, or precluding a rise in costs for monitoring. The city would not need to establish monitoring stations with special equipment and trained personnel. There would have to be financial support to the universities to provide the monitoring equipment, but personnel from the technical departments could take on the task of operating the machines, possibly without adding new staff.

A second advantage would lie in relating city monitoring to the training of students. For example, courses could be offered in urban planning that would include regular and sustained monitoring of basic environmental conditions. Students could do much of the work of collecting and analysing data, and preparing reports. City managers could thus obtain regular reports in considerable detail while a cadre of qualified people is being created.

A third advantage would lie in collecting a wide range of data and putting them together in a useable fashion. This would address the problems we have seen in Cebu and Khon Kaen: data are available in local offices, but they are never brought together with other specialized data to expose urban conditions. Or, as in Khon Kaen, periodic review and use of the data would surely show errors or validity problems that would need to be addressed.

A fourth advantage lies in the leverage this could provide for devolution of authority and more effective local urban planning. Giving urban administrators good information on local conditions would tend to increase the initiative that the city could take for itself. This would put work into the devolution that many central governments seem to wish but also seem unable to implement. In addition, it would give city governments more powerful support for their requests to the central government for support and resources. If such teams and processes were available in a number of cities, this would also give the central government firmer bases on which to make resource allocation decisions to cities.

Finally, the idea of a city-university URBPED Team could provide international organizations, both public and private, with a viable locus for their inputs. International organizations are a vital force for promoting sustainable development, which implies promoting the welfare of both people and the ecosystem, but they need ideas and local groups with which to work. In Faisalabad, Khon Kaen and Cebu City, there are highly qualified local universities and urban administrators who are willing to work with the academics to develop new forms of organization to promote sustainable development. The time is now ripe for taking such initiatives.

Notes

1. See the work of Wackerenagel & Rees, 1997, for another way to think about an open systems urban model. This uses the concept of the ecological footprint, or the amount of productive land required to support both the consumption and the waste production of any population, society or economy.
2. It is now well established, for example, that under many conditions a ten-microgram rise in SPM10 produces a three percent increase in the death rate, with no recognizable threshold (Dockery & Pope, 1994; and Dockery, Schwartz & Pope, 1995)
3. Two excellent examples of this building of multidisciplinary teams to promote development can be found in Taiwan's Joint Commission for Rural Reconstruction, or JCRR (Hough & Ness, 1968), and Malaysia's Rural Development Programme under then Prime Minister Tun Abdul Razak (Ness, 1967).

References

Ahmad, T., Yaqub, M., Iqbal, M. & Ahmad, H. (1990) Biochemical analysis of blood in textile workers, *Punjab Medical Journal*.

—— (1998) Study of SGOT and SGPT in Blood of Textile Workers, Biochemistry.

AUICK (1992) Population Dynamics and Port City Development. Unpublished. Kobe: AUICK.

—— (1997) AUICK: The First Decade, Lessons Learned and Views of the Future of the Asian Urban Information Center of Kobe. Unpublished. Kobe: AUICK.

—— (1997b) Migration and Family Planning: Research Reports for Three Cities. Unpublished. Kobe: AUICK.

Banfield, E. (1958) *The Moral Basis of a Backward Society*. Glencoe, IL: The Free Press.

Bashir, A. (1992) The role of mother and child health care and family planning in promoting family health, *The Gynecologist*, Vol. 3, No. 2 & 3, Dec. 92 & Jan–Feb. 93.

Bashir, A., et al. (1992) Maternal mortality in Faisalabad city, *The Gynecologist*, Vol. 3, No. 2 & 3, Dec. 92 & Jan–Feb. 93.

Berger, P.L. (1972) *Pyramids of Sacrifice*. New York: Basic Books.

Boserup, E. (1965) *The Conditions of Agricultural Growth*. London: Allen and Unwin.

—— (1981) *Population and Technological Change*. Chicago: University of Chicago Press.

—— (1987) Population and technology in pre-industrial Europe, *Population and Development Review*, Vol. 13, No. 4, December, pp. 691–701.

Caldwell, J. (1976) Toward a restatement of demographic transition theory, *Population and Development Review*, Vol. 13, No. 4, pp. 691–701.

Chandler, T. & Fox, G. (1974) *3000 Years of Urban Growth*. New York: Academic Press.

City of Kobe (1989) *A Centennial Tribute of Kobe*. Kobe: City Government.

Coale, A. & Watkins, S.C. (1986) *The Decline of Fertility in Europe*. Princeton: Princeton University Press, p. 484.

Costa, F.J., et al. (Eds.) (1989) *Urbanization in Asia: Spatial Dimensions and Policy Issues*. Honolulu: University of Hawaii Press.

—— (1988) *Asian Urbanization: Problems and Processes*. Berlin: Gebruder Borntraeger.

De Souza, R.-M. (1999) *Household Transportation Use and Urban Air Pollution: A Comparative Analysis of Thailand, Mexico and the United States*. New York: Population Reference Bureau.

De Vries, J. (1984) *European Urbanization 1500–1800*. Cambridge, MA: Harvard University Press.

Dockery, D.W. & Pope, C.A. (1994) Acute respiratory effects of acute air pollution, *Annual Review of Public Health*, pp. 107–132.

Dockery, D.W., Schwartz, J. & Pope, C.A. (1995) Comments from Original Investigators. In *Health Effects Institute, The Phase I Report of the Particle Epidemiology Evaluation Report.* Portland, Or.: Health Effects Institute, pp. 115–122.

Douglass, M. & Friedmann, F. (Eds.) (1998) *Cities for Citizens: Planning and the Rise of Civil Society in a Global Age.* New York: John Wiley & Sons.

Drake, W.D. (1993) Toward Building a Theory of Population Environment Dynamics, A Family of Transitions. In Ness, G.D., Drake, W.D. & Brechin, S.R. (Eds.), *Population-Environment Dynamics: Ideas and Observations.* Ann Arbor: University of Michigan Press, pp. 304–356.

—— (Ed.) (1995) Population-Environment Dynamics: Transitions in Global Change. Unpublished. Ann Arbor: University of Michigan School of Natural Resources.

Eder, N. (1996) *Poisoned Prosperity: Development, Environment and Modernization in South Korea.* Armonk: M.E. Sharpe.

Ehrlich, P. & Ehrlich, A. (1972, 1990) *The Population Bomb.* San Francisco: W.H. Freeman.

Faisalabad Development Authority (FDA) (1994) Faisalabad Master Plan. Unpublished. Faisalabad: FDA.

—— (1993) Environmental Infrastructure Master Plan Study. Unpublished. Faisalabad: Water and Sanitation Agency.

—— (1995) Directorate of Environmental Control, Structural Plan of Faisalabad up to 2000. Unpublished. Faisalabad: FDA.

Food and Agriculture Organization (FAO) (1993) Patterns of Commercial Woodfuel Supply, Distribution and Use in the City and Province of Cebu, Regional Wood Energy Development Program in Asia. GCP/RAS/131/NET. Field Document No. 42, July 1993.

Fenner, B.L. (1985) *Cebu Under the Spanish Flag: An Economic-Social History.* Cebu City: San Carlos Publications, University of San Carlos.

Flieger, W. & Cusi, D.R. (1998) The Mountains of Cebu and their Inhabitants: Measurements & Estimates. East-West Center, Honolulu, and Office of Population Studies and University of San Carlos: Cebu City.

Flieger, W., B. Koppin & Lim, C. (1976) *Geographical Patterns of Internal Migration in the Philippines: 1960–1970.* Manila: National Census and Statistics Office, UNFPA-NCSO Monograph No.5.

Friedman, J. (1998) The Common Good: Assessing the Performance of Cities. In H. Dandiker (Ed.), *City, Space and Globalization: An International Perspective.* Ann Arbor, Michigan: University of Michigan, College of Architecture and Urban Planning, pp. 15–22.

Fuentes, R.U. (1993) Environmental Pollution Management, *Proceedings of the Ninth Philippine Chemistry Congress.* Manila: Philippines Chemistry Congress.

Fuller, T., Peerasit, K., Lightfoot, P. & Rathanamongholmas, S. (1983) *Migration and Development in Modern Thailand.* Bangkok: The Social Science Association of Thailand.

Government of Pakistan (1972) *Agricultural Census.* Islamabad: Agricultural Census Organization.

—— (1981) *Agricultural Census*. Islamabad: Agricultural Census Organization.

—— (1990) *Agricultural Census*. Islamabad: Agricultural Census Organization.

—— (1997) *Economic Survey 1996–97*. Islamabad: Finance Division.

—— (1985) *Hand Book of Population Census Data*. Islamabad: Population Census Organization.

—— (1989) *Pakistan Demographic Survey*. Islamabad: Federal Bureau of Statistics.

—— (1992) *Pakistan Demographic and Health Survey 1990–91*. Islamabad: National Institute of Population Studies.

Government of the Punjab (1993) Punjab Development Statistics. Lohore: Bureau of Statistics.

—— (1994) Punjab Development Statistics. Lahore: Bureau of Statistics.

Government of Thailand (1986) Survey of Migration into the Bangkok Metropolis, and Khon Kaen Province. Bangkok: National Statistical Office.

Hannon, B. & Ruth, M. (1994) *Dynamic Modeling*. New York: Springer Verlag.

Hermalin, A.I. (1995) Aging in Asia: Setting the research foundation, *Asia Pacific Population Research Reports*. Honolulu: East West Center Program on Population.

—— (1998) Comparative Study of the Elderly in Asia, Research Reports. Report no. 98–51. Ann Arbor: University of Michigan Population Studies Center.

Hough, R.L. & Ness, G.D. (1968) Taiwan's Joint Commission on Rural Reconstruction: A Model for Internationally Induced Development, *International Development Review*, Fall, pp. 22–30.

Iqbal, M., et al. (1991) Effect of lead poisoning on some human blood parameters, *Pakistan Medical Journal*, February.

Israel, D.C. (1996) Industrial policy and the environment: The case of the manufacturing sector in Metro Cebu, Philippines, *Journal of Philippine Development*, 42, pp. 365–23.

Kearns, G. (1989) Zivilis or Hygaeia: Urban Public Health and the Epidemiological Transition. In R. Lawson (Ed.), *The Rise and Fall of Great Cities*. London: Belhaven Press, pp. 96–124.

Keyes, C.F. (1987) *Thailand, Buddhist Kingdom as a Modern Nation State*. Boulder, CO.: Westview Press.

—— (1991) *Reshaping Local Worlds: Formal Education and Cultural Change in Rural Southeast Asia*. New Haven, CT: Yale University Southeast Asian Studies.

Kim, E.M. (1997) *Big Business, Strong State: Collusion and Conflict in South Korean Development*. Albany, NY: State University of New York Press.

Koo, H. (Ed.) (1993) *State and Society in Contemporary Korea*. Ithaca, NY: Cornell University Press.

Lawton, R. (Ed.) (1989) *The Rise and Fall of Great Cities*. London: Belhaven Press, p. 185.

Leitmann, J. (1994) *Rapid Urban Environmental Assessment, Vol. 1*, Methodology and Preliminary Findings, Urban Management Project. Washington, DC: The World Bank.

—— (1994) *Rapid Urban Environmental Assessment, Vol. 2*, Tools and Outputs, Urban Management Project. Washington, DC: The World Bank.

—— (1999) *Sustaining Cities: Environmental Planning and Management in Urban Design*. New York: McGraw Hill.

Lightfoot, P., Fuller T. & Kamnuansilpa, P. (1983) Circulation and interpersonal networks linking rural and urban areas: The case of Roi-Et, Northeastern Thailand, Papers of the East-West Population Institute Papers, No. 84. Honolulu, Hawaii: East West Center.

Lim, J.D. & Kim, N.I. (1992) Republic of Korea: Pusan and Mokpo. In AUICK, Population Dynamics and Port City Development: Comparative Analyses of Ten Asian Port Cities. Unpublished. Kobe: AUICK, pp. 201-244.

Livi-Bacci, M. (1992) *A Concise History of World Population*, translated by Carl Ipsen. Cambridge, Massachusetts: Oxford Press.

Lutz, W. (1994) *Population, Development, Environment: Understanding their Interactions in Mauritius*. Berlin: Springer Verlag.

McGee, T.G. & Robinson, I.M. (1995) *The Mego-Urban Regions of Southeast Asia*. Vancouver, BC: University of Vancouver Press.

McKeown, T. & Brown, R.G. (1955) Medical evidence related to English population change in the 18th century, *Population Studies, Vol. IX*.

Meadows, D.H., Meadows, E.L. & Randers, J. (1972) *The Limits to Growth*. London: Pan Books Ltd.

—— (1991) *Beyond the Limits: Confronting Global Collapse and Envisioning a Sustainable Future*. London: Earthscan Press.

Morell, V. (1999) The Sixth Extinction, *National Geographic*, 1995(2), pp. 43–59.

Muramatsu, M. (1984) Afterword: Reflections on Japan from a Political-Ecological Perspective. In Ness & Ando, *The Land is Shrinking*. Baltimore: Johns Hopkins University Press, pp. 189–202.

Ness, G.D. (1967) *Bureaucracy and Rural Development in Malaysia*. Berkeley: University of California Press.

Ness, G.D. & Ando, H. (1984) *The Land is Shrinking: Population Planning in Asia*. Baltimore: Johns Hopkins University Press.

Ness, G.D., Brechin, S.R. & Drake, W. (Eds.) (1993) *Population-Environment Dynamics: Ideas and Observations*. Ann Arbor: University of Michigan Press.

—— (1993) The Long View: Population-Environment Dynamics in Historical Perspective. In Ness, Drake & Brechin (Eds.), *Population Environment Dynamics: Ideas and Observations*. Ann Arbor: University of Michigan Press, pp. 33–56.

—— (1994) *Population and Environment: Frameworks for Analysis*. Madison, WI: The Environment and Natural Resources Training Project (EPAT).

Ness, G.D. & Golay, M. (1997) *Population and Strategies for National Sustainable Development.* London: Earthscan Press.

—— (1997) World Population Growth. In D. Brune, D.V. Chapman, M.D. Gwynne & J.M. Pacyna (Eds.), *The Global Environment: Science Technology and Management.* Oslo: Scandinavian Scientific Publications, Vol. 2, pp. 637–656.

Nishima, H. (Ed.) (1989) *How to Conquer Air Pollution: A Japanese Experience.* New York: Elsivier.

Omran, A.R. (1982) Epidemiological Transition. In J.A. Ross (Ed.), *International Encyclopedia of Population.* New York: Free Press, pp. 172–83.

Overseas Development Administration (1994) Solid Waste Management Strategy Area Upgrading Project Contract Reference: Cntr 932052A. Unpublished.

Pascual, E.M. (1966) *Population Redistribution in the Philippines.* Manila: University of the Philippines.

Philippines (Rep.), National Statistics Office (1992) *1990 Census of Population and Housing.* Report No. 3., Manila.

—— (1994) *National Demographic Survey 1993. Philippines, Manila.*

—— (1997) *1995 Census of Population.* Report No. 2., Manila.

—— (1998) *1995 Census-Based National, Regional, and Provincial Population Projections.* Manila.

Pirenne, H. (1952) *Medieval Cities: Their Origins and the Revival of Trade.* Princeton, NJ: Princeton University Press.

Population Action International (PAI) (1998) *Educating Girls: Gender Gaps and Gains.* Washington DC: PAI.

Population Crisis Committee (1990) *Cities: Life in the World's 100 Largest Cities.* Washington, DC: Population Crisis Committee.

Rabibhadana, A. (1976) The Origin of Thai Society in the Earl Bangkok Period: 1782–1872. *Data Paper.* Ithaca, New York: Cornell University Center for Southeast Asian Studies.

Ruland, J. (1992) *Urban Development in Southeast Asia: Regional Cities and Local Development.* Boulder, Colorado: Westview Press.

Shills, E. (1959) Political development in the new states, *Comparative Studies in Society and History,* Vol. II, 1959–60, pp. 265–292; 379–411.

Siam Society, The (1989) *Culture and Environment in Thailand.* Bangkok: The Siam Society.

Stokes, E. (1959) *The English Utilitarians in India.* Oxford: Clarendon Press.

Suvanajata, T. (1976) Is the Thai social system loosely structured?, *Social Science Review,* 7(1–2).

Takayose, S. (1985) Population Redistribution and the Construction of Port Island and Suma New Town in Kobe. In UNFPA/NUPRI, *Population Redistribution in Planned Port Cities.* Tokyo: Nihon University Population Research Institute.

UN (1996) *World Population Prospects, The 1996 Revision*. New York: United Nations.

UN (1996b) *World Urbanization Prospects, The 1996 Revision*. New York: United Nations.

UNCED (1992) *Agenda 21*. New York, UNDP.

UNDP (1996) *Human Development Report*. New York: United Nations Development Program.

UNDP (1998) *Human Development Report*. New York: United Nations Development Program.

UNFPA (1982) *World Land Use Classification*. New York: UNFDA.

UNFPA (1987) *Report of the Asian Conference on Population and Development in Medium-Sized Cities*. New York, UNFPA.

UNFPA, Cairo (1994) *World Programme of Action of the International Conference on Population and Development*. New York: UNFPA.

UNFPA (1997) *Environment for People: Building Bridges for Sustainable Development*. Papers prepared for the Special Session of the UN General Assembly on UNCED five years after. New York: UNFPA.

Vitusec, P., Ehrlich, P. & Matson, P.A. (1986) Human appropriation of the products of photosynthesis, *Bioscience*, 363(3), pp. 368–373.

Wackernagel, M. & Rees W. (1997) *Our Ecological Footprint: Reducing Human Impact on the Earth*. Gabriola Island, BC, Canada: New Society Publishers.

Walag, E.L. (1984) A study of the seawater intrusion in Cebu and Mandaue: A progress report, *The Philippine Scientist*, 21:123–150.

Weber, M. (1930) *The Protestant Ethic and the Spirit of Capitalism*. New York: Scribners.

—— (1958) *The City*, translated and edited by D. Martindale and G. Neuwirth. Glencoe, IL: The Free Press, p. 242.

Wernstedt, F.L. & Spencer, J.E. (1967). *The Philippine Island World: A Physical, Cultural, and Regional Geography*. Berkeley, University of California Press.

World Bank (1997) *World Development Report*. Washington DC: The World Bank.

World Bank (1998) *World Development Report*. Washington DC: The World Bank.

World Bank (1999) *World Development Report*. Washington, DC: The World Bank.

World Resources Institute (1993) *World Resources*. Washington, DC: World Resources Institute.

Water Resource Center, University of San Carlos (1997) Current Status of Cebu's Water Resources. Cebu City: University of San Carlos, Water Resources Center. Unpublished.

Yamasaki, T. (1992) Japan. In AUICK, Population Dynamics and Port City Development. Unpublished. Kobe: AUICK, pp. 158-200.

Authors

Chanawongse, Dr Krasae, Former Minister of Foreign Affairs
29 Soi Chote-sahai, Prochacheun Rd, Bangsue, Bangkok 10800, Thailand.
Tel: 66 2 587 8811; FAX: 66 2 587 8822

Flieger, Professor Wilhelm, Director, Office of Population Studies
University of San Carlos, Cebu City 6000, The Philippines.
Tel: 63 32 346 0102; FAX 63 32 346 6050; Email: ops@mangga.usc.edu.ph

Iqbal, Dr Kareem, President, MJS Research Institute
B-5, 2nd Floor, Islamic Plaza, Plot # SB-3, Block 13-B, Gulshan-e-Iqbal, Karachi 75300,
Pakistan.
Tel: 92 21 586 5293; FAX: 92 21 568 5584; Email: emesjay@cyber.net.pk

Ejaz, Mr Ali
C/O Department of Rural Sociology, University of Agriculture, Faisalabad, Pakistan.
Email: ijaz@paknet4.ptc.pk

Ejaz, Professor Kishwar, Chair, Department of Rural Sociology
Agricultural University, 4 Al Najaf Colony, Main Road, Faisalabad, Pakistan.
Tel: 92 717 398

Hashimoto, Tsukasa, Manager
AUICK, Kobe International House, 20th Floor, 8-1-6 Goko-dori, Chuo-ku, Kobe 651-0087,
Japan.
Tel: 81 78 291 0641; FAX: 81 78 291 0691; Email:auick@kobe-sc.tao.go.jp

Kamnuansilpa, Professor Peerasit, Associate Dean for Planning and Development, Department of
Sociology, Faculty of Humanities and Social Sciences, Khon Kaen University, Khon Kaen
40002, Thailand.
Tel: 66 43 237 605; FAX: 66 43 237 605; Email: peerasit@kku1.kku.ac.th

Kanemitsu, Mr Kiyoyuki, Executive Diector, AUICK
AUICK, Kobe International House, 20th Floor, 8-1-6 Goko-dori, Chuo-ku, Kobe 651-0087,
Japan.
Tel: 81 78 291 0641; FAX 81 78 291 0691; Email: auick@kobe-sc.tao.go.jp

Koike, Ms Miho
AUICK, Kobe International House, 20th Floor, 8-1-6 Goko-dori, Chuo-ku, Kobe 651-0087,
Japan.
Tel: 81 78 291 0641; FAX: 81 78 291 0691; Email: auick@kobe-sc.tao.go.jp

Lim, Professor Jung Duk, Director: Labor Research Institute; President: Pusan Development
Institute, Pusan National University, 30 Jangjun-Dong 609-735, Pusan Republic of Korea
Tel: 82 51 510 2544; FAX: 82 15 512-7828; Email: jdl777@chollian.net

Low, Mr Michael
7863 Stonehedge Valley, Gregory, MI, 48137
Tel: 1 734 433 0620; Email: mmlow@umich.edu

Ness, Gayl D., Professor Emeritus, Department of Sociology
University of Michgian, Ann Arbor, MI 48109
Tel: 1 734 668 7033; FAX: 1 734 763 6887; Email: gaylness@umich.edu

Techamanee, Yupin, Dean of Humanities and Social Sciences
Khon Kaen University, Khon Kaen 40002, Thailand.
Tel: 66 43 237 605; FAX 66 43 237 605; Email: yupin@kku.ac.th

Wongthanavasu, Professor Supawatanakorn
School of Nursing, Khon Kaen Unviersity, Kon Kaen 40002, Thailand.
Tel: 66 43 237 606; FAX: 66 43 342 007; Email: supawata@kku1.kku.ac.th

Ueda, Mr Kyoji, Director
AUICK, Kobe International House, 20th Floor, 8-1-6 Goko-dori, Chuo-ku, Kobe 651-0087,
Japan.
Tel: 81 78 291 0641; FAX 81 78 291 0691; Email: auick@kobe-sc.tao.go.jp

Index

DATE DUE	
APR 1 7 2000	